THE NEW EMPLOYEE

DEVELOPING A PRODUCTIVE HUMAN RESOURCE

Gordon F. Shea

PRIME SYSTEMS INC.

▲▼ **Addison-Wesley Publishing Company**

Reading, Massachusetts • Menlo Park, California
London • Amsterdam • Don Mills, Ontario • Sydney

658.3124
S53n

Library of Congress Cataloging in Publication Data

Shea, Gordon F   1925-
    The new employee.

    Bibliography: p.
    1.   Employee induction.   2.   Job satisfaction.
3.   Personnel management.   I.   Title.
HF5549.5.I53S5   658.3'124   80-16346
ISBN 0-201-07137-1

m.R.

ISBN 0-201-07137-1
ABCDEFGHIJ-AL-89876543210

To my daughter Laurie Ann Shea whose experience inspired this work;

to the thousands of supervisors, managers, trainers, and personnel specialists who have shared their experience and ideas with me; and

to the millions of new employees each year who might have a happier and more productive working life if their supervisors and trainers were to use some of the ideas in this book.

CONTENTS

FOREWORD

It is amazing that so little has been written about orientation and training for new employees. Considering that this is one event that all people in the work force face at least once, and many face several times, one must consider the effects of such orientation and development efforts.

We could conjecture on the reasons why organizations do not provide adequate orientations. Perhaps, at one time when the Personnel function and the Human Resource Development (HRD) (e.g., training) function were usually together, a certain procedure was assumed. The people on the Personnel side did the processing, and then turned the new employee over to the HRD people. I am not saying that this procedure actually took place, we don't have that evidence. But it is possible that many employers thought that it was happening.

As HRD has assumed broader functions, it is possible that the orientation program is one that has no real home and no sponsor. The results can be found in the numerous examples contained in this book.

In these days, when there is so much concern about cost-benefit and other financial data to justify expenditures, the loss through ineffective or missing orientation and development programs can readily be calculated. Various government and legal requirements have increased the processing part of the orientation experience, but frequently at the cost of reducing the people contact part of the orientation experience.

When employees enter a new work situation, no matter how many years they have been in the work force, they are faced with cultural shock. If the employee were being sent to a foreign country, the implications would be obvious. Yet it is possible to have cultural shock without ever leaving the United States. Read carefully the many examples given in this book of how employees encounter cultural behavior in a new work situation which is different, unreal, and at times bizarre. That is cultural shock. It can turn a carefully recruited and selected new employee into a loss to the organization.

Orientation is more than giving the new employee a manual to read, and more than making sure that the appropriate papers have been signed. It is a process—a continuing process. In this book the reader will get help in understanding when the process begins, and about the continuing efforts that must be made if the orientation is to be helpful to the individual and to the organization.

There is increased concern about Quality of Work Life, humanizing the work place, and social values. Most of what is written deals with those currently in the work, and in a fixed employment situation. The statistics tell us that there is better than a 25 percent turnover in the work force in any one year. That means that a large number of workers (at all levels) are entering a new place of employment annually. Each of them could benefit from the kinds of orientation and development programs discussed in this book.

At one point in the book, an intriguing question is raised. What about the not-new employee? For some, there never was any orientation. For others, it was so far back in their work experience that they are essentially out-of-date. Should there not also be some kind of "re-orientation"?

The responsibility for orientation should not be placed in the Personnel office, or in the HRD unit. The responsibility rests with the immediate supervisor, who should look to the HRD unit for help in planning, implementing, and following up the orientation program. To be successful, orientation must be a joint effort.

The reader will find that throughout the book, Mr. Shea has helped us recognize that orientation is not an event—it is a process.

Dr. Leonard Nadler
George Washington University

PREFACE

My purpose in this work is to focus attention on the often wasted or diminished productive potential of new employees. Through inept, insensitive, and faulty handling by some supervisors, managers, and personnel specialists, the initial interest and enthusiasm usually held by new employees quickly wither and die. New employees almost always seek a job in the hope of bettering their situation in life. When the job is finally won, the new persons are usually a little nervous but eager, and they deeply want to succeed and contribute what they can to their new organization. They want to make it!

Unfortunately, through indifferent treatment, poor planning, and inadequate training, the spark of hope within new employees often goes out—sometimes never to be rekindled. New employees are an expensive and usually valuable and potentially highly productive human resource. We need to treat each new person as such.

This book is written for all those concerned with employee productivity, with the quality of working life, and with the art of supervision and management. It is of special importance to those people in personnel who are responsible for acquiring, orienting, training, and supporting new employees, for it offers many guides in improving the effectiveness of their work. For people in related fields of economics, sociology, and psychology, and for researchers concerned with development of human potential, *The New Employee* probes a heretofore largely neglected important area of human experience. This book is of vital importance to the supervisor or manager who is actually responsible for employee output, for it offers such supervisors, at all levels, a step-by-step process for improving the way new employees are introduced to the job, integrated into the workgroup, trained and developed, and, most importantly, motivated to produce.

The New Employee will serve as a primary professional reference work for those involved in human resource development or personnel work. Placement specialists, educators, management consultants, and professional trainers can benefit from this book.

This work outlines a systems approach which ensures that the valuable human resource embodied in new employees is utilized to the fullest, to benefit both the individual and the organization. It offers supervisors, managers, and personnel specialists a wide variety of specific techniques for ensuring that the bright promise inherent in new employees is indeed captured by the organization. By return token, the new employees should benefit through greater job satisfaction and an improved quality of life at work.

This book is unique in that it draws on the personal life experiences of over two thousand supervisors, managers, and personnel specialists from industrial firms, government agencies, institutions, and service organizations who contributed their ideas and suggestions. The life cycle of new employees from their earliest perceptions of the organization, through the process of recruitment, selection, hiring, training, placement, and development, to the point where they become mature self-actualizing *regular* employees is traced with abundant insights and recommendations. The slant of the book gives special attention to employees who are new to the workforce, but in general the suggestions apply to any employees new to your organization (and even to some employees who have been on the payroll for years). The content is also applicable to employees who have been transferred to new environments.

The standard findings of human resource researchers and writers such as Abraham Maslow, Frederick Herzberg, Douglas Bray, and Gordon Darkenwald are woven through the text as the thoughts of these people illuminate principles or support contentions made herein. I am particularly indebted in this work to the writings of Dr. Lawrence J. Peter and Raymond Hall (*The Peter Principle*), George M. Prince (*The Practice of Creativity*), Joseph Luft and Harry Ingham for their work on the concept of "The Johari Window," David C. Booker's work on Task Analysis and Training, David McClelland's *The Achieving Society,* Douglas McGregor's *The Human Side of Enterprise,* and especially the work of Robert K. Merton, Robert Rosenthal, and Lenore Jacobson on "The Self-Fulfilling Prophecy."

Throughout this book I have taken some rather unconventional viewpoints and some provocative positions surrounding the vital issue of employee productivity. These positions come from over thirty years of experience as a practicing supervisor manager and executive in private firms, government agencies, and institutions. These ideas have been forged in the crucible of freewheeling seminars and workshops for managers where such notions have been subjected to the critical scrutiny of and debate by practical users of these concepts. Those were the people who had to apply them on the job and who in turn demanded practicality above all else. These are ideas in which I strongly believe. The purpose here is not to convert people to a way of thinking, but to stimulate thought and thereby evoke even better ways of working with new employees in the future.

The broad outlines of the book evolved from presenting conferences and seminars on "Making New Employees Productive" (or similar titles) to personnel people and first-line supervisors. I greatly appreciate the contributions made by these people through small group sharing of ideas and from recitation of their own experiences. Most of the examples in the book are drawn from my own experiences as an employee, a supervisor, a manager, and a trainer.

I appreciate the help of Mirga Massey who typed and edited the original manuscript and who contributed many useful suggestions. Dr. Bradford Shea read and improved many of the early chapters. The personal experiences of my daughter, Laurie Ann Shea, as a new employee triggered the resolve to write this book. *The New Employee* is therefore dedicated to Laurie—a highly productive new employee.

Beltsville, Maryland   G. F. S.
August 1980

CHAPTER 1

THE NEW EMPLOYEE—OPPORTUNITY GAINED OR LOST

The new employee offers an unparalleled opportunity to every organization and to every supervisor and manager. Much of the enthusiasm, creativity, and commitment that so characterizes a new employee is lost through inept hiring practices, poor orientation, and ineffective integration of the employee into the work group. There is much that can be done to capture that human potential and at the same time to open vistas of growth and achievement for a fellow human being. We will never have a better time than now—when the employee is new.

An organization has often been compared to an organism. In our case, the analogy might be extended to include the reality that the people resemble the body's cells. Organisms throughout their lives are constantly replacing cells, whether growing, stabilizing, or declining. A characteristic of aging is that survival messages are not picked up by new cells completely, and eventually the organism withers. If we insure that the new employees are provided with constructive messages, nourished properly, and become an active part of the whole, we might be able to rejuvenate the organization in ways we have not yet learned to restore our bodies. Organizations need not grow old and outdated if we keep a fresh flow of healthy replacements moving in to refresh and revitalize the organism. How to keep the flow of new members healthy and productive is the primary concern of this book.

New employees generally seek and accept employment in your organization in the hopes of bettering their situation. They are alert, interested, eager to please, and at the same time nervous, worried, and perhaps a little scared. They intuitively pick up clues about what is acceptable, the tone or climate of the place, and, for better or worse, the work standards that must be met. It is not uncommon for the supervisor or the organization to communicate contradictory behavior patterns, a sense of indifference to people, and low or sloppy standards of performance.

1

OPPORTUNITIES LOST

Try to remember your first day or preferably your first hours on a new job—especially one you acquired when you were young and new to the work force. Go over in your mind the events that occurred and the feelings and thoughts that you had about those events.

Mercifully, perhaps you can't remember much.

Often, when teaching a seminar on "The New Employee—Orientation and On-the-Job Training," I ask the participants (who are primarily practicing supervisors and managers or personnel staff people) to see if they can identify with the following vignette.

On my first morning I arrived thirty minutes early, gave my name to a receptionist, and waited for an hour and a quarter. After watching various well-dressed young people who "worked" beyond the receptionist's gate, drifting from office to office, drinking coffee and discussing last night's game, I began to get a good feel for what this organization was all about. This was a similar scene to one I witnessed several weeks earlier, when I first came in for an interview, except that then it was 2:30 in the afternoon. Their behavior at least seemed consistent.

Finally that morning a young man came to me, introduced himself, and took me into the plant to meet my supervisor. The supervisor looked at me somewhat blankly at first then muttered, "Yeah! That's right, you're coming in this morning." His distracted gaze and manner told me that no planning had been done. "Uh huh, yeah," he said, "now let's see—use this desk over here—and here, read this procedures manual for a while, it'll get you oriented."

After a couple of hours of trying to make sense out of a lot of procedural nonsense that I had no background for understanding nor anything to tie the facts to, my "hero" returned. I had managed at great effort not to fall asleep or at least not to be obvious about it. However, by then he had thought of something to keep me busy—which took all of the mental acumen of a five-year-old.

By this time in my seminars I'm getting enough head-nodding to recognize that at least half of the group can relate to a similar experience in their own life. What of your own real life experience?

At any rate, I came away from the job that day with several distinct impressions, the accuracy of which I had little opportunity to evaluate.

1. The personnel people didn't do much.

2. My boss considered my presence a necessary nuisance—at least on that day.

3. I apparently wasn't very important in the overall scheme of things.

4. I hadn't learned much (that at least was real).

5. I had met a lot of people in the afternoon and they were all jumbled up in my mind.

6. I would never be able to understand or use that procedures manual effectively. (I didn't even know if the manual was essential to my new job.)

7. I wasn't looking forward to the next day.

At dinner that evening when I was asked about the new job by an assemblage of interested figures (my wife and an assortment of in-laws), feelings of inadequacy flooded over me for I could tell them nothing of significance. Every question put me on the spot because I knew little of the operation and almost nothing about my relationship to the things others were doing. In retrospect, I believe my family soon came to the conclusion, that I had tentatively reached, that my new job didn't amount to much.

The next day I buoyed myself up with the thought that the job must be worth something or they wouldn't be paying me for doing it. Later I discovered that even this happy assumption was not necessarily correct. Fortunately, in time, I came to discover that this particular job did have significance, but only after I had lost much of my original enthusiasm and had acquired some questionable work habits (looking busy and sleeping with my eyes open).

Have you had an experience like this? Though your experience may vary from case to case each with its own missed opportunities or positive events, I find that negative incidents are the rule rather than the exception—especially with younger (and more impressionable) employees.

When I ask my seminar participants to list good experiences and bad experiences they had as a new employee, the negative column is generally twice as long as the positive. This may reflect a tendency to focus on our negative experiences, but those may be the most lasting. We behave according to our perceptions and, if the negative impressions are the ones we remember, it is on those that we will form the basis for our future actions.

The important lesson is that new employees are most often looking for an opportunity, open and eager to learn, nervous and worried, and anxious to do well. We will probably never have a better opportunity to develop productive employees.

HOW THE NEW EMPLOYEE IS TAUGHT

Some supervisors have said that many new employees are, in effect, not taught at all. They are just placed on a job and not given any real training. However, my own belief is that even if only by poor example, indifference, or indirection, such neglected employees are indeed taught.

When new employees see people in an organization goofing off, ignoring their responsibilities, or acting indifferent toward others, the new employees are learning at least something about the organization—they *are* being taught. They may choose to disregard the lesson taught, but they nevertheless witness such situations. This is often where new employees "start to go wrong."

In other situations the supervisor or the organization fails to send any signals at all about key aspects of a new employee's job, such as safety or production. In those cases the employees may need to carry standards over from previous experience or make conclusions of their own. Even if the new employees choose to check out the lack of signals from management (a difficult thing to do tactfully when you are new on the job), they often get indifferent or vague responses.

Many years ago, when attending college, I needed a job desperately in order to support my family and to stay in school. I applied for a job in a meat market on the basis of a referral from the University's placement office.

The department manager asked me if I had worked in a meat market before, to which I replied, "Yes, at the B & B market." Since my total experience at the B & B was helping a friend one afternoon grind hamburger and cube cube steaks, it was fortunate that he asked no further questions. The manager told me to get an apron and get out on the counter. So much for evaluation of experience.

The "counter" was an old-fashioned meat counter about eighty feet long with virtually nothing prepackaged. You faced the customers and filled their orders, weighing and pricing items as you went. I got out "on the counter" as far away from the boss as I could get because I knew next to nothing about meat.

I really didn't know veal from pork when seen in their raw state. Previously, I had only encountered these meats already cooked and served on a plate. Here, before me, were seemingly endless trays of several hundred types of meat—all uncooked and in a wide variety of forms. When the customers began giving their orders I often did not know what they were talking about though I had heard most of the words before. Yet, I was highly motivated. I was scared, but I wanted to do a good job—I needed the job desperately.

I solved my dilemma by asking customers if they would like to pick out their meat. They often gazed at me, first with amazement and then with delight. They would then happily march to the right area of the counter and say, "I'll take that one, that one, and that one," pointing to the specific pieces that appealed to them. In turn, I dutifully gave them "that one, that one, and that one." They recognized at once that I was not the type of butcher that was "a slight-of-hand artist" who would palm off fatty and boney pieces "underneath the good stuff" (as they now do with impunity in prepackaged meats). With me, the customers were in charge and they seemed to get a little giddy over the experience.

Thus, the customers taught me the meat business. Though older workers taught me how to eviscerate a chicken or saw the bone on a pork roast, much of my learning was from indirect teaching by the indifferent behavior of the manager.

This story, however, has a more important moral. My survival technique was so successful that I quickly developed a following. A large number of customers began to ask for me to serve them or they waited until I was free. The boss noted this and gave me a raise because I apparently "had a way with the customers." I was thus rewarded "for giving the store away" since it was up to the other countermen to get rid of the inferior cuts any way they could.

I personally expected to eventually begin behaving as a hocus-pocus magician in making the poor cuts disappear from the counter and magically appear in the customer's package. But at this point, I ran into another dilemma.

While the manager rewarded me for giving the customers what they wanted, and the assistant manager demonstrated the "dirty tricks" of the trade, a retired partner of the firm dropped in occasionally and lectured us on how this market had achieved its reputation and success by offering the customers excellent service, high quality meat, and square dealings.

Since no meat is perfect, I now had the option of behaving whichever way I wanted to, and I could point to one leader or the other as the reason for my behavior. How often does the new employee get conflicting messages from management as to what behavior is preferred?

Though this experience occurred more than twenty years ago, I have never had a clear reading on what the manager would have actually preferred that I do about the fat and gristle. Since my survival and success had been built on exceptional service and high-quality product, I was tempted to ignore the economic considerations put forth by the assistant manager who now felt constrained to get rid of more than his fair share of questionable product.

Could it be that many employees are reacting to mixed, variable, or missing signals and trying to do the best they can? Can it be that many employees, particularly new ones, are being taught directly or indirectly to be nonproductive or counterproductive.

WHERE WE START TO GO WRONG

Management people seem to often take the same attitude as parents who fight in front of children on the notion that they are "too young to notice." Yet everything that happens to a new employee is noted, recorded, and possibly used at some point by that person.

Many things that happen to a new employee may be beyond a supervisor's personal control. For example, if you are the supervisor you may have few ways to control the organization's external image, the behavior of people in the personnel department, or their interactions with the work group. But we usually can *influence* such inputs or counteract the negative effects to some degree at least.

I have seen supervisors effectively confront delays in "processing" the new employee, and plan and manage the integrating of the new employee into the work group in a happy and thoughtful way. Unfortunately, I have also seen people "turned off" by their reception, funneled into dead-end jobs, and taught (quite effectively) that negative behavior pays off. The choice, or at least part of it, is up to us.

New employees are not pieces of inert clay, ready to be molded. They are finely-tuned sensing mechanisms who sample the atmosphere of the organization, record observations about the behavior of other employees, interpret verbal and nonverbal clues about acceptable behaviors from the supervisor, and make conscious and subconscious decisions about how to survive and perhaps prosper in this environment.

The supervisor or staff support personnel who interact with new employees often perceive the new "team member" in a positive light, but they often also have problems in doing what they know is right. New employees are often hired long after the increased workload, which justified adding a person to the organization, has been created. This lag often makes it hard for the supervisor to plan adequately and to think through ways to satisfy new employee needs. When stretched thin, the supervisor with a growing workload often feels overwhelmed.

Additionally, the supervisor may be untrained in the art of delegation and in the mechanisms for analyzing the work and training people to do it. Today many supervisors are trained to supervise in general, but they have had little or no introduction to how to make the most of the opportunities offered by the new employee. The supervisor may be well aware that if she or he does not effectively manage the orientation of the new employee, others will do the task instead—perhaps to the detriment of all concerned. Supervisors want to do an effective job, but may not know how to do it.

If you can examine the process by which employees are currently recruited, hired, inducted, oriented, and trained in your organization, and then think about how you would feel as the process took over a significant segment of your life, you might then get some perspective on the problems faced by new employees. In doing this, however, it is helpful if we do not "discount" the needs of new employees. In general, we have been trained to make less of other people's feelings and needs than they deserve, and later to wonder why we get a negative reaction from them. If we are really sensitive and aware, we will generally come to the conclusion that much can be done to make our organization a healthier, happier place for each human being.

AN ACTION PLAN FOR THE NEW EMPLOYEE

We need to ask ourselves, "What do I want from a new employee?" and "How can I do my best to ensure that new employees are motivated and able to give the organization what we want?" We might then ask, but also check out with the new employee, "What does the new employee want and hope for from the job?" Does the employee want this new organization to be a joyous achieving place or does he or she just "expect and want a job"? We can assume, but we can't know before we check it out. We can't meet expectations and aspirations before they are manifest.

Once we have some idea about what the new employee sees in our job opportunity, we need to deal with a series of external and internal factors before the potential of the individual begins to be used.

The organization image The public view of the organization often precedes the first contact, and it may have a positive or negative effect on the person. Everything from the stereotypes affixed to organizations such as yours (i.e., "In government they can't fire you and you never have to work hard" or "Private industry is a jungle") to the company advertising, its buildings, the service facilities available, and even news reports can impact on the new or potential employee. We need to be able to build on the strengths the organization offers or to counteract a negative image (at least within the confines of your working environment).

Recruitment, hiring, and induction Impressions of the pace of the organization, the quality of its work standards, how it views and treats people, and how flexible it is in meeting special human needs cast a long shadow before the organization. Whether this shadow is seen as cooling and refreshing or as gloomy and threatening is largely determined by those who plan and manage such affairs.

Unfortunately, in large firms or agencies much of this work is done by others than those who will later be responsible for the new employee's productivity. Whether these earlier things are done well or poorly often largely determines the primary impact on the new employee. Whether the new person's supervisor can build on a positive impression or must undo a negative one influences how much energy and enthusiasm that supervisor has for the job.

Orientation and on-the-job training Despite how much prior damage has been done to the perceptions of the new employee inside or outside the organization, the supervisor has an opportunity to recoup the losses by effective employee orientation and on-the-job training.

Sad to say, orientation often is left to others outside the supervisor's workgroup. "Company Orientation" often consists of a whirlwind faculties tour and an introduction to some eighty-seven people who are important. On-the-job training often means "no training" and the employee is left to "pick up things" as they come along. What this overwhelmed and baffled employee is sure of is that "I'll never get on top of this job."

Integration into the workgroup Workgroup integration is also often handled badly. New employees are often quickly introduced to the other employees and then left to their own devices for establishing relationships with the others. Feelings of uncertainty, isolation, and fear are quite common as they struggle for acceptance and belonging.

In order to adapt, the employees try to absorb group norms, establish an identity, and gain some status in the workgroup. It seems that as often as not, these goals are achieved by searching for the lowest common denominator. The group, on the other hand, sets standards (high or low), influences behavior, and metes out punishments and rewards according to the degree to which new employees conform. One might well wonder whether or not a supervisor's influence on new employees is primary or secondary.

Motivation and employee development The greatest opportunity for motivation and employee development is cast in the first few hours of employment. If the employees can do something that they can sink their teeth into, if they can learn something that they can tell their friends at home (and thereby enhance their status), if they can earn a pat on the back, if they can gain a sense of accomplishment in some small way, they will be off on the right foot.

These first impressions of themselves, the organization, and the supervisor, are vital for long-term growth and development. "As the twig is bent so grows the tree."

WHAT CAN I DO?

The answer to this question depends a great deal upon our job. If we are a recruiter, a supervisor, or a trainer, we can do our job well. If we write copy for recruitment ads, present formal organization-wide programs, or simply receive people when they come to apply for a job, we can do a good job.

Doing a good job in all of these cases means being sensitive and aware of the needs of new employees, and to provide innovative and effective ways for them to meet their needs so that they can and will meet the organization's needs as time goes on. If we maintain high standards of professionalism, treat people considerately and fairly, and plan and manage our jobs well, we can do much to encourage new employees to be productive.

Fortunately in addition to the negative stories I've mentioned earlier, I've also been treated well by some supervisors and organizations.

I've seen advertising copy that presented clear and honest statements. I've been given realistic and fair job standards. I've been treated courteously and efficiently with little waiting. I've been introduced to my job and other workgroup members on a planned and effective basis. I've been truthfully counseled about opportunities and job requirements, and I've been made to feel a part of a winning team. I can guarantee that those supervisors and those organizations got a good return on their small *extra* investment in me as a new employee. This latter approach is what this book is all about.

This book offers practical, tried, and proven methods for developing productive new employees. It also strives to encourage your creativity in designing effective ingenious ways to increase productivity in new employees.

ONE MORE QUESTION!

When do new employees become old employees? New employees start to become old employees when they fit into the environment for better or worse. When they start influencing newcomers and passing on good behaviors or poor, we often begin to recognize the aging process. When the employees begin to be set in their ways, we no longer have new employees. Perhaps if we do our job well, that day may never come. Perhaps we can keep their perspective on the job as sharp and as fresh as on that very first morning.

STUDY QUESTIONS

1. List at least three reasons why it is particularly important to plan and organize for the arrival of a new employee on his or her first day of work.

2. Try to recall some of the negative experiences you encountered your first day on a job.

3. Make a quick list of good experiences and bad experiences you've had in entering on a job. Which list is longer? Why?

4. List some of the indirect learning experiences you had when working as a new employee, where the lesson taught was probably different than the one management assumed was being taught.

5. Identify some of the coping mechanisms (ways of surviving) in a job used when you were a new employee, or some coping mechanisms you've seen others use. Were they successful in maintaining employment?

6. Think of the new employees you've been responsible for in one way or another. Have they been taught negative or unproductive behavior by anyone in the organization? Expressions such as, "They do it over there," or "Practice what you preach" often reflect the reality that the employee has been ill taught through the examples of others.

7. In developing an action plan for a new employee, what questions should we ask ourselves?

8. Name five critical internal and external factors affecting the new employee action plan.

9. What can I do? Make a list of contributions you can make in your job to the successful acquisition, orientation, integration, and training of a new employee.

CHAPTER 2

THE PRODUCTIVITY CRUNCH

We should all be concerned about the future because we have to spend the rest of our lives there. (Charles F. Kettering, from *Seeds For Thought*.)

We all have a stake in productivity—short term and long term. Productivity influences the level of our economic well-being, the rising or falling rate of inflation, and the quality and effectiveness of the services we receive in our consumer-oriented society. The new employee, if properly managed and supported, can do much to increase our society's overall productivity.

Webster defines productivity as "the ability or capacity to produce; the abundance or richness of output; the physical output per unit of productive effort." Further, the dictionary specifically defines productivity as "the ability of land to produce a given yield of a particular crop; the degree of effectiveness of industrial management in utilizing the facilities for production; esp. the effectiveness in utilizing labor and equipment." Based on these statements, it would not be too far afield to include the "output of service" per unit of time and other resources expended by personnel in government agencies, institutions, and service firms. If we can translate people, equipment, facilities, and other resources into units of money, we can state that productivity is what we hope we are getting for our money expended.

In more recent times we have begun to consider measuring quality as well as quantity in evaluating productivity. This is of particular concern as we reach a high level of material affluence and become increasingly concerned with the quality of life. Quality and the effectiveness of our output is also of prime concern as a higher proportion of our transactions with others become service-oriented in such areas as health, personal care, and regulation.

WHAT DIFFERENCE DOES IT MAKE?

In our *almost* "post-industrial" society the work force is increasingly changing from one of "production workers" (be they farm or factory) to one of service personnel (maintenance, research, administration, etc.). These service workers are also likely to be performing tasks that cannot be measured nor evaluated easily. The future therefore becomes a large question mark, and it is on the future that today's new employee will have the greatest impact. "What are we getting for our money?" is increasingly the big question.

Some economists claim we are getting less and less for our money today. They produce figures to show that traditional service jobs have made lower productivity gains than manufacturing jobs. For the decade ending in 1977, U.S. productivity increased overall by 1.6 percent annually, while laundry and cleaning services workers gained only 0.8 percent. Similarly, motel and hotel workers' productivity gained only 0.9 percent. In 1978, while the U.S. growth in productivity was less than 1 percent, manufacturing showed productivity gains of 2.7 percent, thereby presumably fingering service workers as the culprits in our productivity decline.

However, even in manufacturing, the trend is not too clear. Despite its 1978 showing, manufacturing, which had been averaging a 2.7 percent annual productivity gain from 1947 to 1966, slipped to an average of 1.9 percent between 1973 and 1978. The most significant fact is that there has been a great boom in service-producing jobs in the last thirty years. In three decades, service jobs have jumped 120 percent as against 30 percent for manufacturing. Today, 60 percent of all working Americans are employed in service jobs.

The gap between manufacturing and service employment is getting larger. Growth in manufacturing jobs has largely stabilized, while private services are growing faster than ever. Department of Labor figures indicate that over 85 percent of all job increases in the 1970s have been in the service industries. Today and in the coming years, young people will find their most abundant job opportunities in the service industries.

Even more startling is that the greatest part of the millions of service jobs that have been created since World War II have not been counted in the productivity figures. This is because the government's official productivity figures only reflect the private sector of our economy. The government (which now accounts for 16 percent of all nonfarm jobs) and nonprofit fields such as education and health care are not counted in most official figures. Standard productivity measures are not very helpful in calculating whether government and nonprofit service organizations improve life or degrade it. It is against this background of uncertainty that questions of productivity or service improvements are argued.

Yet today there is a public "hue and cry" arising over productivity losses. The effect of lowered productivity, *at least as it is perceived,* is seen in the rising costs of government, services, and goods. This has led the public to experiment with untested remedies and ill-considered emotional backlash tactics such as Proposition 13. Yet, when inflation soars almost uncontrollably, people seek desperate remedies. When our material standard of living seems to be declining, when services are delayed or bungled, when we get inadequate and incompetent responses from professionals and government alike, people sometimes turn nasty and do damaging things. They at least lose faith.

The question reduces itself to: Do we have any responsibility to try to make new employees as productive as possible? The answer, if we seek an improved quality of life in our society, is "yes."

WHAT CAN I DO?

Is the responsibility of attempting to make new employees as productive as possible an individual and/or a group responsibility? When it comes down to it, we can ask ourselves, "What do I want from myself, from my job, and from society? How can I do my part?" Of all the ways we can take a personal hand in our future, few opportunities offer as much potential for productiviity increase qualitatively and quantitatively as the new employee.

Whether tax dollars are wasted by indifference, excessive socializing, or make-work projects in the future, will be greatly influenced by the way new employees are trained to function today. Whether we encounter insulting service workers, unmotivated sales personnel, or incompetent performance in any area, will often depend upon the quality of supervision and the degree to which supervisors motivate new employees and imbue them with high standards.

I remember an old German anecdote about a ship's captain who called down into the hold of a ship asking, "Max, what are you doing?" "Nothing," came the answer. The next question was directed to Franz. "Franz, what are you doing?" "I'm helping Max," came the reply. Sometimes it seems that our entire work force is helping Max. Though we really know better, we all have our moments of frustration. The great question is where did Franz and Max learn their work habits and when? Perhaps we are the victims of inflation and public resentment because we fail to do our *full* job and fail to ask the *unthinkable question.*

The unthinkable question for many supervisors, staff personnel, and managers at all levels (particularly in service and support areas) is simply: *Is the new employee really needed?*

This leads to a whole series of subordinate questions. What would happen if the new employee did not come to work for the organization? Would it make any real difference? Are we just filling a job slot or are we getting a *real* job done? What, if anything, would happen if the job we were filling were abolished? Granted that if the new employee were not hired and brought aboard, certain chores would not get done, but would it really matter if they didn't? The answer in a surprising number of cases would be "no!"

A story is told of a captain in Pharaoh's army who was in charge of one thousand slaves who were harnessed to a great block of stone. Their job was to haul the stone up a ramp to a pyramid. Part way up the ramp the group stopped and seemed unable to move the block further. The story goes that the captain then executed every other slave. The remaining slaves got the block to the top.

Much as we might deplore the captain's management techniques and system of motivation, it demonstrates that we seldom know what we can do until we have to do it.

Supervisors frequently request additional employees based on the amount of work to be done without ever asking what, if anything, would happen if some of that work didn't get done. How do we really know if the work waiting to be done really contributes *value* to the organization? This question is largely unthinkable because we seem to automatically assume that if work is waiting to be done, it *has* to be done.

A prime example of work that was of questionable value occurred years ago when I was a new civilian employee of the Air Force working as a Documents Control Officer. The work of my unit was to process incoming classified and unclassified documents and to file them according to their related countries. I was new to the security system and very concerned to compromise no classified matter. I had heard about an incident where maintenance workers discovered a secret document in the elevator shaft, and the FBI and other security agents were crawling all over the place to identify and punish the person responsible.

I had been on the job about ten days when an assistant and I went to the security vault to select the next batches of documents for processing. We laid the packages of documents out on the floor in sequence only to find to our horror that some 80,000 secret documents were missing.

If the FBI had been upset about one document, what would they do to me for losing 80,000? After checking and rechecking, I finally decided to throw myself on the mercy of my boss. In the meantime some of my panic had subsided because I had been able to talk to a security officer who had some film stored in the vault. That person said it was possible that some of our documents had been destroyed inadvertently when they had burned some film.

To my amazement my boss took the whole affair quite calmly. He simply asked if we might be able to get the other security officer to state in writing that some of our documents were burned along with their film. The person did this, and we merely attached a list of the missing items to the statement and filed it. The crisis was over and I could breathe again.

However, the real answer to the tranquility displayed by my boss was to emerge slowly. I discovered that the missing documents were called "coal mine" reports. These reports came in batches of 200 each—two copies of each document, sequenced by number. They were then separated. One copy was filed and the other copy was listed on the "burn sheet" for destruction. Once opened, each document had to be listed separately since the package had been disturbed. When the documents were received, only the first and last document in the package had to be listed. This "burn" procedure required a lot of typing and overloaded our unit.

The crisis came some weeks later when the units which used these reports requested a substantial increase in staff based on an enormous backlog of unprocessed reports. I also asked for another typist. The manager was most upset because the staff requests from the units would have doubled their personnel.

Slowly the light dawned. My boss knew that these reports were virtually worthless, and, while modest staff increases could be explained, in no way could he justify doubling his number.

I then examined the "coal mine" reports. They were reports by prisoners of war in the USSR during World War II who had been assigned to work at a saw mill or salt mine in some remote part of the USSR. The job of our organization was to identify mapable features for aeronautical charts and provide coordinates for those features. The "coal mine" reports gave *no mapable features.*

Earlier I had requested that our liaison at the Pentagon secure only one copy of each report rather than two, but such a suggestion was received with horror. I was told, "If we change the system, we might not get any!" I didn't see the sense of this, but I went along with it until I realized that if we hadn't gotten any it wouldn't have made any difference except for a substantial reduction in workload.

After that, I simply listed two sets of documents by packaged serial number on the "burn roster" and turned them over to the security officer to dispose of them. Each day we hauled out mail sacks full of useless documents until our files were nearly bare. We did this under the very noses of those who were dreaming of unbounded empires that they would someday rule. In about three months we had burned about 250,000 documents. The backlog was gone and we were easily able to provide service on those documents which had value.

The empire builders didn't even know that their empires had vanished until I had published a short story about the events. By then I was long gone! If we had not disposed of those worthless documents I'm sure some poor clerk would be processing them to this day. I also suspect that those documents which were already in the files at the time I arrived are still there.

How did this come about in the first place? I suspect that someone made the decision that all POW's returning from the USSR had to be interviewed. Accordingly, records had to be made and filed. Since something of value might occasionally crop up, *all* records had to be kept. Eventually, copies crept into our system because somebody either didn't know their job or wanted a backlog for some ulterior purpose. At any rate, I'm sure my unit saved the country quite a bit of money at no loss in value. Later, but several years overdue, the agency abolished that whole operation.

Though this may be an extreme (though true) example, a lot of people in government and industry would be shocked and indignant if anyone suggested that anything they were doing was unnecessary.

How do we actually know how many people we need? Managers and supervisors at many levels are often not clued into the plans, goals, and objectives of the organization. They are simply assigned projects or tasks and expected to perform them without question. Is it any surprise that no one asks, "Does this work really need to be done?" More often we just assume that the work we are processing needs to be done.

There is a great need in all organizations for some form of a Management by Objectives program that works. We need to increasingly focus on the goals and purposes of the organization as it exists in a changing world. As new needs evolve, we all should focus on what my job or my organization unit contributes to achieving those goals.

It is common for supervisors who sense that their subordinates are overloaded to think in terms of adding employees. However, seldom does the supervisor look for ways to stretch the existing labor force or budget. Few are familiar with work simplification and methods improvement techniques. Few can analyze work flow effectively. Few can do an effective job of employee load forecasting. Until these and related human resource analysis techniques are used more widely and more effectively, we may not be able to answer truthfully, "How many people do I need?"

The table of organization is not cast in concrete, but neither is it a sponge to sop up all loose productivity. Because this book is focused on the new employee, we will not deal at length with productivity improvement techniques (such as employee load forecasting), but only mention them here to spur thinking about "the unthinkable question." Have we ever tried to stretch our available people power in order to get the job done? I have seen where stretching became a positive motivation because it gave the people a chance to show what they can do.

One last aspect of "the unthinkable question" remains. Would you be punished *in any way* if you did not fill a job slot? The chances are good that the answer would be in the affirmative. The statement, "If I don't fill the job slot I'll lose it" strikes sympathetic fears in the heart of every bureaucrat whether he or she is employed in private industry, a nonprofit organization, or a government agency. The fear of getting caught short of people at a later date is only part of the problem. The tendency of personnel departments to rate employees' job levels according to how many people they supervise, the complexity of their work, and the level of their job classification provides a positive incentive to ignore productivity and "go with the numbers." Since your boss, his or her boss, and so on up the ladder also depends on those numbers, you may indeed be punished (and not only by the system) if you do not maintain the size and scope of your empire. This problem exists in and out of government.

It not only takes courage to opt for productivity over numbers, the question before each individual is: "Can I afford to put group (public) interest ahead of my own—especially since my sacrifice would probably not change the outcome?" The incentives for numbers simply may be too high.

Is it any wonder then that when a new employee is hired the supervisor may not know what to do with the person? Could this lead to indifference as to how employees are oriented and trained? We need incentives for management that are not just based on numbers.

PRODUCTIVITY AND THE NEW EMPLOYEE

Whether or not we are playing a shell game with the new employee (a question only you can answer), there are a number of things that we can do that offer hope for increased productivity. We will explore many of those ideas in this book. In many ways, though, this subject will never be completed for there will always be new and innovative ways to make the new employee productive.

People start a new job with many options. They can choose between the many models of behavior which they will emulate and they can absorb or reject various standards of behavior. They can only choose, however, if the options are open and made known to them. I remember hearing a supervisor say to a new employee, "All you have to do around here is be sure that you show up on time everyday." Is it any wonder that this organization had a high turnover rate along with low productivity? We can all do better than that!

STUDY QUESTIONS

1. How does the dictionary define productivity? Develop your own definition—one that suits you and your situation. The definition should be simple enough to keep clearly in your mind as you go about your job.

2. In what ways is the work force changing in our *almost* "post-industrial society"?

3. How do increases in service workers compare to those in manufacturing? What are the implications of these changes for the future?

4. How does the new employee affect this question of productivity and the quality of life?

5. What is "the unthinkable question"? What implications would a thorough use of the unthinkable question have on the question of productivity and the quality of life?

6. How does a workable "Management by Objectives" system relate to deciding if certain work really is necessary?

7. Name four human resource analysis techniques that, if applied, would help you decide how many people you need.

8. List two disincentives for asking the unthinkable question.

CHAPTER 3

ORGANIZATION
AND IMAGE—FIRST
IMPRESSIONS

How do new employees view their new organization? Surprisingly, the answer
may lie in impressions made years, even decades, earlier.

EARLY PERCEPTIONS

People do not have to be very old before they start picking up comments from
their elders about the federal or local government, or how people are treated in
a hospital, or thoughts concerning the nature of private industry or "factory
work." If a family has a tradition of being school teachers or working for the
county, attitudes, opinions, and perceptions tend to float through the family
freely. If a particular firm, or occupation, or institution dominates the local
economy (a company town, a mining town, or a college town), people will acquire a great deal of subjective data about local feelings and perceptions about
"that work" or "that organization."

A group of us young raw recruits were on a drill field in Mississippi one
day when one of us made a mistake. "How long have you been in this man's
Army, soldier?" asked the drill sergeant in sarcastic rhetoric. "All my life!"
replied the recruit without humor.

He had indeed been born in an Army hospital and grew up on one or another military base until the day of his enlistment. The Army had never been
far from his consciousness. Then, as a new recruit, he was still in the Army he
had been in all of his life. For once the sergeant did not have a rejoinder, and
he set out again to put us through our paces.

Those who apply to a particular organization for employment or those
who fail to apply have often been influenced by other people's perceptions of
that organization. People frequently enter an organization with preconceived
notions about how hard they will be expected to work, how much they'll be expected to produce, and how much opportunity they'll have for advancement.
Expressions such as: "You'll never make much money but you'll always have

19

a job," "I can retire after twenty years," "That's a hot organization," or "The sky's the limit with that outfit" reflect preconceived expectations. For staff personnel or the supervisor interested in ensuring that a new employee is productive, this past conditioning can be of great importance.

Early impressions are often the more lasting ones. It is not uncommon to hear people late in life recite their early views on organizations and vividly remember how hard they sought employment with a given organization or how hard they fought to escape a destiny of lifetime employment with a given mine or mill. Literature is replete with examples of struggle to enter or avoid employment of certain types.

I grew up in a mill town and, from a very early age, I was determined—at any cost—to avoid what I perceived as a lifetime of drudgery in those grim dirty steel mills and factories. Given my early economic circumstances, the prevalence of factory work in my area, and my lack of special talents, factory work seemed inevitable. The only choice seemed to be between dirty factories and relatively clean ones—and the dirty ones seemed most likely because generations of people with talents equal to mine had wound up there.

The specter of gaunt, grey, windowless, silent factories also engraved an impression on my mind during the 1930s. It seemed private industry could not be trusted to provide reliable employment in periods of economic downturn. I wanted more for my family than sporadic employment and the humiliation and degradation of being unable to meet my obligations. Government service, on the other hand, offered respectability, permanence, and challenge. As soon as I finished college I left a job in a steel mill and took a job with the federal government. The roots of that decision can be traced to impressions made upon me when I was about seven years old.

Ironically I found the work in the government stimulating, but the environment was stifling. Later I worked in an electronics firm as a production engineer and found factories, in the advanced technology fields at least, to be challenging and exciting. Circumstance and curiosity had shown me both sides of the coin, but for many people career expectations and anticipated employment patterns greatly influence where they will end up, what they'll be doing, and how well they'll be doing it.

It is my suggestion that you take a minute to reflect on what brought you to your current position and to what degree preconceived notions and perceptions entered into the choices you made. Might not the same kind of considerations be true for others?

Whether these early perceptions are an asset or a liability to the supervisor or staff specialist responsible for dealing with a new employee, they are likely to have a bearing on the person's personal productivity. None of these factors or attitudes are unchangeable, but they may need to be brought out into the open and discussed fully when they are likely to affect expectations or performance. The organization's representatives need to clearly communicate their expectations and then watch for verbal and nonverbal clues to see if there is a reasonable match with the perspective employee's expectations. Often, if people merely have a chance to talk out their early expectations, they can resolve a problem themselves, if one existed, or reinforce their enthusiasm for the organization if they had positive expectations

THE ORGANIZATION IMAGE

You may be a part of such a small organization (a neighborhood jewelry store or a local print shop, etc.), that has little in the way of an organization image except for the way you appear in the eyes of people passing by. Yet people might still think of the company as part of "private enterprise," and your organization gains or loses from the mystique associated with those two words. In many cases, people may apply for employment at your establishment only because you are convenient, or because they saw a sign in your window, or because they heard of the job through friends. Even in those cases, the image you project in the local community can have a bearing on the performance of the new employee. Gossip, your reputation for fair dealing, and the amount of apparent turnover can alter people's perceptions of the business.

In larger organizations, the problem is infinitely more complex. People join your organization for their own purposes, not yours. They are trying to meet their needs first. The organization's needs come second, and then only in order to ensure that their own needs get met on a continuing basis.

Talk about loyalty to the organization is largely nonsense. Such loyalty, if it exists at all, develops after a long and mutually satisfying relationship. Loyalty has to be earned. It is not inherent in the relationship. And, to be effective, loyalty has to be truly a two-way street. People identify best with organizations that treat them well, offer reasonable continuity, satisfy their social and belonging needs, enhance their self-respect, and offer opportunities for growth and development. People generally also like to be identified with an organization that offers them some hope of pride and some esteem in the eyes of others.

Think of your own feelings about your present or past employers on that account.

Listed below are some factors which affect an organization's image. You could probably add more items based on your personal experience.

1. How many people are in the organization?

2. What is the economic impact of the organization on the local community? Does it dominate or is it prominent?

3. What type of press coverage has the organization gotten?

    a. Its labor relations image?

    b. Its reputation for honesty and fair dealings?

      c. Its impact on environmental matters (if any)?

      d. Its history of strikes and labor disputes?

4. What type of advertising if any does it do? Locally or nationally?

5. Are its products or services well respected?

6. To what degree does it or its top management get involved in community affairs?

7. Through what media (TV, newspapers, magazines, etc.) are people most likely to first learn about the organization?

Interesting as these insights might be, much of the image of the organizational unit you belong to may be formed in response to the image of the larger organization, such as with a multinational corporation. The classification of organizations to which your company or institution may belong could also influence its image. Your organization may also be so small that it does not significantly impact on anyone but its customers or the people it serves. The principal concern about organization image is that it tends to create stereotypes, and these stereotypes *may* need to be dealt with if the new employee is to maximize productivity. We are looking here mainly for mismatches between the organization's needs and the new employee's expectations about what type of behavior or productivity is expected in the new job. If the new employee anticipates easy-going socialization to fill most of the day, then that person might need to be disabused of the idea rapidly. Other types of mismatches can be equally detrimental and may need to be explored at the time of hiring or, if it is too late for that, as early as possible in the relationship.

Organizational Impact

When an organization is large enough to impact on people in the community fairly often or with individuals on an almost daily basis, as with some utilities or government agencies, the impact is often created by the lowest-level employees in the organization. No amount of public relations chatter can compensate for the snippy clerk or the drunken service employee who calls at your home.

Often the real image of the organization, as far as the consumer, client, or citizen is concerned, may be formed by the lowest paid, most obvious employee. A work crew in the neighborhood using foul language, engaging in horseplay, and behaving dangerously can create a lasting impact on any citizen. The state, city, or county highway department may be judged more severely for potholes in the road than for publicity related to bribe taking in the organization. People often tend to judge the whole organization by the behavior of an inefficient flagman or flagwoman who is slowing down traffic rather than by the miles of well maintained roads. The same is true with service people who have poor telephone manners.

I have often been impressed by the reality that organizations sometimes pay the least to those people who contact the public the most. They also frequently provide the least real training to those people, and experience the greatest turnover in those jobs. This is certainly not always the case, but it does happen. Store clerks are usually taught to run a cash register, but often they are not taught how to interact effectively with an irate customer.

Some organizations receive such negative publicity that even the employees disassociate themselves with the company. For example, some maintenance crews for a major sewer and water utility told homeowners that they were from the gas company since the symbol on their truck was ambiguous.

Identification with a proud and respected organization can scarcely help but promote productivity. No one gets much kick out of being on a losing team.

RECRUITMENT AND SELECTION PROCESSES
AFFECT EMPLOYEE EXPECTATIONS

Every recruiter is a salesperson for the organization in more ways than one. Not only are they trying to attract prospective employees but their whole demeanor conveys impressions about the organization they represent. Do they schedule appointments effectively and keep them? Do they conduct brief effective interviews? Do they adhere closely to a schedule or do they show flexibility and creativity when faced with problems? Every recruiter should, insofar as possible, serve as a microcosm of the total organization, reflecting its values, its personality, and its methods of doing business.

I have seen poorly trained company recruiters at colleges selling their organization to graduating seniors by extravagant claims that could never be met. I wonder if their management followed up on the turnover statistics related to these high pressure jobs. Just when such recruits might begin to become productive in the organization, the exodus of the disillusioned would begin.

Though initial recruitment is usually a staff function, supervisors may get involved at least in creating the job specifications. It seems that supervisors and personnel people are often in cahoots in overspecifying job requirements—sometimes to the point where, if they got the person they sought, that person would soon become bored with the job and leave. Overspecification can be seen as a way of reducing the chance for error, but it often achieves just the opposite. Sometimes credentialism (specifying college, degrees, etc.) almost guarantees failure because the job does not match the requirements and consequently cannot meet the recruit's expectations.

For recruitment purposes, an effective job specification should begin with a detailed analysis of the tasks to be done, and the Knowledge, Skills, Abilities, and Decisions (KSADs) that those tasks require. In later chapters we will deal with the mechanism of such a determination, but, in the meantime, personnel people and supervisors will continue to list requirements unrelated to the actual job to be performed and no one will be the wiser. Oddly enough, people in decision-making positions in many organizations fail to recognize that if academic degrees are required for a job, the person filling the position expects to be able to use that knowledge and will be disappointed in a job that does not really require such know-how.

The Supreme Court has ruled that testing for jobs will be nondiscriminatory and job-related, but even today this injunction is often violated. Tests have long been a way of overspecifying job requirements, and this overspecification often leads to boredom and diffident behavior.

Certainly there are many competent recruiters and many realistic supervisors who work hand in hand to achieve success, but there are also many who just don't make it. In my gloomier moments, I stand convinced that if an old literary device could actually be played out in real life the end result would be disaster. We are all familiar with the plot where the caliph of Bagdad or some historic king changes into rags and wanders through the kingdom to see how well his laws and generosity are actually carried out. In the end, all turns out well.

Today, I'm afraid that story would not have a happy ending. If Henry Ford, or Alfred P. Sloan, or any other great captain of American industry were to return to this earth to work in their enterprise to see how their business fared, they would never get through the front door. Personnel would have no slot labeled "entrepreneur." Creativity, enterprise, hard work, and ingenuity do not show up well on resumes. It sometimes seems that even the shadow of real productivity is screened out of many organizations. I wonder how many people started their own enterprise because they did not fit other people's precast assembly-line molds.

Realistic job specifications and effective job matching are the keys to solid recruitment. The individual supervisor must determine who is most suitable since only the supervisor is responsible for productivity and only the supervisor can determine how much authority for decision making the new employee will be allowed. Again we see that employees' perceptions of what the work will be like are often cast much earlier than their appearance on the job. The organization that sets the employee up for disappointments is asking for problems.

By the time people appear at the door of an organization to search for work, they often have their concepts and notions about the organization pretty well formed. The supervisor's job at this point is to detect such attitudes and to undo the negative perceptions and to reinforce the positive attitudes—no small job to say the least.

In a broader sense we need to decide what each of us can do to project a positive organizational image and counter any negative aspects. Mainly this will come about only through deeds, large and small.

STUDY QUESTIONS

1. Think back to your first or second regular job. List the impressions, feelings, and knowledge you had about that organization before you began your first contact with that organization. How did you first hear about the organization? What did you perceive that the organization offered you that influenced you to make contact?

2. How did such impressions, knowledge, and feelings affect how you made contact with the organization and the approach you used?

3. You probably had a mixture of feelings and thoughts about that organization. List the positive factors and negative factors as they appeared to you at that time.

4. Where did you gain those positive or negative feelings you experienced before you began work? Was it from family? friends? counselors? general knowledge in your neighborhood? gossip among your peers?

5. What was your primary motive for approaching that organization? Was it just to have income or were the reasons more complex?

6. What types of personal needs did you *expect* that organization to fill? What needs did you *hope* that organization would fill?

7. Think of some organizations that you would have or did avoid applying to because of negative impressions you held about that organization. What were these impressions and how could they have been avoided?

8. Try to visualize what impressions your current organization is likely to be having on prospective employees. List positive and negative aspects of that image as they are likely to affect recruitment, selection, and employee performance. How can the organization build on its strengths and overcome its weaknesses?

9. Are there likely to be mismatches between the new employee's perception of what working will be like in your organization and the expectations of management for that employee? How serious is the mismatch likely to be? How can we bring the new or prospective employee closer to realistic expectations?

10. In the eyes of the customer or the public, who is making the greatest and most lasting impression on them as far as your organization is concerned?

CHAPTER 4

RECRUITMENT AND SELECTION

The director of a large branch of a national service organization has hired six top-notch, bright, aggressive young executive trainees as his assistant in the last eight years. He spent weeks searching each of them out, going through dozens of applicants and interviewing exhaustively to ensure that he found someone with initiative and energy, someone who truly represented the ideal of the young American executive on the way up. All have quit in frustration and disgust.

This man was playing a psychological game. (Games in this context are not fun games. They are negative pay-off subconscious manipulations that reinforce the game players' negative feelings about themselves, another person, or everyone in general.) To each candidate, the director offered opportunities to grow and develop, a chance to show initiative and speedy movement up in the organization. As work began, however, each new person soon discovered a system of repressive regulations, a boss who kept each of them working on routine projects, and a great reluctance on the part of the director to relinquish any authority or approve any decisions made by his new assistant. All six of the new employees had been "bear-trapped."

The "bear-trapper" sucks a person in with promises or come-ons which have real potential, but when the victim is within the cage, the bear-trapper reneges on all promises.

When hiring workers, the bear-trapper sends messages of *just trust me.* Bear-trappers appear to be nice people who are attentive, polite, friendly, and

---

Note: The purpose of this chapter is not to teach good recruitment and selection procedures and techniques. There are many good sources of information on those subjects already available. Here I wish to focus on the implications of those subjects on the productivity of the new employee, and to deal with more fundamental issues about how to match the job and the person through the recruitment and selection process.

often very confidential. But most of all, bear-trappers make promises ("the bait") which are either explicit or implied:

"You'll only be on this job for a little while."

"You've got a great future here."

"You'll get a chance to show what you can do."

"In three months you'll get a raise."

"You'll have a chance to work on your own research projects."

"We offer lots of opportunities for promotion."

When the trap has fallen, the smiling interviewer shrugs and says, "That's the way the ball bounces," as though to say, "What do you expect from me?"

Eventually the employee finds that people seem to have forgotten the promises, or that the internal organization realities are not as described and no amount of reminding does any good.

In larger organizations the bear-trapper is often not the one who is expected to deliver on the promises, though the bear-trapper is almost never confronted by those who *are* expected to deliver. This can lead to the conclusion that the whole organization is a bear-trapping conspiracy, and often it is—though perhaps not consciously.

Years ago I attended a convention for Electronic and Electrical Engineers in New York, partly to pick up new equipment ideas for some production problems we were having. I also went because the convention served as a job mart, and I was looking for an escape from a division of a major producer of equipment for the Industrial Controls field. I had gone to work for the division when it was an independent research and development organization. Shortly thereafter it was acquired by a larger firm. Yet, for two years it had kept its promises, offered great growth potential, and had been generous in its rewards. I was looking again for that type of place because recently a new general manager had turned the place into a concentration camp. He squelched initiative and made some decisions I was convinced would eventually destroy us.

At the convention, I picked up one of those career opportunities books where firms list display ads for recruitment purposes. I had read several dozen large ads and must have been getting jaded when all of a sudden my eyes landed on one that brought me fully alert. As I avidly skimmed the columns, I was concluding that this is my kind of place. It offered everything I wanted: opportunity, challenge, rewards, a great location, high salaries—and then I reached the bottom. It was my present employer.

I had been aware of the power, the effectiveness, and the occasional outright dishonesty of advertising copy, but never had I seen its naked might used so forcefully. To describe my dungeon in such sparkling terms stunned me. I have never fully trusted advertising copywriters since.

Was the company bear-trapping? Yes, I believe so. Though the ad probably reflected the general manager's image of his division, and the ad writer had probably never been inside the facility, it was a type of subconscious bear-trapping since the promises made were not able to match existing reality. That is the real danger in bear-trapping. The person baiting the trap is not assessing the long-term consequences of the deception, or worse, not recognizing the deception by not checking out the reality of the promises against what actually happens in the organization. The chances are good that sometime in your life or career you, too, have been bear-trapped.

Why does bear-trapping occur? Primarily it occurs because the recruiter (whether a supervisor, the advertising manager, or an actual field recruiter) fails to assess the long-term consequences of bear-trapping. Recruiters of all types are frequently faced with an immediate need to fill a slot or meet a quota. They buy now and pay later. Even those who are recruiting to meet the organization's long-term needs, such as management trainees, research interns, or high-level executives, paint false and misleading pictures of organization reality—half fantasy and half hope.

THE RUINATION OF THE NEW EMPLOYEE

When a person joins an organization, the act usually involves considerable personal, financial, and social investment. These commitments should not be considered lightly by the organization.

Usually new recruits have accepted to work for a given income, perhaps even a lower salary, with prospects for improvement. They often hope for opportunity and eventually greater gain. Often they move to a new location, thereby cutting themselves off from family, friends, and the network of information sources previously available to them. They have put their personal social status on the line—and have probably relayed those organizational promises to their family and friends. They have agreed to commit at least a portion of their working lives to the new organization. They have accepted the risks of failure and disappointment that a new job entails. They will experience the discomfort of adjusting to new people, new surroundings, and new work methods. They will, for a while at least, limit their options of undoing the employment agreement and going elsewhere.

When the new employees find themselves caged and the bait withdrawn, is it any surprise that they turn hostile?

Often the new employee has invested so much in the new job that withdrawal is not considered feasible, at least for the present. When this is the case, the real tragedy begins to unfold. If the new employee is fool enough to keep insisting that an individual or the organization live up to its agreements, the bear-trapper begins to perceive the new employee as a nuisance, a complainer, a boor. Subconsciously the bear-trapper enjoys the control that he or she has over the new employee now that the new employee has been rendered impotent or inadequate. Bear-trapping, especially if the victim seems strong, self-reliant, and capable, bolsters the bear-trapper's pathetic self-esteem.

In turn, the new employee retaliates by goofing off, looking busy, by-passing, hiding, letting things slide, withholding information, starting rumors, filing grievances, socializing excessively, forming cliques, and possibly even sabotaging operations. Often these techniques for coping with betrayal are subconscious and, since there is no positive motivation, the employee's productivity suffers seemingly without cause. When I've been asked to interview people who were labeled as unsatisfactory performers, I found the following two factors in over half of the cases:

1. At some time in their career—most often at the beginning—the employees' performance was very satisfactory, but a decline set in after a long period of time.

2. They have been bear-trapped at one time or another—though they didn't call it that. They were deceived by promises, implied or stated, that were not carried out.

THE ISSUE OF DEADWOOD

Bear-trapping leads logically to the issue of Deadwood.

When people speak derisively of organizational deadwood (those employees who have indeed retired at full salary and still clutter up the organization), they generally speak of trying to get *rid* of the deadwood rather than *preventing* its development.

Curiously we don't hire deadwood. There are no advertisements in the newspaper or a professional journal saying, "Wanted: Deadwood. All non-producers apply to XYZ Corporation to get easy, well-paying jobs. No responsibilities, no work requirements, no prior experience needed. Live a happy life until retirement. Some retirement benefits available almost at once."

If we don't hire deadwood, then where does it come from? I suspect in almost all cases the organization personnel are busy producing it. It is my strong belief that cultivating deadwood is an organizational do-it-yourself project, and that a vast variety of organizational personnel—ranging from recruiters to deadwood Dick's immediate supervisors—contribute their time and energy to the project. It may even start with the PR people who construct the organization's image—or possibly with the personnel department.

If you were to try to identify *in advance* which people from a randomly chosen group of newly hired employees were likely to become deadwood in the next ten to twenty years (assuming they stayed around that long), who would you pick? When I ask that question of supervisors and managers in my seminars I find that the majority focus on the passive employee who just wants to get along and who doesn't show any initiative.

I disagree. Instead, I place myself with the usual minority that identifies as potential deadwood the creative, energetic, dynamic employee who pushes for change and improvement. It is that individual who most likely will be squashed or caged by the mediocre supervisor who doesn't want anybody to rock the boat. Such a supervisor unimaginatively gives out the interesting work to the old tried and true workhorse, maintains the status quo, and doesn't want to get involved in employees' personal matters.

I don't believe that the passive, compliant employee is likely to become deadwood because she or he will do what the boss says to do and will get along fine. Though such individuals are seldom motivated, they generally do want to do what is required and stay out of trouble. People who are truly inadequate to do the job are seldom, if ever, hired. And if they are employed, they seldom last through the probationary period.

If, on the other hand, the new employee is ambitious and aggressive and gets in trouble with management by showing initiative, yet feels constrained to hold onto the job in hand, that employee has to cope somehow. This person often gives up and retreats into a shell—eventually to be labeled "deadwood." There are, of course, other causes, such as senility, but becoming an organizational vegetable is not natural, and we should hunt for reasons.

How can we provide a better job-match—or rematching if conditions change over time—so that the person newly hired, promoted, or transferred does not, in time, become deadwood? I have several suggestions for all personnel involved in the recruitment and selection process:

1. Stop selling the organization so hard. Listen to what each candidate for a job is saying about himself or herself—their hopes, fears, and concerns—as well as to the recitation of their technical or managerial accomplishments.

2. Be more careful with job specifications. Ensure that the supervisor for whom the person will be working is being straight about the level of authority the new employee will enjoy, the variety of tasks the person will perform, and the existing and potential opportunities that will be realized on the job.

3. Stop talking in vague generalities. Get down to specifics.

4. Be sure there is no potential for bear-trapping. Document promises, follow up on them, and confront the bear-trapper if one is uncovered. Before hiring, ask the candidate to state clearly (even in writing) his or her understanding of the promises made by the organization.

5. Realistically assess the long-term implications of the job and the organization possibilities for fulfilling the individual's needs. An organization's recruiter cannot do an effective job without input from the advanced planning group of the organization.

6. Do not overspecify the educational or experience requirements of the job. I would guess that a fair portion of the jobs requiring a college education could be done better by a person with a high school education and a few weeks of quality training. Overspecification often aimed at reducing the chance of selecting the wrong person often achieves the

opposite. The better educated may be able to grasp the job quicker, but that in itself can more quickly lead to frustration if the job does not amount to much.

7. If prehire testing is used, ensure that it is truly job-related. The Assessment Center method of selecting employees for large organizations should be considered more closely. This technique for providing realistic opportunities for the applicant to demonstrate the skills that will actually be used on the job may need tailoring to fit a given situation, but it increases the chances of a good job-employee match.

8. Do not be overly impressed by credentials. The skills displayed in acquiring credentials may have little relationship to those actually to be used on the job. The knowledge and experience gained in acquiring specific credentials may be very helpful in performing the job, but not necessarily. If a realistic certification testing program preceded the award of the credentials, such as preparation of a master's thesis or an architectural project, the thesis or project should be examined rather than the certification produced.

9. Try to arrange a trial period of employment if possible. This does not mean a probationary period, but instead an opportunity to do the work for a while without either party making a long-term commitment. If such a trial is possible, ensure that the prospective employee is fully involved in planning the experience (as to schedule, learning experiences, etc.), otherwise full commitment to the trial is usually missing.

10. Ensure that the prospective supervisor has the final say in hiring the new employee, otherwise the supervisor may not make the commitment necessary to ensure a healthy interpersonal relationship or on-the-job success.

OTHER PROBLEMS IN PERSONNEL SELECTION

When the Personnel Department or a selection panel chooses a new employee it relieves the supervisor of any real responsibility for making the employee a success. If the new employee is imposed on the supervisor it often prejudices the relationship, unless some accident of chemistry allows the supervisor and subordinate to come together. It is often random chance and the reality that a wide variety of people can do any job to a reasonable level of proficiency that enables supervisors, who are not personally commited to the employment of a specific new employee, to accept the employee and not sabotage her or him.

Staff people in the Personnel Department often argue with this contention, but their arguments are undercut because they seldom have any idea of what an employee could do if motivated, trained, and supported as opposed to what they are actually doing. If the supervisor acquiesces in the selection, accepts the employee's level of performance, and doesn't try to fire or transfer the employee, the recruiter assumes that they have a successful placement. The personnel department seldom follows up enough on new employees to know for sure.

We know that in the past many supervisors have discriminated and have rewritten job specifications to select their friends, and they have gotten their organizations in trouble with the EEO laws by doing so. Such people bear watching. But if people in a supervisory role are to be responsible for productivity, they must reasonably control the means to achieve that productivity.

Except in very small organizations, it is impractical for the supervisor to recruit. It is seldom, however, impractical for the supervisor to select. In the selection process it may be quite proper for a staff organization (serving higher-level management) to act as watchdog, and ensure that the selection process serves the legal and long-term obligations of the organization.

To take away the responsibility for selection from the supervisor (as selection panels sometimes do) often ensures that the new employee will not receive the support and help needed for job success because the supervisor is resentful. This approach allows the supervisor to cop out and say, "What can you expect? I'm stuck with this person—there's nothing I can do." The role of a watchdog is to guard the house, not manage it.

Personnel staff members can veto (in the name of higher-level authority), but they should not be allowed to select. They can find qualified people, they can arrange situations where the new employee can demonstrate his or her skills, they can provide training and support. If they do these things well, the supervisor will be hard put to defend his or her rejection of a good potential employee.

Much has been done in recent years through training and education to make supervisors more aware of their subconscious biases, to train them in achieving effective interpersonal relations, and to broaden their perspective on their role in meeting the overall goals and objectives of the organization in a responsible manner. We need to build on these personal development efforts and return decision-making responsibility to the supervisor.

A great problem, particularly with lower-level supervisors, is their feeling of impotency, of victimization, of despair. If they engage in harmful, biased, or self-serving behaviors, they need to be effectively confronted. But they do not need to be relieved of their responsibility for "making things happen."

Supervisors need to take their responsibility for proper selection much more seriously. We need management systems that reward high performance so that the supervisors are careful to select people who can *and will* produce. Supervisors need to know more about what makes new employees successful and how to mutually work for their joint success. More honest selection will also benefit new employees, for it benefits no one to be "set-up" for failure.

Perspective employees can contribute to the process of successful recruitment and selection by asking themselves what they are really looking for in the short term and in the long term. With such goals firmly in mind, candidates should frame questions for the recruiter and for the supervisor that will enable them to determine if this organization, this job, and this supervisor is likely to contribute to meeting their needs. It does employees no good to be bear-trapped or misplaced. The candidates should ask some other personal questions: Should I really take this job? Am I being bear-trapped? What are my motives in considering this job? What do I need out of this situation?

THE QUESTION OF SELECTION PANELS

I have been concerned for many years about the tendency for line management (particularly in government and academic institutions) to abdicate their responsibility for selection and turn the task over to selection panels.

The selection panel will not supervise the new employee. Qualifications are job specific, not abstract, nor are organizational objectives abstract. These things are very personal to the relationship between supervisor and subordinate. When a group of people talk to an employee (up to thirty-five panel members in one absurd situation I witnessed—imagine the cost of that decision), they know little about the specific job under consideration and even less about the personal chemistry that will exist between the two people who will have to work together. They can talk abstraction and assorted nonsense—and probably will since they personally have no real stake riding on the outcome.

I find selection panels a "set-up" for failure. The supervisor may very well dislike the selectee and set out to prove him or her incompetent—not a difficult task to do once they decide that the new employee won't cut the mustard. We need better supervisory training, some of it focused on selection and the training of new employees. If that were done, perhaps we could get back to a more responsible method of selection.

Each of you might seriously ask yourself: Is the recruitment and selection process used in my organization helping or hindering the prospective employee and consequently the organization's ability to acquire productive new employees?

STUDY QUESTIONS

1. Describe the psychological game of "bear-trapping."

2. Name some of the people in the organization who possibly could be "bear-trapping" the new employee.

3. Identify several of the types of investment most new employees make in an organization when they accept a position.

4. What are the long-term consequences of successful "bear-trapping" to the hiring organization?

5. Name some of the ways the new employee retaliates for being "bear-trapped."

6. Name some of the ways an organization tends to attract potential "deadwood."

7. How does the lack of decision-making authority in the supervisor tend to set up the new employee for failure?

CHAPTER 5

ASSESSING THE PROSPECTIVE EMPLOYEE'S KNOWLEDGE, SKILLS, AND ABILITIES

The most difficult task facing the candidates for a position is to convince the personnel interviewer or supervisor sitting across the desk or table that they can do the job better than other applicants. The other side of the same task from the supervisor's or interviewer's position is to ensure that they get the person with best possible combinations of knowledge, skills, and abilities to carry out the job under discussion. From the candidates' position, they are engaged in a selling job, and the people in the organization are attempting to be artful buyers. From this point of view, the problem seems rather direct and relatively simple—a series of tasks dependent upon the skills of the people involved. In some ways, the problem is more complicated.

Seldom will the needs of either side of the transaction be satisfied unless the deal concluded provides a good match between person and job. Thus, each party generally has a mutual goal—to ensure that any agreement they enter into satisfies both parties. I say "generally" because there are some temporary situations that exist where the needs of one of the parties can be met without meeting the needs of the other, but often there is deception or dishonesty at play in such situations. The employee who takes what is supposed to be a long-term job to meet immediate needs and then quits after accumulating enough money is one example. Another example is when a company hires for a temporary overload without informing the new employee, and then begins laying off when the work slackens.

However, in most cases the participants know, if only intuitively, that the best deal for them is not a good deal unless it is also a good deal for the other side. People who think otherwise are only fooling themselves.

DEVELOPING WIN/WIN PLACEMENTS

Applicants are selling themselves, and often want or need a job badly. However, in most cases a poor match between them and the job will not meet their long-term needs, and may actually set them back. "Selling" themselves successfully may be a disaster if they aren't careful. If the job doesn't work out, they may feel committed to stay a while so that they don't appear to be "job hoppers." This compulsion leads not only to wretchedness, but delays attainment of career goals. Also, the prospective employees may be giving up an existing job and, now in the new situation, may face discharge or poor performance ratings. Prospective employees need to know in advance, as much as possible, that they will be successful on the job. Individuals may try to get a desirable job, while not being sure that they can carry it off if they are employed, but do so in the *hope* that they can succeed. However, there may be ways to avoid that risk with little chance of loss.

The organization has a similar need, but in many ways its problem is even more complex. Job success or failure can be dependent on a wide variety of factors. The employee's ability to perform the task adequately may only be part of the problem. The organizational climate, interpersonal relations, the social content of the job, the levels of decision making, the quality of training, and a host of other factors affect the quality of the placement, and many of these factors are not under the control of those who make the decision to hire. The organization's greatest hazard may be a focus on satisfying short-term needs (filling the slot) rather than meeting the organization's long-term needs.

By not dealing straight with each other and by focusing on getting the best deal they can make, both sides in the employee selection process may set up the conditions for a lose/lose relationship. Most of us can sympathize with a person who needs a job and takes a long-term risk for a short-term gain in the hopes that everything will turn out alright. We can also sympathize with the employment specialist who is under pressure to fill a slot and really can't be sure who is the best candidate for the job, or even if any of them will succeed, but has to make a decision and fudges a bit to get the most likely candidate. However, in either case, both parties need more understanding of the job and the person in order to make the best possible choice under the circumstances.

We need to recognize from an organizational point of view that people can be almost infinitely complex and resourceful. Despite what I am about to say about assessment centers, etc., some human beings can figure out ways to be successful despite incredible odds, and no test devised by humankind can be totally accurate when predicting job success or failure. We should humbly recognize that we know so little about human psychology today that a person who is subconsciously dedicated to failure will figure out a way to fail despite our best efforts, and that a person insistent on success will get outside all assessments and somehow figure out a way to succeed.

The best we can hope to do is: (1) reduce our risk of failure to a reasonable degree (where further efforts at assessing job success run into diminishing returns) and then give the person a chance to show what she or he can do, and (2) both sides provide as much information as they possibly can to the other side relevant to the job and the individual's duties to be done so that both parties can effectively design the best possible relationship.

At least three times in my career people have proposed approaches to getting acquainted and mutually learning if I could do the job. These approaches were creative and told us things about each other that we could learn in no other way.

1. I had applied for a job as a writer/editor with a major trade publication. After lengthy discussion and much soul searching, the editor proposed that, instead of hiring me outright, I prepare an article on assignment with a short deadline on a subject in my field. If the assignment was carried out satisfactorily, I'd get paid for the article and subsequently hired. However, this assignment convinced me that writing to a schedule was not my cup of tea.

2. When I was in high school, a foreman recognized that I was uncertain about accepting a position in his department as inspector because I liked my present job. He suggested that I work for two weeks on the second shift in his department so that I didn't have to give up my present position until I was sure. I decided to stay with the first job, but I always appreciated the opportunity he offered me.

3. The third opportunity came from a Foundation executive. We had both agreed that neither of us could tell for certain whether I would like the job he was offering, or that I would be successful in carrying out the complex managerial duties involved. We brainstormed a variety of approaches to working together without full commitment on either side and decided on a two-step approach: He would hire me as a consultant through my present employer to work on several short-term projects. If that process worked out to our mutual satisfaction, I would take a leave of absense and try the job on a full-time basis. My current employer was agreeable, and the arrangement worked out satisfactorily and met everyone's needs—a win/win arrangement all around.

In all of these examples, my employer had full on-the-job assessment of my skills and knowledge, and I had a chance to see how well I liked the job—job assessment, if you wish. The variety of approaches shows a small sampling of the imaginative ways a mutual employee/employer assessment can work—perhaps the ideal situation. In many cases, however, such a mutual trial period is not feasible, though I believe it could be done far more often than we think it can.

When trial assessments are not feasible, there is still often a need for the organization to know more about the employee than references and credentials will show. Likewise, the employee needs to know more about the job than can be determined by asking interviewers questions and a quick trip through the facility.

MUTUAL ASSESSMENT

Assessment of an applicant and the job is generally weighted in favor of the organization. The cultural attitude, "We've got the *job* to offer—you're only one of many applicants," reflects an almost subconscious view of inherent organizational superiority and power. Historically, people not only were more abundant than jobs, they needed them desperately and often had little to offer that some other person didn't have, hence, the almost hysterical emphasis on experience—the one thing that could give an applicant the edge on another. Therefore, the organization appraised the applicant and the applicant had better not get uppity and ask too many questions or that truly precious job would go to someone else. There is still much of that attitude hanging about. Where jobs are scarce and prospective employees abundant, this attitude is still functional. The feeling that the organization's rights have primacy over the employee's rights may not only be historically out of date, but it can thwart achievement of organizational goals if we are not careful.

If people are not treated as full partners in the placement process, they develop coping mechanisms to keep their options open. Experienced personnel people are well aware of these coping mechanisms, but are often unable to control them. The employee coping mechanisms often account for many unsuccessful placements. Increasingly, as people become more specialized and valuable, as social systems protect people from the severe consequences of unemployment, and as people become more mobile and sophisticated, we need to involve them successfully in the placement process on a win/win basis.

In recent decades organizations have come a long way in developing techniques for assessing the potential of individuals, but because of this archaic feeling of organizational awe often felt by the prospective employee, and because this feeling is often reinforced by interviewers and prospective supervisors (often by punishing behavior), the employee often does not or cannot fully assess the organization, and a poor placement results. The organization often controls a great deal of the information, and candidates who ask difficult questions may be punished by not being hired.

Organizations still face the very practical problem of needing to assess skills and aptitudes in order to fill specific job vacancies. Prospective employees also need to know more about the nature of the work to be done in order to avoid error in accepting a job offer. There are a variety of ways applicants can get to know the work and the organization can get to know the individuals and their abilities. Performance testing and the Assessment Center

Method (ACM) are two fairly common ways, though even here results can get distorted if we are not careful.

THE ART OF ASSESSMENT

The assessment of human skills and potential comes in three varieties.

Things a person has already done. The primary problem here is getting the person to reveal herself or himself, testing out the level of performance and keeping track of those bits of skills and knowledge so that the individual can be matched against organizational needs and opportunities. These are in the realms of "real sharing" and "meaningful feedback." In this area nothing of potential value should be overlooked. "I've just been a housewife" often mocks a varied career, rich with experience in planning, organizing, directing, coordinating, and controlling a complex (though usually small) organization. There is also bound to be a lot of experience in problem solving, decision making, and creative human development. Service industries at least can use much of that background.

Things a person might be able to do if given a chance. Since these things are mostly in the area of undeveloped potential, neither the individual nor anyone else will know until it is tried. In this, we should not discount people nor their abilities. The only fair way is to give them a chance to try it out—support them and see what happens. If you expect failure, you will probably get it. If you expect success, you will often be delighted with the results. Later in this book when we discuss delegation of authority and related concepts we will deal with some of the ways of managing that type of human development.

Things people claim to be able to do or complex abilities they may already possess which are job-related. This category of skills and knowledge can be subdivided into two categories: (1) the assessment of visible and direct skills and/or knowledge such as the ability to type or take shorthand, and (2) the possession of a complex variety of skills that interrelate in performing a specific job.

Performance Testing

For category (1) the primary concern today is to ensure that the criteria used for selecting applicants or promoting personnel is clearly job-related. In the past, much irrelevant material, such as IQ tests, have been used to screen out people. Today, Equal Employment Opportunity and affirmative action requirements focus on proving that any testing used in qualifying people does have a direct relationship to the work the person would be doing. A typing test for a clerk typist, where speed and accuracy is directly measurable and is clearly part of the job the person will perform, gives us a way of testing the relevance of the test.

In other jobs where performance testing is less common, yet where the employer wants to hire or promote people of demonstrated skill or knowledge, the situation is more complex. Here we tend to focus on performance testing which can give more reliable results than most common written or oral tests.

Effective performance testing usually starts with identifying the specific tasks that the person holding the job will do. Then the Knowledge, Skills, Abilities, and Decisions (KSADs) that are needed to perform each task are identified and defined. A test is established that will measure those specific KSADs required for that particular task and not others. If the candidate performs the relevant tasks according to consistent, fair, and equal standards, the person qualifies. Later chapters dealing with task analysis techniques and setting training objectives will detail this type of measurable performance. One type of testing which is performance-oriented and deals with a complex set of skills, knowledge, and behaviors is the assessment center method used to estimate the likelihood of success in complex jobs such as sales or management.

Assessment Centers

The Assessment Center Method (ACM) was first employed in the United States by the Office of Strategic Services during World War II to train intelligence operatives to handle assignments behind enemy lines. The assessment system simulated conditions as they might occur behind enemy lines. Candidates were required to perform a series of tasks under simulated stress conditions, and their performance was evaluated by trained observers. The well-documented[1] phenomenal success of this effort led business executives in the 1950s to use the Assessment Center Method to select and promote managers and sales personnel.

Where success in a job is dependent upon a complex set of interrelated behaviors, and where prediction of success likelihood is important to the organizations (because of the costs of failures or errors in judgment), the ACM has much to offer. The Assessment Center Method is a proven technique used by several hundred companies, government agencies, and institutions to improve the selection and promotion procedure for key positions which require a diverse set of skills and abilities. The Assessment Center Method has paid considerable dividends in reducing training costs (you don't have to train successful candidates in things they have already proven they can do), thus avoiding costly mismatching of people and jobs and reducing the likelihood of management mistakes in choosing people. Lately, particularly in government offices, ACM has been used to identify job-related behavioral strengths or weaknesses

---

[1]OSS Assessment Staff, *Assessment of Men* (New York: Rinehart, 1948) and *Fortune Magazine,* "A Good Man is Hard to Find" (March 1946): 62.

of current employees and supervisors (such as the ability to delegate authority effectively) so that supportive or compensatory training and development opportunities can be offered.

In many higher-level or more complex jobs, such as that of supervisor or manager, the ability to display a wide range of appropriate behaviors under stress conditions is more critical than purely technical knowledge or skills. The Assessment Center itself is an "away from the job" experience where a dozen or more candidates (usually in groups of six) meet at a training site to perform a series of situational exercises and tests, alone and in conjunction with the team. These exercises accurately reflect, for example, managerial on-the-job demands and bring out the skills directly demanded in actual on-the-job performance. Participants are observed and evaluated by several trained assessors who develop written reports on each person's performance.

The exercises and tests used in an Assessment Center derive from the job-related behaviors to be assessed. These behaviors are identified during a detailed analysis of the tasks actually performed by incumbents already in the kind of position for which the candidate is being considered. From an analysis of the tasks that the prospective jobholder would be expected to perform, the required skills are identified. Exercises are then either designed to measure the performance of those skills, or selected from standard exercises used in other organizations which meet the same skill measurement objectives. Sometimes the matter of relevance of the tests to the peculiarities of the employing organization (i.e., the telephone industry or a chemical plant) is important, sometimes it is not.

Typical exercises for managerial participants, especially where training and development efforts will follow the Assessment Center rather than selection or promotion is concerned, might be:

1. An *In-Basket* presents typical management problems to the individual assessee in the form of memos, reports, notes, records of telephone calls, etc., which might come across a manager's desk in a given day. How the assessee handles those details will be appraised. Such a test is used to determine the person's ability to plan and organize work, make decisions, attend to details, perceive the significance of some items, and delegate work.

2. A *Management Game* is used in a group context so that the assessors can view each individual in relation to interpersonal behavior in dimensions such as leadership, decisiveness, resistance to stress, ability to plan and organize work, and social sensitivity. The Management Game is structured so that special business experience and knowledge is hardly relevant, consequently, no one participant will have any advantage over the other. This game is designed to measure interpersonal and work skills, not business knowledge.

3. A *Leaderless Group Discussion* has participants acting as a board or committee with a preassigned decision to reach. Often, each participant is assigned a role or point of view which they are to push. In such cases the dimensions which are to be assessed might include oral communications skills, leadership, planning and organizing ability, resistance to stress, interpersonal sensitivity, judgment, and the ability to influence others.

4. An *Interview* between each participant and an assessor team might last for an hour or two. The interview may be based on a personal history blank filled in by the candidate before arriving at the Center, or on a set of standardized questions asked by the assessors. The purpose of this interview is not to gather personal data, but to focus on how the person handles the questions and how the person views himself or herself. Some behaviors parallel those observed elsewhere in the Center process, such as oral communications and personal impact. But here the aim is primarily toward ascertaining the person's level of aspiration and expectations about her or his future, advancement motivation, the importance of job security, goal flexibility, and range of interests.

5. *Miscellaneous Methods* may include such items as paper and pencil tests (if math, for instance, was a job requirement), motivational tests, "the irate citizen phone call," and the "problem analysis test." These measure a wide range of dimensions, including desire to hold a leadership role, assertiveness, and independence.[2]

When the Assessment Center is cost effective (the expense of such an effort is outweighed by the gains), the ACM is a powerful management tool. One of the principal advantages is that it assesses a person's likelihood of success against actual job requirements and not against abstract or subjective criteria that have little relevance to actual job performance. As such, it has been used as a method of meeting EEO and Affirmative Action requirements.

For the prospective new employee, effective, job-related assessment has three powerful advantages: (1) The new employee will have a realistic view of the behaviors required on the new job (and as such, ACM performs a type of training function). (2) It will be fair and relevant and most likely will be seen as such. (3) The candidate for the job can more realistically appraise personal interest in the job being offered. There is also the possibility that, if used correctly, even successful candidates for a job will have had some areas of weakness identified so that personally or through the employing organization the individual can take steps to strengthen those areas. Even when a candidate

[2]Based on Dr. Douglas Bray's, *The Assessment Center Method Training and Development Handbook,* 2nd ed. (McGraw-Hill, 1976), chapter 16. Dr. Bray pioneered the development of the Assessment Center Method in 1956 and is now Director of Management Selection and Development Research for The American Telephone and Telegraph Company.

fails, some organizations will provide feedback to the candidate so that the person can take steps to overcome weaknesses that were revealed by the Assessment Center.

STUDY QUESTIONS

1. Why is it important that each side in a placement ensure that the other side gets their needs met, as well as each party ensuring that they get their own needs met?

2. Why can we never be totally sure that a person will succeed or fail in a given job? What factors are involved?

3. In assessing the likelihood of job success for a new employee, what are two things we can hope to accomplish, and what two things can we try to do to accomplish these ends?

4. What are the advantages and disadvantages of "trial employment" situations?

5. Where in your organization does the concept of organizational primacy over individual needs manifest itself? Try to think of other places that you have encountered that attitude.

6. Name the three varieties of assessment.

7. Try to identify three types of performance testing used in your organization (or which could be used in your organization other than those listed in this chapter).

8. Describe the origins and uses of Assessment Centers.

9. What is the key element of the Assessment Center?

10. Name five types of exercises used in a managerial Assessment Center.

11. For the prospective employee, what two powerful advantages does a realistic Assessment Center experience provide?

CHAPTER 6

THE ACT OF EMPLOYMENT

The act of employment should be an act of celebration, a joyous occasion, a time of good feelings. For many people it is. The new employee may actually celebrate by going out to dinner, by toasting the new beginning, by doing something else special for the evening—the occasion seldom goes by unmarked. There may be apprehension and doubts connected with the new job, but for now they are set aside while the person reflects on how the new situation promises to improve over what it was before.

In the organization, however, there is often a sigh of relief that the slot is filled or that one more quota has been met. There may be good feelings if the match of job and person is a good one, but often the supervisor merely grunts and turns to other business. If the position has been a difficult one to fill, or if the job has been open for a long time, the work may be backed up and the supervisor has plenty of other things to think about. The sense of relief is understandable, but it could be that by being blasé we miss opportunities. It could be also that we have seen employees turn out badly and therefore we tend to "wait and see" rather than to celebrate. But an employer could also presume oneself to be better off than before the person was hired, so why not celebrate at least a little? If the expectation of failure can produce failure, could the "wait and see" attitude tilt us toward failure? If we are not deeply committed to the new employee's success, we might not do as much as possible to guarantee that success.

Have you ever thought of sending a card of welcome and congratulations to the new person on your staff? Could an announcement be sent to the person's home? Could you organize a short informal coffee klatch with the workgroup when the new employee is hired? "Too much" you might say, but the question remains: How else can you sanctify the act of employment so that your mutual commitment is launched on a joyful beginning?

THE COMMENCEMENT

The act of employing a person is a serious business, and it is usually regarded as such by all the parties concerned. Yet, the behavior of the participants often belies that assumed concern, with negative results for both the new employee and the organization.

Hiring is done in a variety of ways, from a phone call to a very formal letter of employment offer. Day laborers are often picked up at curbside by contractors who ride by looking for the most likely workers in groups of unemployed men. Temporary secretaries or school teachers may get their daily assignments over the telephone from a central office. At the other end of the scale, civil service employees get formal letters offering a specific job which requires a formal response. Executives are often asked to sign a legal contract to seal their acceptance of employment. Most of us fall somewhere in between. That is, we get a verbal notification which often includes final negotiations for wages and conditions and a formal notice from the personnel office to confirm the verbal agreement already made. What is implied in the employment agreement? What is understood? What are the results? How does the agreement and the final act of employment affect the new employee and the organization? There is no easy and definite way to say for sure, but there are a number of things that should be looked at by every organization engaged in hiring new employees.

THE ACT OF HIRING

Joanne B. was called from a shower by an incessantly ringing phone in mid-morning as she was getting ready to go out for an interview.

"Hello."

"Miss Joanne B.?"

"Yes?" she replied.

"Where the hell have you been? I've been waiting for you for over an hour. I've got a lot of work to get out and you're leaving me in a lurch. You were supposed to start at 9 A.M. When will you be here?"

By the time Joanne unscrambled that communication, she knew that her caller had assumed that she had been hired and was to start that morning. She had been interviewed by the firm twice, but to her knowledge she had never been offered a job and certainly she had not yet accepted one.

Later she discovered that a sad-looking letter that she had decided was a piece of junk mail contained not an offer of a job, but a notice to report to work on such and such a day and time. There had been no final conversations, and not even the starting salary had been clearly identified. The letter did not ask for a reply or indicate that one was needed.

After the tonguelashing she had received from her "new" boss and the sloppiness of the letter, Joanne decided she'd really rather work elsewhere.

Over the years, I have discovered that many people know little about their new job or the organization, and sometimes they didn't even know what salary they were getting. Incredible as it may seem, accepting a job without knowing precisely what the income will be is not very unusual. The lack of knowledge on starting salary seems most common among very young people and very old people. This, I think, is because they often want the job so badly they will take almost anything. Additionally, an underlying assumption is that either the job pays the legal minimum or the employer at least has to offer something that would attract people. I have known some people who are surprised that neither assumption held true in their case. Also, especially the young person with little work experience may be so overawed by the organization that they view asking questions about salary and fringe benefits as ungracious and as not showing a deep enough interest in getting the job. When employees are in doubt about any of the important aspects of employment, their concern for these aspects distracts them from job concentration and diverts their energies. It also encourages them to seek out data and advice from other workers. Often they get much misinformation and gossip.

New employees need a clear-cut understanding of their relation with the organization and of the agreement they are entering into when they accept employment.

THE EMPLOYMENT CONTRACT

An employment agreement can range in form from a simple handshake over a verbal agreement to a legal contract spelling out in great detail the specific terms and conditions of employment. The complexity of the agreement and how it is sealed tends to be closely related to the amount of salary involved and the complexity of the new employee's duties. Laborers may not even get a handshake, executives may have a battery of lawyers draw up the agreement. But in any case, *every* employment agreement carries with it legal obligations and is, therefore, in one form or another, an employment contract.

Difficult as it may be, verbal agreements can be enforced. Many organizations avoid the formal letter of employment because of an unwillingness to make a real commitment, others fail to do so out of indifference. Many people hire casually ("If this person doesn't work out I'll get another one") and then find out that they made commitments they hadn't bargained for.

The number of legal and contractual agreements an organization commits itself to are wide-ranging and sometimes overpowering. Few supervisors, managers, and personnel people are trained to appreciate the breadth of the organization's commitments.

A partial list of legal entanglements an organization may be caught up in at the time of employment include:

1. Equal Employment Opportunity laws

2. Wage and hour laws

3. Income tax laws

4. Labor relations laws (arbitration, grievances, Union membership, etc.)

5. Social Security laws

6. Workman's Compensation laws

7. Insurance laws

8. Security regulations

9. Occupational health and safety laws

10. Pension and trust fund laws

Also, depending on the type of organization, government, or private business, there may be aspects of civil service laws and regulations. These legal obligations may also come in federal, state, county, or municipal varieties. Nor can we avoid the ramifications of a union contract if one exists. Finally, we have the ultimate recourse of the employee suing the organization if the employee feels she or he has been treated unfairly or illegally.

Employees accepting a job seldom realize the legal implications of their commitment to a job. If they are to know these implications at all, they have to be trained. Handling government classified material and reporting requirements of government agencies are examples of these implications.

When you add to the foregoing, the reality that the organization and its chief executives are held legally responsible for the acts of their subordinates, the legal implications of the employment contract seem enormously overpowering. The employment *contract,* and it is a contract even if nothing is put into writing, is not a thing to be taken lightly. In the orientation and training of the new employee, the seriousness of this *contract* is often overlooked. Is it any surprise that new employees often take their job less than seriously?

THE EMPLOYMENT AGREEMENT

Outside of the legal aspects of the actual or implied contract that the employee is offered is the nature of the basic *agreement* between the employee and the organization. This understanding or *agreement* may be of greater fundamental importance to both the individual and the organization than the formal or implied contract. This agreement is the basis of personal commitment. This is the item that leads to job success or failure. This is where the parties feel that justice is achieved or denied, this is where true equity is involved.

The key to any successful *agreement* is that the parties involved get their needs met as well as possible within the context of their relationship. To keep an employment agreement from unraveling, both sides need to know clearly what they are to receive and what they are to give. They also need to know how to renegotiate the agreement if conditions change after employment. Without a full sense of understanding and a sense of fairness about the agreement, neither side is likely to feel fully committed to the success of the agreement.

The basis of any legal contract is that there is at least some degree of reciprocity. A completely one-sided contract is legally unenforceable, and in no way is such a document (written or not) an agreement.

Each side has to receive something, a return in kind, for what it is giving up. The closer an agreement comes to equal return or equal sharing, the more likely the courts are to conclude that mutual dependence or mutual influence existed when the agreement was shaped. Justice involves at least a degree of equity. Unions were created by workers to balance the power of the organization and to achieve equity. When equity becomes unbalanced, the laws and the courts are frequently called upon to redress that imbalance.

With an employment "agreement," the sense of equity or justice is even more critical. One of the best arguments for an effective program of wage and salary administration is that it strives to achieve equity. When jobs are scarce and applicants are plentiful, an organization can get employees at less than a fair wage. But employees often have a finely tuned sense of the going rate or what is right and wrong, and they can adjust their output to meet their income—thus achieving equity in their own way. How often have you heard, "For what they pay me around here, what can you expect?"? The converse is also true. When the employee does not really earn his or her income there is a tendency to withhold raises and promotions and perhaps terminate employment. Employers or employees who expect to get away with a seriously inequitable agreement are usually deluding themselves.

Marriage is a contract, but even more than a contract it is an agreement. Many people tend not to take the *contract* too seriously unless a legal separation or divorce is impending. A short reflection on the behavior of many married couples will bear out my contention.

The *agreement* in marriage—that is, the understanding implicit in marriage—is taken very seriously. Some of this agreement is stated explicitly ("I'll love you forever") and this part also might not be taken too seriously in some cases. However, the implicit aspects, such as each person's role and the types of decisions each will make, is often considered too obvious to even discuss. Several marriage counselors have told me that the greatest source of trouble in marriages involve those *assumptions* that the partners make about themselves and about each other. These are the hidden assumptions that never come out in discussion until they are violated. These hidden assumptions are often subconscious and unaware, for they constitute that great body of beliefs we grow up with that are just taken for granted ("That's the way things are"). Though we operate as if such assumptions are total truth, we don't consciously mention them until they are violated or challenged.

At the time of employment, both the organization and the new employee frequently have assumptions they are laying upon each other without ever making themselves clear. They are assuming the best, and when they are disappointed they can feel injured, lamenting, "Why does this always happen to me?"

At the risk of overdoing the details of the agreement, all assumptions should be checked out before the act of employment occurs. Failure to do so sets up the relationship for an unproductive future. Unasked questions such as, how much authority will I have? what specific objectives will I be expected to accomplish? how serious is lateness or socializing considered? often come home to haunt the person who takes the job under one set of assumptions and finds that his or her new supervisor, or the organization as a whole, is operating on a different set.

Assumptions the organization makes about the new employee may be just as harmful. Good interviewers often dig out clashes in values, objectives, and habits—clashes that need to be resolved before a serious tender of employment is made. However, there are some culturally-based assumptions, such as an employee's desire for income and security, that they do not probe as deeply as they might. I am not suggesting that differences in values, goals, and habits make for an untenable situation. I am merely suggesting that insofar as possible, the offer of employment and its acceptance should be done with eyes open wide.

Making the agreement explicit in detail may seem to be making too much of a good thing. Overdetailing seems comparable to treating candidates like children, but unless we are quite explicit we can never be sure that we truly have a good match. Is your message clear? Is it complete?

I am much encouraged by the fact that many young people are preparing marriage agreements that spell out their future roles and relationships more clearly. This may take the so-called romance out of marriage, but I suspect it is a more sound basis for marriage than the traditional generalities that have led to so many divorces. In a society where custom and tradition are dominant, assumptions may work well. In our highly complex, socially mobile society of today, a mismatch of assumptions can easily take place. Both parties of an employment contract need to invest the time and effort required to check out their assumptions with each other. Failure to do so is a set-up for an unhappy relationship.

The act of employment is the sealing of the agreement. Since this act of sealing the agreement is often done in a hurry—after a long and careful review of the candidates, or, from the employee's point of view, after looking at a variety of job opportunities[1]—we may overlook a lot of important details. Our unspoken assumptions about what this specific act of employment implies may be very important details.

---

[1] It is a curious cultural heritage that we speak of job opportunities, but seldom of hiring opportunities. In our mental processes we still place employment high on our scale of values and regard the hiring, perhaps even of a first-class producer, as though we were doing him or her a favor.

WHEN THE AGREEMENT IS REACHED

What has been said, verbally or in writing, concerning the employment agreement is only part of the story. Questions about whether the organization should offer a written contract, a formal written offer of employment, or a verbal offer are matters of judgment, but each has its own impact on the new employee. It is not so much what the agreement says or implies, the key element is what the employee *infers* from the agreement. Written offers leave less to the imagination, but the whole process of applicant interaction with the organization up to the time of hiring influences the employee's view of the agreement.

Most recruiters are quite good at picking up clues as to whether or not the prospective employee will be a good employee. Questions about how much notice the present employer will need and how much notice the applicant plans to give, elicit feedback on how considerate the candidate is of the current employer, which sends a message that "this organization expects to be treated with consideration if you ever leave here." Likewise, when trying to arrive at a mutually agreeable starting date, we communicate how considerate or inconsiderate the organization is of the candidate's needs and concerns.

At this point, when the pressure of interviewing is off, an agreement to hire has been reached, and only the details of acceptance and start remain to be settled, the organization sometimes gets into trouble.

Once the critical point of acceptance is reached when the future new employee has reached her or his Rubicon, the employer often muffs the job. At this critical point, the emotional level is high, and often neither side listens as carefully as it might. Often the message coming back to the employer is embodied in clues and cues that the candidate is experiencing difficulty. At this point, we tend to deal with facts rather than feelings, and we may fail to pick up the most critical data in the message—the feelings. We need to use reflective feedback techniques to act as a sounding board so that the applicant can work through problems and resolve them. If the candidate needs help or information we may be able to supply it, but primarily we need to help the person solve any problems so that we do not get "no shows," renegotiation problems, or a new employee who is distracted by unresolved problems. Once the offer has been made, the next transaction may be very important. At this point we will get more information from listening than we will from probing and questioning.

These final concerns of the employee should not be discounted any more than organizational concerns should be discounted. Some of these concerns may be disposed of, others may not. At this point, neither party should feel so committed that they cannot back off the deal. At the same time, minor irritants resulting from unattended concerns can fester and undo the positive aspects of an otherwise effective recruitment and placement effort. We should be willing to invest time and effort to resolve the issues created by the actual act of employment.

SEALING THE AGREEMENT

There is something attractive and intriguing about the red plastic seal of molten wax applied to letters in the days before envelopes, and in the impression made in the wax that identified the originator of the message and confirmed her or his responsibility for what was written there. In sealing the employment agreement we put our imprint on it as surely as an ancient ring or stamp could ever do. We also have an opportunity equal to or exceeding that of any ancient king to proclaim our intentions and our commitment to that agreement.

When I was inducted into the Army, they took down a lot of information about me—my hometown, where I went to school, etc.—data that I thought was pretty worthless but needed by the bureaucracy to justify their existence. To my surprise, everytime I graduated from a technical school or received a promotion, an announcement of it appeared in my hometown newspaper. The colleges I attended did the same. In time, I began to perceive two results of this effort. First, it increased my personal sense of identification with the organization, for I knew that others, my family and friends, were also identifying me closely with those organizations and I somewhat felt an obligation to meet their expectations. Second, the organization was getting free publicity which would keep the organization's name before the public and aid in later recruitment (since the emphasis was on good things that were happening to people).

Later, I encountered firms that sent out similar announcements or press releases to professional journals and trade magazines as well as to local and hometown papers when I was hired. I was not that big a deal, but they never failed to get their name and my name before the public. One New York company even put an ad in the *Wall Street Journal* announcing that I was joining their firm. I don't know about the impact that ad had on the industry they were serving, but my friends had to rein me down from the ceiling where I was floating.

About this time I began to realize that not only did such efforts communicate to the public that they were a growing dynamic organization, but that the company was trying to interest those who knew me personally. This was not because those people were so numerous or powerful, it was simply that my sense of worth and success was now being identified with the success of that organization. Leaving or failing suddenly became less of a viable alternative to me. The company was announcing its commitment with me, could I do less? The act of employment was now complete.

STUDY QUESTIONS

1. How do most people feel when accepting a new job? How did you feel when you accepted previous jobs? How does the employing personnel often feel?

2. Why is a clear-cut understanding of new employees' relationship with the organization they are entering and the employment contract so vital?

3. Develop your own list of the legal and semi-legal commitments your organization is making when it hires a new employee.

4. What is the difference between the formal or implied *contract* and the understanding or "agreement" between the employee and the organization (and vice versa)?

5. List five assumptions the prospective employee may be making that are seldom made explicit, and then list five assumptions management personnel may be making about an employment agreement that they are also not likely to make explicit.

6. What is the critical point in the hiring process when the employer is least likely to be paying attention to verbal and nonverbal clues from the prospective employee? What can we do at this critical juncture if we are in the employer role?

7. How can the organization effectively "seal" the employment agreement?

CHAPTER 7

THAT CRITICAL
FIRST DAY

Before reading this chapter it might be a good idea for you to conduct an exercise. Visualize your own situation and assume that:

1. You are a supervisor of a potential new employee operating in a specific environment and filling a specific job vacancy, or

2. You are a staff specialist concerned about new employee hiring, orientation, training, or some other area of new employee development, or

3. You are a new employee concerned with starting out on the right foot, or

4. You are a manager at any level concerned with employee productivity and human resource development.

PERSONAL PLANNING EXERCISE

Take paper and pen and frame answers to the following questions according to your own situation. Interpret the questions according to your own special needs and interests.

1. What things would the new employee need to know about this new environment that would make her or him comfortable in the surroundings? (List all the things you can think of.)

2. What impressions and impact would I want to make on the new employee that first day? (Or what impressions I would like to receive if I were the new employee?) (Try not to worry about the "how to" in this question at the moment—focus on the "what.")

3. What *key* policies and procedures must the employee be aware of the first day so that mistakes will not be made on the second day? (Don't plan too far ahead and stick to vital issues only.)

4. What specific things can I do to ensure that the person will begin to know her or his fellow employees without feeling overwhelmed? (List as many as practical for that first day.)

5. What special things (their own desk, work area, etc.) can I do to make the person feel physically comfortable, welcome, and secure?

6. What job-related tasks can I reasonably teach the person to do well that first day so to provide a sense of accomplishment? (No more than three things, and one may be sufficient.)

7. What positive experience can I provide for the new employee that the person could talk about to the "folks at home"? (This item should relate to enhancing the domestic or social status or prestige of the person—something that could make her or him feel valued or significant in the job situation.)

8. *For Supervisors:* How can I ensure that I will be available most of the time on the new employee's first day to ensure personal attention and to convey a clear message that he or she is an important addition to the work team?

The foregoing certainly seems like a lot of work to go through, and it very well may be, but once the questions are answered and the plans are laid, they can be filed for future use whenever a new employee is to be inducted into the workgroup. The effort can also be looked at as an investment that is bound to provide a great return on each new employee in the years to come.

On the following pages are a number of ideas and suggestions made by supervisors, managers, staff specialists, and professional trainers related to orientation and training which you might wish to use to supplement your lists and notes. They are provided after you have been asked to work through your own analysis so as to encourage you to consider each item on its own merit and not just grab at someone else's ready-made answers. Each situation is unique and must be dealt with as such, so use whatever is useful in meeting your needs.

In preparing your lists, one thing you should be careful not to do is to *assume.* Many supervisors *assume* that the personnel office has taken care of many of the things the new employee needs to know, when in fact they have not. Conversely, personnel people often *assume* that supervisors will take care of such basic facts of orientation as lunch periods, breaks, location of facilities, etc., when indeed history clearly indicates that even these elementary items are often overlooked.

One long-time state employee told the following story, which I have no reason to doubt since I've heard variations on the central theme so often.

She had been asked at the initial interview why she wanted the job. She replied that she needed the money. After a few more sentences, she was sent home with the phrase, "We will call you if we can use you." Two weeks later she received a letter asking her to come in. Since she had not spoken to anyone about a specific job, she assumed that she was there for another interview. When she arrived she was taken to a table in a remote back room. She was seated at a table that was covered with newspapers and told that this is where she would work. This was the first clue that she was hired, and she didn't even know how much she would be paid.

She sat by the covered table until someone (a co-worker it turned out to be) eventually asked if she was going to lunch. She followed the crowd to a lunch room and hurried back to make sure she was not late. It was three days before she found out the actual length of the lunch period. In the afternoon, a clerk finally gave her some papers to alphabetize and her working career was officially launched. The next morning, the newspapers had been removed from her table only to be replaced by cleaner bags. On the third day, she met her supervisor.

One might blame the employee for passivity, but an organization can be awesome to a new employee. From her viewpoint, at least she had a job of sorts and she was glad for that reason. Such treatment can also lead an employee to quickly assume the defensive position ("I only work here") and to conclude that "if they want me to do something in return for the money they are paying me they should tell me what they want me to do."

IDEAS TO CONSIDER

When I was a new supervisor with Litton Industries the personnel department would send a form, consisting of two and a half sheets, along with each new employee. The half-sheet presented a list of specific things that the supervisor was to inform the employee of by the end of the first day. At the end of that day the employee was to sign the sheet attesting that she or he had been informed of the items. The supervisor would then sign and date the sheet and return it to personnel (for filing in the employee's personnel jacket).

The first full sheet was a list of information items the supervisor was to convey to the employee by the end of the first week. It was handled in the same fashion. The second full sheet listed items to be covered by the supervisor by the end of the first month.

As a supervisor at that time I found the lists invaluable. Though part of the purpose of the lists may have been to ensure against a supervisory slip-up, to me it was a programmed training tool and I much appreciated its help. Since I found the timing and interval of those forms appropriate, I have organized this chapter and the next two chapters on the same time frame.

The following ideas are arranged in the same order as the exercise questions, and provide possible ideas that can be used to ensure that a new employee gets off to as good a start as possible toward becoming a productive employee. Some of these ideas came from my own experience, but even more came from the experience of training course participants I have had over the years. Some items seem obvious, but I have often seen them over-looked—perhaps for just that reason.

Need to Know—Orientation for the First Day

According to Webster, the verb "to orient" means "To set right by adjusting to facts or principles, to acquaint with the existing situation, to ascertain the bearings of and to put into correct position or relation." In dealing with the orientation items, I use the supervisor's point of view because no one has as much influence on the new employee as the supervisor.

Need to Know:

1. Special words and terms used by the workgroup

2. Working hours

3. Breaks and lunch hours

4. Location of facilities
   a. Restrooms
   b. Public telephones
   c. Eating places

5. Health and safety considerations
   a. Physical safety procedures
   b. Fire escapes
   c. Exits (layout of building)
   d. Procedures for fire drills
   e. First-aid kits
   f. Nursing station (if such is available)
   g. Facts on how and where to report fires or other emergencies (A small card listing emergency numbers and other critical data might be supplied so that the person can affix it to his or her desk or workplace.)

6. Pay days and how the person will be paid

7. Location of work area (if this is not clear in the job context)

8. Information on *when, where,* and *how* they will receive *formal* organizational orientation (if any)

9. Who and when to call in case of illness, tardiness, etc. (including office phone numbers)

10. Information on parking, bus stops, car pooling, etc.

11. How to operate the phone system

    a. How to be reached from the outside (in case an emergency arises at home)

    b. How to answer the phone in that particular work area

12. Who to go to for supplies and other equipment

As can be seen, this represents quite a bit of detail to be absorbed by one individual in one day. When the key procedures are added, as well as introductions to co-workers and the introduction to on-the-job training, we skirt close to the point of overload.

Because of the unproductive possibility of mentally swamping the new employee, the preceding items should be scheduled throughout the day in order to allow for gradual absorption. In some organizations, a physical walk-through tour with key locations and facilities pointed out, helps give the over-all framework needed for filling in the pieces. It is like having the edge pieces of a puzzle put in place first. Having names, phone numbers, etc., typed on a card the employee can carry for a day or so is also often helpful.

In thinking back over the jobs I have had in three decades, many times few of the above items were covered—especially the health and safety items. I guess I'm lucky (and so were a lot of other people) that no emergencies arose that first day or for many days thereafter.

Impressions and Impact

Perhaps one of the key things to impress upon the employee is that you, the supervisor, *at least* know what you are doing, you have planned ahead, and you have specific objectives to be achieved.

Employees (new or old) learn, whether we wish it or not. If we are disorganized, indifferent, or sloppy in our approach, the employee will absorb these standards. No amount of future lecturing will erase these standards ("If he or she does it, why can't I?").

There may be other *prime* impressions you want to make on the employee related to your work situation such as "no smoking" in a chemical plant, or the "buddy system" when conducting police patrols in dangerous areas, but whatever they are, pick the *primary* one or two for the first day in order to avoid overload. Too many "very important items" can lead to the employee discounting everything he or she has been taught.

Key Policies, Procedures, and Rules

It was said earlier that key policies and procedures in the first day context relate to those things necessary to keep out of trouble on the second day. Also remember to not plan too far ahead in this regard and stick to vital issues only.

Again we relate specifically to the problems of confusion and overload. Typical items might include:

1. Basic security requirements and procedures for handling classified material (if such is involved) to the degree which will ensure the new employee does not incur a violation

2. "Leave policy," including how to report such leave

3. Rules for receiving and making personal calls

4. Dress code (if required) and behavior unique to that department or operation

Physical and Emotional Comfort

The new employee is likely to be tense and "uptight," so a sincere warm welcome is certainly in order. Whether the person feels comfortable in coming to the supervisor with problems in the future is often subconsciously decided at that first moment of meeting.

Planning ahead for the arrival of new employees also demonstrates concern. A clean work place of their own, possibly with their name affixed (even if done crudely), is an effective welcome. Keys ready in advance (if appropriate) signifies that the new employees are well enough thought of to be worth some advanced planning. If they are to have extensive outside contacts, business cards might be ordered in advance and available when new employees arrive. Or, if personalization (nicknames, etc.) is allowed, the order for cards might be taken that first day. Information as to who to go to for different kinds of answers or for guidance when the supervisor is gone also offers substantial reassurance to new employees. An informal chat exploring interests beyond the job or professional considerations is often a good idea for breaks or lunch (if the supervisor feels natural and comfortable doing such) and can do much to put new people at ease. Even asking them for their preferences in supplies shows a concern and warmth. (Once, when I first opened my desk drawer as a new employee there was a small card saying "Welcome" which listed the names of my secretary, my new supervisor and all of my coworkers. For all of that day I felt so good I was walking two feet off the ground. That organization provided some of the best experiences of my working life.)

Physical comfort, within the confines of the work environment, might also be considered. Heat, light, air conditioning, and other relatively fixed considerations may still allow for meeting individual needs or preferences if thought is given beforehand. Preparing their work area ahead of time with supplies, materials, and equipment enables new employees to be productive "early on." Involving other personnel in getting ready for new arrivals often gives them a stake in the new persons' ability to easily enter the work environment. Physical comfort in types of chairs, lamps, etc., may be constrained by the budget and physical resources available, but planning ahead can maximize opportunities for new employees' comfort and convenience.

None of this is coddling new employees—though perhaps it offers opportunities for better treatment than when we arrived at a new job. Not having supplies, or minor irritants in physical conditions, as well as tension and stress can all impede productivity. Prior planning can reduce these irritants so that new employees can get on with the job.

Some Work-Related Accomplishments

Perhaps the most difficult thing to attain on the first day is to involve new employees deeply enough in the job to allow them to experience some sense of achievement. If the employees are highly experienced, especially on jobs requiring skills such as typist, auto mechanic, printer, or assembler, they may only need proper equipment and the opportunity to demonstrate those skills. If, however, the employees are untrained or unfamiliar with the equipment used or product produced, more care and planning may be required.

Work-related accomplishment is not likely to be achieved on a work item that is totally new to the employees, though some offices or work sites do contain easy-to-master devices, such as some duplicators, or singular tasks which the new people can master quickly. The new employees will feel good if they can demonstrate their competence or go home feeling that they now know something they didn't know when they started that morning.

Another source of ideas is the new employee themselves. After a chat about the kinds of tasks that are done in that environment, the supervisor might inquire about things that the employees have done before (especially about items that are not on their application forms or resume) and felt good about. If the employees can demonstrate some prior knowledge or skill that is relevant to the new operation they are encountering, this will often suffice to give them that sense of accomplishment.

One work group I supervised developed a long list of things we commonly did in our office that required relatively little learning to master, but would make new people feel they had learned something. This included changing paper supplies in the copier, making blueprints, identifying drawing sizes by sight, ordering supplies, transferring calls on our intercom system, outlining the technical reports we wrote, learning the major components of our filing system, proofreading with a counterpart, and many more.

None of these tasks are very profound or complex, but that is just the point. People often come away from their first day on a new job with such a jumble of impressions that it is hard to identify even a single thing that has been learned. With all of the other details to be absorbed during the first day, one clear-cut task which has been learned is refreshing.

The items new people can absorb in the first day is somewhat related to their previous experiences. Start in an area in which they are comfortable, and ensure that they are successful in anything they try. It is important to build a pattern of success, accomplishment and productivity. Failure abuses the self-image and sets new employees up for future failure. The first day's learning should be well planned, produce success, and make the employees feel good about their new environment and the people who manage it.

Integrating the New Employee into the Workgroup

It has always seemed strange to me that groups often produce elaborate going away parties for work associates who are retiring, transferring, or accepting new jobs—people they will probably seldom or never see again—and yet do absolutely nothing overtly to welcome a new employee with whom they will probably be working for years to come.

The supervisor will often introduce a new employee to the workgroup and to a variety of outsiders as well (especially if taking the employee on a tour)—probably to far more people than any one person can remember in a day. At lunch time, a new person may be left to his or her own devices, or perhaps asked to join a group almost as an afterthought. Sometimes a new employee isn't even informed as to when it is time for lunch.

Most of the successful ideas that have been suggested to me over the years about how to successfully integrate new employees into the workgroup relate to involving workgroup members in the welcoming and support process.

Senior employees sometimes use the introduction of new employees as an opportunity to "size up" the new people, or to baffle and confuse them by tricks such as sending them for a "pipe stretcher." Such negative behavior on the part of the in-group should be confronted effectively, but steps can also be taken to assure that such unfriendly evaluations and abusive situations do not occur.

While many fortunate supervisors have no need to worry about negative behaviors on the part of workgroup members, they still often fail to maximize the supportive first-day opportunities for integrating employees into the group. Some ideas for first-day encounters which might be considered are:

1. Plan the introductions (both number and type) so as not to be overwhelming. Introduce primarily those with whom the person will have repeated contact during the first day or two.

2. Include nicknames and other terms of affection, if appropriate and if both parties feel comfortable with the use of such.

3. Give the new person a list of names of those they will meet so that they can strengthen their retention of the names.

4. Explain to the new employee, in general terms, how their work will fit into or relate to the work of others.

5. Identify the person the new employee can go to for help if the supervisor is absent.

6. Designate buddies to serve as "helping friends" during breaks and at lunch time.

7. Introduce the person to someone who can be helpful in providing the new employee with information on car pools, special interest groups, bus schedules, and transportation information.

8. None of these suggestions can take the place of getting the workgroup involved in making the new person feel comfortable and accepted.

There are also some techniques for increasing organizational awareness of the new employee, including:

1. Publish the person's name, picture, and background facts (especially hometowns and current community) in the company newsletter if one is published.

2. Notify outside contacts, clients, customers, etc., of the new person's arrival.

3. Briefly introduce the new person to the coworkers at a short meeting so that they will know the person and so that those who are inclined to be friendly can later come forward to help the new person.

4. Identify people in the group that have special knowledge, contacts, or information that could be of value or interest to the new employee.

You may already have many of these ideas on the personal list you made when you read about the personal planning exercise at the beginning of this chapter. You also may want to supplement your list. The main point is to get the person feeling at home as soon as possible so that she or he will be ready to learn and develop, without feeling uncertain about how well-accepted they are.

Enhanced Social Status or Prestige

Trying to offer new employees an opportunity to feel valued and significant in the job situation can be related to either enhanced social prestige within the workgroup, or with the folks at home, or both.

One thing I've witnessed that increases a new employee's social status flows out of the friendly chats that can occur that first day. If someone is proud of their bowling or tennis score, or speaks of belonging to certain clubs or a church, introducing that person to people of like interests can greatly enhance the sense of social acceptance and worth. Often, giving a person a chance to demonstrate an area of special competence early in the game can also give the new employee a chance to talk about her or his work experiences when they get home.

It should be apparent that we can structure checklists of things we can do to get new employees off to a good start. These checklists can be used to move the employees more rapidly and more surely toward a productive future, a future which will benefit the supervisor, the organization, and the new employees, for the future of all are subtly intertwined.

Your checklists, ideas, and guidelines will have to be unique for each situation. Each new employee also represents a unique opportunity. Only you can design a list to fit your situation and the new person with whom you are to interact. It is my hope that you will not be sloppy or casual, and that good things will grow from your relationship—for both of you.

Making Yourself Available

One thing remains for the supervisor before the first day arrives—how to make yourself available to ensure that the new employee gets off on the right foot.

Many supervisors have jobs where they interact with a variety of people on an almost continuous basis. They attend long and drawn-out meetings, they get a lot of phone calls, they make a multitude of decisions large and small all day long, and they experience frequent interruptions. They seldom feel in control of their contacts, consequently, they have a hard time setting aside enough time to really work with the new employee.

Most often, however, setting aside time to work with newly hired people is an investment that can pay big dividends. Their feelings of worth, the sense they make of things going on about them, and the ease and comfort with which they adjust to the new environment are all importantly related to being able to interact with their new supervisor in a relaxed and fruitful manner.

I am not necessarily talking about the supervisor spending the whole day with the new group member—that might be too intense and overpowering. It also might not provide the new person with an opportunity to reflect on and absorb the data and sensations being received. An hour or two at the beginning, the sharing of breaks and the lunch hour, and an hour or so at the end of the day might be sufficient. However, for the rest of the day the supervisor should be readily and easily accessible for questions and requests.

Questions and requests should not be viewed negatively for they show initiative and a problem-solving orientation. Questions that appear silly seldom are from the asker's point of view, and they are often an attempt to orient oneself. Also, problems that might be easily resolved in a relaxed atmosphere may be hard to manage under stress. The tension often experienced by the new employee will best dissolve when given thorough and patient responses. Impatience or annoyance shown early in a relationship tends to produce passivity and "doing only what is necessary"—the enemy of high productivity.

Basically, however, the issue of being available that first day is largely one of preplanning and preaction. What would happen on a normal day (not one when a new employee is to arrive) if you were to become ill? What happens when you go on a vacation? Isn't it strange that the place probably continues to operate anyway? What if you were to be invisible for one day, what would go on? That last question might be too frightening to contemplate. But seriously, ask yourself the following questions:

1. Who is trained or being trained to take over many of my supervisory duties while I invest my time in the new employee today? (If the answer is no one, then you and the organization are potentially in a lot of trouble. We'll deal with the issue of delegation later.)

2. Who can attend meetings in my place? (Or could I take the new employee with me to a meeting? Would it be worthwhile?)

3. Who else can answer my phone calls and follow up on requests?

4. Which requests *must* I deal with today? (Could I use these few necessary items as a chance to show the new employee what goes on around here?)

5. Have I previously notified other people (including my supervisor) that I won't be available today, except for serious emergencies?

6. Do I have someone available who can work with, help, guide, and train the new employee for the short periods when I am not available?

As we can see from these questions, "being available" is normally a matter of effective planning and taking the necessary steps to carry out the plan. At the end of the first day, ask yourself how you would be thinking, feeling, and acting if you were the new employee. Then check out the reality of your perception with the new employee.

At this time you might want to go back to the exercise suggested at the start of this chapter and add anything from the preceding pages, or add any new ideas you have had that you might find useful.

STUDY QUESTIONS

1. What are the eight key questions that need to be asked about the preparation for each new employee on his or her first day?

2. Which of the eight questions have you had responsibility for, or an effect upon, prior to reading this chapter?

3. Which of these eight items do you consider most important in your present organization when dealing with the new employee? Why?

4. Why is it important that neither the supervisor of the new employee nor the personnel department people who affect the new person assume that the other has handled any or all of the eight key questions?

5. Identify the twelve primary "need to know" items that the new employee should be oriented to on the first day. Which are critical in your present organization?

6. What is the primary "impression and impact" likely to be made on a new employee in your organization?

7. What key policies, procedures, and rules might *reasonably* be communicated to and absorbed by the new employee in your organizational unit on the first day?

8. What *specific* factors do you consider to be most important in your department in each of the areas of:

   a. physical and emotional comfort

   b. opportunities for work-related accomplishments

   c. integrating the new employee into the work group

   d. enhanced social status or prestige

9. List five things you can plan to do in order to make yourself available to give close attention to the new employee on her or his first day.

CHAPTER 8

BY THE END OF
THE FIRST WEEK

Years ago I read a squib in the *Reader's Digest* about a woman who approached a famous child psychologist after he gave a brilliant speech on his subject.

"When should I start training my son?" she asked.

"How old is the child?" he responded.

"Six," she replied.

"Lady—hurry home, you are six years late!"

We may not be six years late, but it is often late in the game before we seriously begin to train new employees. Serious training should begin within the first week and be well advanced by the end of it.

"Day One" laid the foundation for a good beginning, but hardly less important are days two, three, four, and five. Each day as the first week progresses should ensure some growth in self-assurance, comfort, and productivity. The details to be covered by the supervisor each subsequent day may be fewer, but they are just as important. We want to keep the new person's interest, curiosity, and enthusiasm at a high level. We want to begin to strengthen the process of good work habits. We want to interchange with the new employee on a level that will produce good productive results for both of us.

PLANNING THE REST OF THE WEEK

At this point it might be well to repeat a version of the exercise suggested in the previous chapter. Ask yourself the following questions, but pause after asking each and list all the things or ideas that you can think of that will relate to each question.

I have asked groups of supervisors and staff personnel to answer these questions in groups composed of people in occupations as diverse as police, nursing, manufacturing, utilities, office, and military intelligence. Different backgrounds and needs produced some different items on each list, but other items were very common. Later in the chapter some of the common items are given for you to consider in applying to your situation. However, you are more likely to touch the unique aspects of your own job if you answer each problem alone first and then supplement your product with ideas from this book and perhaps from discussions with your peers.

Question 1. What additional things does the new employee need to know by the end of the first week? After you develop your final list, you can schedule the things to be learned over the remaining four days of the week. Try to avoid concerning yourself with scheduling until you have a complete list. Trying to dream up items and sequencing and scheduling them at the same time causes confusion and impedes the creative process. Develop your list first, sequence the items second, and finally schedule them. Also ask yourself what learning from the first day may benefit from reinforcement. Reexamine your lists from the first day and see what was too complex or diverse to be easily absorbed in the first day, and then add it to your list for the first week.

Question 2. What key policies and procedures can I hope to convey during this week? Those items that come closest to the employee, such as fringe benefits, and those which are most critical in job success are best handled now. Never is the employee likely to be more attentive than she or he will be this week. As far as job performance is concerned, the most lasting, enduring impressions will be made during the first week. Critical personal and job incidents may be remembered longer, but these will probably be the exceptions. The things communicated in the first five days will probably be regarded as "the rule." List those that are important in your organization.

Question 3. What impressions or impacts do I want to introduce or reinforce? This list may now be shorter, but it should be kept in a positive vein. By keeping the answers to this question clearly before you, you will avoid negative behaviors and examples.

Question 4. What else can I do to help further integrate the new employee into the workgroup and the larger organization successfully? By the end of the first week, social relationships will have begun to firm up. For better or worse, the new employee will have a fairly good idea of how the other employees regard her or him, and chances are good that the level of social comfort will be high or low. While the period of social adjustment may go on for quite some time, many employees feel "left out" by the end of the first week and opportunity has been lost. List ideas on what you can do to prevent this loss.

Question 5. What work-related sense of accomplishment can be experienced by the new employee? Nearly every job worthy of the name, except perhaps in the most highly complex ones, should offer a solid emotional pay-off by the end of a week. Whether the person is offered a chance to do a piece of work alone, or whether the person is allowed to work as a full member of an achieving team will be much influenced by the kind of work available, the experience and skills of the new employee, and most of all, by the ingenuity and creativity of the supervisor who can structure work assignments to include challenge. List opportunities for such experiences that exist in your bailiwick.

Question 6. What types of counseling are needed; how much should I do and when? It is important for the supervisor and for the employee to get together from time to time to talk about progress and problems. The main planning problem for the supervisor will be to list the things the new employee needs feedback on, and how much information relevant to those things should be imparted. Then the scheduling part can be worked in with your other commitments.

Question 7. How can I make myself available to work with the new employee? Effective time management is a tough game, but it often involves solving small problems before they become big ones. Hours invested this week in the new employee may save hundreds of hours in the weeks and years to come. Assess the tasks to be done in connection with the new employee, estimate the time required, schedule it, and then live by the schedule. This investment will produce surprisingly gratifying dividends.

The Need to Know (Questions 1 and 2)

A check-off sheet for the first week might include:

1. Convey a general statement of organization objectives to the new employee.

2. Conduct a *general* review of key policies and procedures on an item-by-item basis.

3. Provide a one-to-one presentation on those fringe benefits that will affect the employee, and provide any available written material on those benefits.

4. Specify the general parameters of the new employee's job, especially as it interrelates to other people and their jobs.

5. Sketch a brief overview of the organization's structure.

6. Provide additional details on safety (specific and work-related), and schedule safety training if it is an issue in your organization.

7. Present general information on personal growth and training opportunities available through the organization, as well as information on promotional procedures.

8. Review the new employee's job description, including the scope of authority and how this can be increased.

9. Introduce the department's or the supervisor's own special policies and procedures (if any).

10. Detail the probationary and disciplinary procedures (if any).

11. List information related to special forms, appropriate reference materials, and similar details that the employee needs to know (written notes on such might be helpful).

12. Provide information on special problems:

    a. If classified information is at stake, the new employee will need a rapid introduction to basic security procedures, and perhaps scheduled training at a later date,

    b. If a formal orientation or facilities tour is offered, designate where and when the employee will be involved,

    c. If rights of the employee is an issue, items related to grievances, Equal Employment Opportunity, etc., should be covered.

As you can see from the foregoing list (augmented perhaps by items special to your needs), there is plenty for the supervisor to do during that first week, even if nothing else came up. Hence, careful planning to cover the items adequately without overwhelming or boring the new employee is important—spaced learning on such heavy subjects is vital. Some material may well carry over into subsequent weeks, but a start on nearly all of them should begin during the first week. How to make it all interesting might be a real challenge.

Impressions and Impacts (Question 3)

The story is told of a messenger who brought bad news to the king and was beheaded by the displeased monarch as his reward. After that, the king had a hard time finding volunteer messengers. Those who were pressed into service tended to fudge the facts to make bad news sound like good news. The king probably never knew he was in trouble until the enemy was within the palace.

I often find supervisors behaving much like that ancient king. By abrupt, threatening, judgmental, or punishing behavior, they make it very difficult for the employee to approach with a problem. Remember, to a new employee, a supervisor is often seen as a very powerful person. If we want subordinates to feel free to discuss (and then resolve) problems, we must be open, easy to approach, and supportive in our behavior. If the focus is on problem solving rather than evaluation—especially during this critical early period—a relationship can be built that will enhance the quality of life for both parties and ensure future productivity. No other impression may be more vital.

The impression of a well organized, planned way of doing business also needs to be reinforced.

Further Integration into the Workgroup and the Organization (Question 4)

Part of the process of getting bearings in a new workgroup, and in the larger organization, relates to information and how well the employee gets to know the people she or he will be working with. Below are listed some items which are *informational* and *social*. All need to be dealt with creatively and effectively.

Informational:

1. Who will supervise when the supervisor is gone (if not dealt with on first day)?

2. Who will provide direction and training—(if not clear from the first day)?

3. Include more information on coworkers' names (how they prefer to be referred to, nicknames, etc.).

4. Supplement data on coworkers' functions and responsibilities (such information should be spaced over the week so as not to be confusing).

5. In large and complex organizations a gradual tour of the facilities on a planned and scheduled basis can be helpful. One new area at a time can be visited—not all at once.

6. Plan introductions on contacts outside the department, with lists of names, locations, and phone numbers to reinforce learning.

7. In large and specialized organizations, particularly in government agencies, the meaning of strange words, special terms, and acronyms can be very helpful (providing an employee with a list can speed the person's learning if these terms are numerous).

Social:

1. Ask coworkers to share in the introductory process, on a planned basis. Areas where coworkers can help include:
   a. Help in preparing for the new person's arrival. Discover what each person feels comfortable in contributing and encourage the group to come up with constructive ideas.
   b. The buddy system should be used for lunches and breaks during the first week.
   c. Have coworkers (on a volunteer basis) introduce the new person to people who can provide services to the new person inside and outside the department.

2. Schedule one or two informal get-togethers where workgroup members are identified by their special talents.

3. Share knowledge of the new employee's special interests, accomplishments, and outside activities with the workgroup in a supportive fashion.

Many of these approaches may be far too complicated for your situation, but parts of them may be useful. The degree to which special efforts are required are often related to the complexity and diversity of the work being done, and to the magnitude of the organization structure. Some of the items would probably occur in the natural process of employee adjustment, but then they might not. The supervisor needs to consider whether they should be left to random chance or be planned. The new employee and the workgroup itself will eventually reach an accommodation of sorts. Do you want to influence this accommodation? Only you need to estimate what type of influence the workgroup will have on the employee—for better or worse.

Work-Related Sense of Accomplishment (Question 5)

With sufficient advanced planning most supervisors can structure one or more work assignments that can allow new employees to demonstrate their competence, their prior knowledge, or their ability to learn quickly within the first week. A great deal depends upon the nature of the work available, and the employees' prior background, but with the application of wit and imagination most supervisors can find a challenge or two for each individual.

For the first week, the most important issue may be that an effort must be made to resist the temptation to cook up things just to keep the new employee busy. The new employee will see through such a sham and value his or her work accordingly. Whatever the employee does, it should produce *something* of value.

The new employee will generally recognize that her or his contribution to a new job will be limited at first, and so they will not be surprised if the supervisor assigns low priority work, however, it should not be make-work. Repairing parts, moving files, or reducing a backlog of low priority work is understandable, but digging post holes and filling them up again—just to keep busy—insults a person. Often, make-work demonstrates a lack of planning, and it may leave a bad taste in the employee's mouth.

Another way that a new employee's sense of worth can be enhanced early in a new relationship is to provide quick, constructive, and detailed feedback on job performance and job accomplishments. Here the emphasis should be on the positive accomplishments of the employee as much as possible.

Early in the relationship the supervisor needs to begin the career-long process of providing the new employee with information about the match or mismatch between job requirements and job performance. During the first week this information will be very limited, unless the work is simple or the person highly enough skilled to begin performing adequately at once.

When providing feedback on performance, we should strive mightily to be *informative* rather than evaluative, *descriptive* rather than judgmental, *factual* rather than vague. The expression, "You're coming along fine," communicates little of value and may be actually misleading. We need to give honest, *specific* information *as the performance occurs.* "You produced several hundred units this week with a three percent rework factor. This is well within normal limits for a new employee." Also, "I'm satisfied with your work," would do much to reassure a new employee. I often think that supervisors are vague on performance feedback because they do not have really explicit standards and norms. The issue of feedback, while often not too critical the first week, becomes very critical the following weeks. Information on quality standards can be just as valuable as quantity data.

Primarily during the first week we want to ensure that we do as much as possible to make new employees productive and guarantee that they do not settle into a rut.[1]

Counseling and Developing Subordinates (Question 6)

Few supervisors seem well trained in the art of counseling. They often give advice rather than information, discount or disregard information the subordinate is supplying, and try to rescue when help is not necessarily needed. The aim of all supervisory counseling is to *facilitate* subordinates solving their own problems, to encourage growth and development, and to help subordinates become independent, mature problem solvers.

Unfortunately, in recent years many personnel people and supervisors have confused counseling with disciplining and evaluating subordinates. When counseling is used as a tool to manipulate a subordinate into behaving in a way desired by the supervisor, it is no longer counseling.

According to the dictionary, counseling is "the act of exchanging ideas; act of talking things over; give advice to; recommend." These words imply a freedom or equality on the part of the other person and the right to reject the advice or recommendations on the part of the person being counseled.

Professional counselors recognize that counseling is for the benefit and development of the counselee, not the counselor. Modern counselors also recognize that the principal value of counseling is to allow for and help the employee to talk out or work through the emotional barriers to problem solving so that decisions can be made *by the counselee.* As such, they recognize that giving advice is seldom valid or helpful. The counselee knows more about his or her problem than anyone else, consequently, the person who "owns the problem" is best qualified to solve the problem. This means that the super-

---

[1]In hospitals and other crisis-oriented situations a useful technique to achieve several objectives at once might be to conduct a well planned and well executed simulated or dry-run for an emergency. This can help integrate the new employee into the workgroup and the role he or she will play in crisis. Also, the employee receives vital job training.

visor should listen to the employee's problems as skillfully as possible and only offer *information* or *permission* when it is asked for. How one goes about doing this well is a considerable art, but it primarily involves very good listening.

In dealing with the new employee, the supervisor should:

1. Listen to the concerns of the new employee, especially on the morning of the second day and in the evenings of the next few days.

2. Make an effort to pick up on verbal and nonverbal clues that the new employee is having a problem, and offer to listen when such clues are detected.

3. Help when possible, but do not get involved in rescuing (taking over responsibility for solving the problem).

4. Do not brush off or discount concerns of the other person. (The person wouldn't be bringing up the problem if it wasn't important to him or her. To judge otherwise would be judging that person to be a fool.)

The most important aspect of these considerations is that the person who sends signals or clearly states a problem is providing the supervisor with data on what is bothering that person. It should be treated with the respect that human information deserves. If that information is dismissed or discounted (making less of the data than it deserves), the new employee may later withhold such information, which often places the supervisor in the dark.

The new employee probably needs effective counseling more during this first week of employment than any other period of her or his career (except for crisis situations), for it is now that the major adjustments of the person to the job are occurring. Depending on the circumstances, the new employee also may be faced with family adjustments, external problems (i.e., new location, new housing, etc.), and a whole new environment, as well as job-related problems. Effective help from the supervisor and personnel people may never be more badly needed.[2]

Making Yourself Available (Question 7)

Supervisors may still face the problem of being overworked, for they are often short-handed, and the new employee is not yet productive. Consequently, there is often a tendency to give a new employee some relatively trivial monotonous assignment and leave her or him there "until things get straightened out."

This lack of investment in the new employee often delays the day when the supervisor can easily assign complex tasks, and it may significantly delay the

---

[2]One issue that may be of vital concern to new employees is money. New employees often need money badly. We should do all we can to ensure that they get paid on time and are promptly reimbursed for moving expenses, etc., if such is appropriate. If the organization allows for advances against salary, the employees may need to know this.

time when "things get straightened out." The postponement or avoidance of training can be a counterproductive effort.

Often, as a person's apprehension about a new job diminishes, enthusiasm also may lessen. Many jobs as they are structured do not have real challenge. If we give even duller assignments as time goes on, the new employee may conclude that nothing new is likely to happen. Techniques for building challenge into the job will be discussed later, but basically the assignments of the first week should contain challenge if at all possible.

Making ourselves available also involves planning ahead to work with the new employee, and it begins long before the new person's arrival. One important time in the first week to be available is for the "idea conference."

THE IDEA CONFERENCE

You'll never have another chance like this one! During the first week, new employees see the new job, the people, the organization, and the environment through fresh and wondering eyes. They will be learning at a terrific pace. They will be asking questions, overtly or covertly, about nearly everything. It is now that the employees will be calling upon every bit of experience, every single fact, every creative idea in their repertoire in the striving for job success.

Before that interest, that energy, that know-how, withers and fades, we need to capture it for later use. The Idea Conference is an effort to benefit from new employees' prior experience, their data bank, and their creative inquiry.

Early in the week we should let new employees know that we are interested in their ideas about how internal operations, methods and procedures, and work processing and flow could be improved, simplified, rearranged, or combined. We should also let them know that we will schedule a personal meeting at the end of each of the next four weeks. At that meeting, we would like to note or record any suggestions or ideas that they have for methods improvements, work simplification, or cost reduction. Also, at the end of the month we will hold a "Creativity–Problem Solving Conference" with all workgroup members to try to implement or use the new employee's ideas.

You might ask the new employees to jot down any ideas they have, anything that they know from their prior experience that might be helpful, and any current operations which seem less effective than they might be. No pressure should be put upon the new people to produce ideas since that creates tension and worry and impedes creative thought.

At these weekly conferences it is important for the supervisor to serve *only* as a recorder. No evaluation or criticism should be made of any idea. Also, it is bad policy to defend any current practices or to explain why you do things the way you do, unless the new employees ask specific and direct questions which can be given specific and direct answers. All suggestions should be dealt with in the monthly meeting, and any reaction, except for recording the employees' statements, can tend to cut off the free flow of their contributions.

If new employees seem critical of you, the workgroup, or current practices, there is no value in reacting negatively. Many people have long established critical habits and here these habits are not the subject of concern. We
want their suggestions and, at the moment, all else is secondary. Often, they
will come to realize that such criticism is unwarranted. The best way we can get
their ideas is to be neutral and simply record their ideas.

FINAL DETAILS

At the end of the first week, we need to wrap up a few loose ends, among
them:

1. What can be expected next week, especially anything that will be different.

2. Summarize what has been accomplished in this week.

3. Complete your first week check-off sheet.

4. Answer new employees' questions and provide assistance as needed.

If even a substantial proportion of these plans are carried out, you will
have moved much closer to achieving the goal of developing productive employees.

STUDY QUESTIONS

1. What are the seven questions that lead to effectively planning learning
   experiences for the new employee during the first week on the job?

2. From the "need to know" list given in the text (questions 1 and 2),
   which three are most important in your job area?

3. On the lists related to integrating the new employee into the workgroup
   and into the organization, choose the three most important items under
   both *Informational* and *Social* in your particular job area.

4. How in your workgroup and with the type of work you manage might
   a new employee attain a work-related sense of accomplishment during
   the first week of employment?

5. What are the four essential elements of effective counseling?

6. What types of problems should the supervisor encourage the new employee to deal with when preparing for the Idea Conference?

7. What four final details should be dealt with toward the end of the first
   week?

CHAPTER 9

THE THIRTY-DAY CHECKPOINT

As the first month progresses, new employees should comfortably settle into a productive pattern of job performance. Personal knowledge of the organization and of its objectives and problems should be growing. Their job-related contacts with others should be spreading toward the outer edges of their short-range needs. The employees will probably begin to focus on their long-term relationship with the organization and the mutual benefits to be gained by each. These people should begin to develop firm bearings and a strong sense of belonging. They are on the way to becoming full team members. The challenges should be coming at a rate and level sufficient to stimulate and stretch the employees.

Also, in most jobs, if planning and training have been adequate, new employees should be generating enough work or services to be evaluated, to some degree at least. Objective feedback on this performance is very important. Both the amount and quality of the feedback during this first month can have a considerable impact on the new employees' perceptions of themselves and of the job.

For most jobs, feedback on performance can start much earlier in the month, and this pattern can be reinforced by a more formal (but usually unofficial) presentation at the end of the first month. However, in providing information to employees on their productivity, it is important to remember five items:

1. Standards should be realistic, clear cut, objective (the same type of standards would apply to any employee), and previously communicated to and explained to each new employee.

2. Assess the *person's performance—not the person* (we are all considerably more than our jobs and none of us can assess the whole person).

3. Be as descriptive (rather than evaluative) as possible.

4. Appraisal comments should relate directly to the standards.

5. After presenting *data,* listen carefully and do not dismiss or discount the employee's comments—you may learn a great deal.

Substantially more detailed comments and suggestions on performance feedback will be given in a later chapter. The main point to remember here is that feedback should start early, be specific, and occur close to the time the performance occurs. Above all, it should be descriptive rather than evaluative.

THE PERSONAL PLANNING EXERCISE

Again it might be helpful for you to take pencil and paper and list the things that the new employee should have a grasp of by the end of the first month, in connection with *your organization.*

The basic questions are similar to those asked earlier, but the answers may be less precise because the settling-in process has progressed considerably and the person's needs are becoming more long term and general.

Question 1. What additional things does the new employee need to know by the end of the first month? After listing the things that come to you immediately, you might want to review your earlier lists for items that naturally extend into a longer-term process.

Question 2. What policies and procedures affect the new employee or could affect job performances? If a policy and procedures manual exists, the index can be examined to ensure a complete listing.

Question 3. What impressions or models do I want to reinforce? This is a particularly challenging area, for maintaining consistency is difficult. It is also difficult to incorporate organizational values into a human being, however indirect the process.

Question 4. What specific tasks can I assign which will allow the individual to grow? If you examine or list all of the tasks performed by members of the immediate workgroup, you can often structure at least the simpler ones into interesting and challenging assignments.

Question 5. What can I do to ensure a broadening pattern of delegation of authority and decision making over the way tasks are performed? Since supervisors should concentrate on getting the job done (the what versus the how), they should search for opportunities to share even their own tasks with subordinates.

Question 6. What are my work-related training objectives which are to be met within this month? By the very fact that we are dealing with the culmination of a thirty-day period, many of the things to be learned and mastered by the new employee involve more general items such as policies and procedures, and more items which are specific to the nature of the job being performed by the incumbent. In this chapter we will not deal with each of the previous questions specifically, but will deal with general issues because much of what you have on your list will be related to your particular organization and the job the new employee holds.

SUPPLEMENTAL IDEAS

In addition to the items you came up with on your list, there might be some additional things that could be useful.

Need to Know by the End of the First Month (Question 1)

Participants in my seminars have listed these items:

a. *A general knowledge of personnel policies, especially benefits.*

b. *The performance appraisal system, including a view of the focus to be used, the items on the form (how they are marked and how the formal system operates), and especially how appraisal is related to raises.* Many supervisors and many organizations balk at voluntarily revealing such data since the employee is usually scheduled for appraisal only once a year. But this secretive approach may be self-defeating. The employee learns of the system from other employees anyway and seldom has any way to check out the reality of what the coworkers are saying. Since a significant part of the employee's future will be affected by this system, it is only a matter of leveling with the employee to reveal the system—there should be no surprises. A positive factor favoring revelation is the "Santa Claus" effect—behavior tends to improve about the time "Santa Claus" (i.e., raise time) is about to arrive. By early revelation the employee can keep in mind what he or she will be evaluated upon and positive habits can be developed during the employee's formative period.

c. *The general flow of work through the organization, especially what creates the need for the employee's product or service, what precedes the employee's function, and what follows it.* In many cases this flow is readily apparent, even obvious, but in many companies employees perform only a part of a much larger task. Not understanding their particular role in the overall production of goods or services often leads to a feeling of insignificance, unspoken questions about job value, and a diminishing sense of self-worth.

d. *A working knowledge of the organization structure and an understanding of how rigid the structure is.* This means more than awareness of the organization chart and how the immediate unit relates to other units. This working knowledge involves an understanding of how to get things done in this particular organization. People used to inflexible organization structures will often not take advantage of cross-departmental transfer of resources or of special ways to resolve interorganizational conflicts. People need a clear knowledge of who can help them solve certain problems and what informal methods are available to get assistance when needed. Clever, innovative individuals often can manage to get the job done in spite of the organization structure.

e. *The schedule of formal orientation offered by the organization, if one exists.*

f. *The person should be able to recognize the names and faces of key people throughout the organization.* While the number and types of individuals that need to be recognized will vary with the job, knowing who's who seems to be an important part of our sense of importance and security. This "nice-to-know" aspect of organizational orientation goes far beyond the range of personal introductions. When an individual is able to point out an important person in the organization to a coworker, or recognize that person's picture in the local paper, the event seems to often enhance the person's sense of being socially "in," and it creates a feeling of identification with the organization. I feel that this aspect of creating a sense of organizational belonging is often underrated.

g. *Knowledge of career ladders and related training opportunities.* By the end of the first month, the employee is usually beginning to feel comfortable enough in the environment to begin to wonder about what the future might bring, and to consider how she or he might begin to prepare for it. Keeping the employee looking forward (assuming opportunities for growth and development do exist in your organization) promotes a high level of interest and the motivation to do better.

h. *Requirements for career advancement.* Organizations that have formed career ladders and well-defined progression paths have a relatively easy time of conveying this information. However, this information is often not conveyed until the employee asks for it. "If they want it badly enough they'll come to me" is all too often an unexpressed supervisory attitude. This statement also assumes that the supervisor is the only source of information.

Aside from the reality that *employee passivity* may lead to the organization not having a variety of trained and certified people to take over any vacant job, such *supervisory passivity* can lead to other negative consequences. The new employee often gets distorted and false information from coworkers. We must ensure that the employee gets adequate information and that the requirements for career advancement (inside or outside that organizational unit) are clearly understood. This topic deserves a special conference, specifically devoted to this subject, within the first thirty days of the person's employment. If the organization has no formal system, or if the jobs available do not require credentials, the conference could be very short. In Waste Water Treatment Facilities where plant operators often have a long and arduous training and education process, as well as a succession of credentials to be acquired,

I've seen this type of conference go on for an hour or two. In that utility, the organization also prepared a packet of information on the courses required and the steps to be taken in order to become a full plant operator. This orderly approach virtually ensures that employee time and effort is used productively.

i. *Details on the length and procedural aspects of the probationary period.* This topic will be covered more completely in the next chapter, but an effective rundown of your organization's approach to the probationary period should be explained *in detail* by the end of the first month.

j. *Organizationally specific items.* For example, if secret classified matter is handled by your organization, detailed training should be performed within the first month. Additionally, an item such as employee safety is more critical in some organizations than others.

Policies and Procedures (Question 2)

Having suffered through many company "briefings" on policies and procedures, I cannot remember a one that was either effective or interesting. Being a light sleeper (during daylight hours), the snoring of the group had always kept me awake—at least fitfully so.

What we laughingly called "briefings" seemed to come in one of three varieties:

1. A specialist droned on and on about some obscure, vague point.

2. A hotshot with a variety of graphs and charts swamped us with data (that person at least kept us awake).

3. Staff people used the briefings as a tool to sell their particular organizational activity—though they probably alienated more people than they converted through their dull, drab performance and obvious hucksterism.

If none of these have been your experience, you have been one of the lucky few. However, it is important that employees learn and be able to use those standard operating policies and procedures that affect them personally and which impinge upon their job duties. The distinctions between policies and procedures and how to convey the information they contain may be helpful.

Organizational policies represent a primary way in which the organization communicates to its employees those items that are of primary concern to the organization. Policies represent the practical wisdom of the organization—its plan of action, its way of management. Policies change, but in the interim employees need to coordinate their activities with the organization's policies. They can hardly do this successfully in the long run if they do not know what those policies are or have vague or inaccurate perceptions of those policies.

Organizational procedures are intended as guidelines for managing or conducting the business of the agency, institution, or firm. Theoretically, they represent tried and true ways of doing things that have proven successful in achieving the organizational goals. At their foundation, procedures are an effort to pass on the experience and the prior problem-solving achievements of the group. They are intended to be helpful, to conserve energy and resources, and to produce consistency of end product or service. Problems arise when procedures are published and perceived to be cast in concrete. Procedures become problems when they institutionalize archaic methods, thwart goal achievement, defeat innovation, compound organizational structures, and slow the process of productivity. *At the least,* people need to know the nature of operating procedures so that they can use them when helpful (and subvert them successfully—may heaven forgive me—when necessary) to achieve organizational goals.

Unfortunately, at least from a teaching viewpoint, organizational policies and procedures are written to conform to a format established for the policy and procedural manual. The essential points for the new employee to know, understand, and use are often buried in the rhetoric of the policy or procedure.

I have found two primary approaches helpful in teaching new employees the essence of specific policies and procedures and how to interpret them. The first method includes the following:

1. Since new employees generally arrive one at a time, I have identified the important policies or procedures that need to be conveyed, scheduled each item at the rate of one a day during the first month, and dealt with that subject in a one-to-one conference on the scheduled day.

2. I have shared the schedule and the policy and procedures manual with the new employee and allowed the employee time to read the item scheduled for the next day.

3. I have asked the employee to read the policy aloud to both of us (this act may seem strange, but it often gives the employee new insight into the policy) and to give her or his interpretation. This is in no way to be considered a test for the employee, it is an *evaluation free* act. It doesn't matter what viewpoint the employee expresses at this time—we want to ensure that the employee leaves the meeting with useful knowledge and does not feel "under the gun" when expressing an understanding of the item.

4. Prior to the meeting, I have identified the key points and concerns that should be understood about the policy, and during the meeting I have shared these with the new employee.

5. The new employee and I discuss each item until both of us feel comfortable that the new employee fully understands the policy or procedure and can use it as needed.

Often this training process takes only five to ten minutes on each item, and this discussion can often be combined with other meetings. Closely related policies and procedures, especially descriptions of fringe benefits, can be combined in a single session as long as overloading the new employee does not occur.

This personalized detailed step-by-step training approach takes time and effort, but it virtually guarantees results. This method also often brought *me* up to date on changes, enhanced my insights on occasion, and represented an investment in a subordinate which paid off.

Larger organizations often collect new employees into groups and try to orient them as to policies and procedures all at one time. This second method works well, as long as:

1. The person's supervisor is aware of what items are covered and those that are not, so that compensatory efforts can be made.

2. The presenters realize that little is gained from any verbal presentation on a given subject, particularly on items such as policies and procedures, that exceeds five minutes (although additional time would be allowed for questions and answers).

3. Small group discussion, effective visuals, and solid illustrative examples are used to make the learning process more stimulating.

Thoughts on Questions 3, 4, 5, and 6

If you carried out the exercise suggested earlier in this chapter some ideas in the following questions have probably been generated.

Question 3. What impressions or models do I want to reinforce?

Question 4. What specific tasks can I assign which will allow the individual to grow?

Question 5. What can I do to ensure a broadening pattern of delegation of authority and decision making over the way tasks are performed?

Question 6. What are my work-related training objectives which are to be met within the month?

These questions cannot be easily answered in general since they are all job specific and must flow out of the job the new employee is hired to fill. Future chapters will provide some suggested methods of answering these questions as they relate to the individual tasks each person is to perform. However, it is up to the supervisor, perhaps with the help of staff specialists, to come up with specific approaches to gaining from these possibilities. Efforts by groups of supervisors to talk over ways to accomplish these ends have often lead to brainstorming a wide variety of possibilities.

THE CREATIVITY CONFERENCE PAYOFF

In the previous chapter the Idea Conference was suggested as a way of recording ideas, suggestions, and even problems perceived by new employees. Its purpose was to capture the often fleeting ideas that new people develop when applying their previous experience in a new environment. In that conference it was suggested that for the first four weekly sessions the supervisor merely record the thoughts of new employees, with only enough interchange to ensure that the supervisor understood their comments.

The purpose of the Idea Conference was not only to develop ideas to improve operations but, to demonstrate an interest in new employees, in their ideas, and in the contribution that they can make to the organization. On the other hand, if we are one of those dead-eye, "shoot from the hip" marksmen who get satisfaction in blowing ideas out of the air, or if we are from the legion of "abominable no men" or "no women," the employees will soon learn not to bring up ideas—for it is better to have no ideas than to see them smothered by others at birth. The key function of the Idea Conference is to make ideas work.

At the end of the first month the supervisor should get together individually with new employees and try to sort out the ideas of record. The task is usually two-fold: (1) updating or allowing the employees to modify their ideas in light of current knowledge (though the employees should be encouraged not to shoot down their own ideas and to focus on strengthening the idea of making it more acceptable to others), and (2) categorizing the ideas, as to the difficulty of implementation and the degree to which the ideas affect others.

Usually a new employee's ideas fall into three categories:

1. *Items that are simple and direct.* Primarily these can be implemented by the supervisor and affect no one else significantly. These involve such things as relocating furniture, acquiring labor-saving devices which fall within budgeted funds, and/or just allowing the employee to change the methods of carrying out tasks. These ideas need not necessarily wait for the month's end meeting, but it is important to express appreciation for the idea to the employee at some point. A review of the success of some of those ideas (since the supervisor has a list of them) can improve the new employee's morale.
   Ideas in this category which are unworkable are rare, but when such is the case, the new employee will usually see that fact clearly by the end of the first month and abandon the ideas willingly. Where their impracticality is not perceived, we should listen carefully for there may be more to the idea than we realize. The focus here is not on preserving the status quo, but on using as many ideas as possible.
2. *Items that affect another person or the allocation of resources.* These ideas often require creative negotiation with the affected person(s) or inclusion of the item in a budget request. Such suggestion may take

more time and often require the ongoing support of the supervisor. Often the affected people can be brought into the decision-making process to ensure that their needs are also met by the proposed change. Examples of this type of idea might involve new work methods by others in the workgroup, the acquisition of capital equipment, or the spending of considerable amounts of money. All avenues for making such ideas practical and usable should be explored.

3. *Complex ideas that affect the whole workgroup affects outside contacts or which involve a significant challenge to the status quo.* Such complex ideas often require considerable cooperation from others to implement and to make them operable after implementation. Group meetings often turn into shooting galleries for new ideas—especially those of new employees since to accept a new person's ideas is often perceived as implied criticism of past group performance ("Why didn't *they* come up with this idea?") The supervisor will be sorely tried to make such ideas workable and acceptable. A variety of the nonevaluative rules of brainstorming, spectrum policy, and other techniques for maximizing the creative potential of the new employee will be covered in Chapter 14 on The Creativity Conference.

STUDY QUESTIONS

1. Name the five elements of effective informal performance appraisal.

2. What six questions should we ask ourselves when planning for the first month of a new employee's performance?

3. List the ten suggestions made by trainees when asked to plan for a new employee's first month on the job.

4. What are the five approaches suggested as being helpful when teaching new employees the essence of specific policies and procedures?

5. Explain the meaning and operation of the Creativity Conference.

6. What are the three general classifications of a new employee's ideas?

7. What steps can *you* take to help implement the new employee's new ideas?

CHAPTER 10

THE PROBATIONARY PERIOD

The probationary period is an arbitrary period of time, chosen by the organization, in which the organization attempts to assess a new individual's performance and determine whether or not that person will make a satisfactory long-term employee. If the organization's judgment of the new employee is negative, they generally discharge the employee without much compunction, and then set about to find another employee to fill the job slot. This is a very formal way of saying that for some period, the new employee's head is on the block.

This position is not the most conducive to getting the job done, though some supervisors are convinced that people work best with the sword of Damocles suspended above the employee's head by a single hair. On the other hand, managers and supervisors who recognize that the pressure of the probationary period may impede the adjustment period and distract from the employee's concentration, are often at a loss to come up with an alternative. They often feel strongly that they need an understood and accepted out if the employee proves to be mismatched to the job.

Also, in a very real sense the organization is also on probation for an indefinite period, though few supervisors or managers consciously deal with this side of the problem. Supervisors often regard a relatively new employee's decision to leave the organization as a personal affront, and they frequently try to punish the departing employee for such audacity. It is as though individual rights do not equal organizational rights.

The main advantage of a probationary period from the new employee's viewpoint is the common assumption, usually made by both the employee and the organization, that once the period is over the employee has earned the right to stay with the organization on a "more or less" permanent basis. Sometimes "more or less" means forever, and sometimes it means as long as *average* or *satisfactory* work is performed. A lot of what "more or less" means (and it is seldom explicit) depends on the type of organization, the degree of freedom its management has to be arbitrary, and the traditions of the organization.

The main advantage of a probationary period from the organization's point of view seems to be that it gives management one guilt-free transaction. It is very difficult to determine beforehand whether or not a person can do a specific job and whether or not the individual *will* do what management wants, even when the new employee *is* competent. Consequently, it is reasonable for an organization to want a try-out period before offering even an implied assurance of continued employment.

The real difficulty I find with the probationary period is that a curious change of behavior often occurs once the probationary period is over.

Some firms have a blanket ninety-day probationary period. Unsatisfactory employees are supposed to be gone by the ninety-first day. While I have seen some new employees disappear before the ninety days are up, the others who remain often turn strange. It is not unknown to have a new employee call in sick on the ninety-first day. The crowds at the water cooler seem to swell. Post-starting-time discussion of last night's TV program or baseball game seems to have a new, very active participant. The overall pace may slacken perceptibly as the new employee breathes a deep sight of relief and settles in for the long haul.

Whether or not the passing of the probationary period is noted or not by the organization, the group, or the individual, it still has significance. A luncheon, a silver watch, or a formal induction ceremony might have value in marking this rite of passage. At least in primitive societies initiates had to prove themselves with feats that demonstrated their competence, strength, and daring before acceptance into the tribe. Can we ask less?

It is not that a probationary period is necessarily a bad thing or even that it doesn't produce all of the benefits anticipated. The probationary period should be a positive constructive period while new employees learn productive work habits and get a chance to demonstrate their skills.

I contend that if the probationary period is designed to suit the work, if it is treated as a period of *mutual* adjustment between the new employee and the organization, and if the learning experiences are progressive and challenging, it can work wonders for the organization and for the individual. If used purposefully, the probationary period can demonstrate to both parties whether or not a good match exists; both sides will know whether or not the relationship should continue. One measure of successful probation should be that neither side is surprised by what happens at the conclusion of the probationary period.

BACKGROUND OF THE PROBATIONARY PERIOD

Probationary periods have lasted from a few minutes (in factories) to a dozen or so years (in academic institutions). In general, when the probationary period is long, the commitment to the employee who survives it tends to be stronger—though there is no certainty of this.

In some organizations (even those which have a written policy on the subject), probation is a very casual thing, often not even noted by supervisors unless they wish to make a recommendation for discharge. In others, such as a unionized factory, every employee who completes probation is feted by fellow employees as an athlete who has successfully completed the management obstacle course.

In most organizations and for most people it seems that the probationary period is regarded as a peripheral threat, but one not to be taken too seriously if (1) the new employee is working satisfactorily, and (2) the new employee is getting along with the boss. In those last two statements, however, may lay the seeds for difficulties to be encountered later. The inducements in many organizations may be structured so as to guarantee that the employee focuses on pleasing the boss (rather than rocking the boat with innovative ideas). Even where work performance is carefully measured, the emphasis is usually placed on achieving "satisfactory" performance.

"IN" GROUP PROBATION

The relationship of the employee to management is not the only way in which a probationary period operates. The idea that the "in" group, be it family, community, club, or peer group, needs a time to observe the behavior of a candidate for membership before fully accepting her or him into full membership seems to be a very basic need. In a similar manner, the workgroup feels it offers much to the outsider—and a large part of a group's self-image is based on an assumed desirability of membership. This superior self-image is a powerful and necessary element in group cohesiveness, and membership in the group is not a privilege to be lightly given out.

This need for informal (peer) group acceptance is no small thing. With the employing organization often viewed as being very powerful and perhaps overwhelming, acceptance by coworkers and integration into their society often seems to be the only counterbalance. Friendly acceptance and social support by peers also sometimes seems the only relief from arbitrary and autocratic management. The group can offer aid and protection for the individual. In other less critical situations the group can offer friendship and pleasant conversation.

STRUCTURE OF THE PROBATIONARY PERIOD

Management often establishes the length of the probationary period based on the dominate type of work performed in that organization. Sophisticated personnel people often set various probationary time periods for the different types of skills required to do the work. The more complex the work, the longer the probationary period. The function of measurability (or the lack of measurability) of the skills also influences the period specified. Basically the question is how long does it take (in this job) for new employees to demonstrate competence and show what types of work habits they possess? Experience in a wide variety of organizations (business, government, and industry) show that thirty days to a year is common. Those jobs with the less complex skills slide toward the lower end, and complex jobs such as research work tends toward the other extreme.

But, as often as not, the standards of measuring job success are not often communicated effectively by the supervisor when needed. It is fairly common for new employees to learn the details of the probationary period from other employees—a very imperfect way.

How should the probationary period be structured? One quite clear answer is that if those suggestions under the previous chapters related to the end of the first day, the first week, and the first month are followed where applicable, much of what needs to be done during the probationary period will have been accomplished. Those things will have already structured much of what needs to be covered before the employees can feel at home and demonstrate their abilities. Also, much of what I'll call training "in the operation of the organization" will have been accomplished.

It is at this point that it is helpful for those representing the organization in dealing with new employees to turn inward and reflect on some basic issues.

1. Have you structured the learning of tasks so that the employees have been exposed to at least a *representative sampling* of all of the tasks they will be expected to perform on the job?

2. Have the new employees been given sufficient time to learn those tasks and to demonstrate their ability to handle them?

3. Have the learning experiences been structured progressively and in an obviously logical sequence so that the individuals know what comes next or how each item fits into the larger job?

4. Have the new employees been given adequate opportunity to demonstrate their degree of mastery of the work?

5. Have the employees been given the opportunity to innovate or to handle emergencies or to solve problems on the job (even if the problem-solving opportunities are only simulated, i.e., because of health or safety reasons, for example)?

6. Are the results measurable and have those measures been communicated to the employees?

7. Has adequate objective feedback been given to the new employees, and have opportunities for correcting errors been allowed?

8. Have you focused on making the new employees a success, or have you simply tried to evaluate them?

9. Can the employees tell clearly the basis for assessing successful job performance, and have they been permitted or encouraged to feed back this information so that you can check it out? (If they haven't fed back their information, how can you be really sure that they understand?)

10. Does the job appraisal criteria refer objectively, specifically, and clearly to the tasks to be performed?

Unless we, as supervisors, can answer those questions positively and with confidence, we may not have structured the probationary period in a way that is helpful to the organization or to the new employee. Basically we need to ask ourselves what should the probationary period achieve and what should be accomplished by the end of the probationary period in order to be fair to the person and to the organization.

TOWARD A TWO-WAY PROBATIONARY PERIOD

The probationary period has to be a two-way proposition or the results are unhealthy. If new employees hold onto a job they dislike just to have a paycheck or to attain security, the results will seldom be the best possible. If the organization holds onto an employee just because of "satisfactory" performance, it may be cheating its constituents. Unfortunately, the job market performs imperfectly and people get into the "wrong" job fairly often. The new employees have a hard time establishing equity often because:

1. They need a job and any job is better than no job.
2. They are beset by primal fears of inadequacy and insecurity, and they lack self-confidence.
3. They feel limited by geography, skills, experience, education, or family considerations.
4. They do not have access to clear, accurate, and complete information about the nature and workings of the job.
5. They have not gotten in touch with themselves enough to be even reasonably sure that they know what they want out of the job.
6. They have not set accurate and complete short- and long-term personal job objectives.

For the more experienced, sophisticated "new" employee (new to a particular organization), items 5 and 6 may no longer be any great issue. Though for the suddenly unemployed or those considering a mid-life career change, the issues may be quite important. At any rate, the preceding considerations can make it difficult for a new employee to consciously consider the organization to be on probation, except as it meets their needs for income and continuity. Long after the probationary period is over, items such as social satisfaction, the need for recognition, and the hunger for a sense of worth and accomplishment may become major items. By then, the employee may be too well shackled by the golden handcuffs of security, social acceptance, and routine to consider termination.

It might be a more satisfying situation if new employees could consciously withhold a part of their commitment to the organization until they see if the organization is meeting its commitments and obligations. This need not mean a holding back on productivity (for the new people can't judge an organization unless they give it their best shot), but rather keeping options open so that the employees feel free to leave without prejudice if things simply devolve into a job/person mismatch. Unfortunately, our culture, our sense of self, and even our upbringing often insist that we make a commitment to the organization and stick by that commitment regardless of the consequences.

From an organizational point of view, such a suggestion may sound treasonous, for the organization *does* invest considerable time and money in the new employee, so shouldn't that investment produce a sense of loyalty or at least commitment? Unfortunately, it often does, or at least it produces a sense of obligation. That sense of obligation often extends to include family, friends, and all those that have been told about the new job. People may sometimes be meeting the expectations of others by holding onto a job rather than being truly committed to it. Often this is a false commitment, for it sometimes ensures that neither the organization nor the individual meet their real needs.

It should be realized that new employees also make an investment in the relationship of a new job. It is a significant portion of their most vital resource—a segment of the time of their life. Six months in the wrong job may be better than six years, but even that six months can never be regained. Also, new people may be striving to learn things that will have no further relevance to them if they were to change jobs. It must be recognized and accepted that new employees make as large an investment in a new job as the organization.

In essence, I am suggesting that the vital ingredient of all contracts, especially in the contract of employment, be observed—the ingredient of equity. Jobs have for so long been so scarce and highly regarded that the notion of equity has largely been muted in employment contracts. Consequently, since employees have often implicitly if not expressly been denied equity, they often feel little actual sense of responsibility for what happens in the work environment. "That's their problem" has so long been subconsciously accepted in some organizations that mediocre performance has often become the norm. I sometimes wonder how much unionization and on-the-job resentment stems subconsciously from this lack of equity—at least as equity is perceived by the employee.

The organization's side of this argument has been so well elucidated (and probably generally accepted) that it needs little elaboration. The existence of a probationary period in itself implies that the organization has reserved for itself a way of dealing with employee/position mismatch—an out—which allows them to terminate without guilt. I suggest that we accept that the employee has the same right.

The existence of employees' right to a good match with their job is inherent in a free society. But far more than that, employees will accept responsibility for making sure that the match is right only if they feel free to negotiate the agreement or repudiate it in the same way that the organization does. Responsible behavior flows best from freedom, not from control, and I doubt if the probationary period will ever be a real success until the conditions are equitable and the agreement mutual.

It still remains a problem, however, that employees seldom see the agreement as equitable because of the differences in relative power between themselves and the organization. Fortunately, as workers become more specialized, as high levels of education and skills grow more common in the work force and people as well as machines come to be more versatile and capable, as our society becomes more technologically complex, and as litigation becomes more common, this sense of equity is spreading. The more the organization needs a particular individual, the more likely equity is to be achieved.

As a society we also need to stop regarding a job change as a negative thing, and to stop putting people down for making such a change. Considerable mediocre performance might be avoided by voluntary job changes. While the organization dislikes making an investment in training individuals and then having them leave, the probationary period enables both parties to assess the situation and decide whether further investment will be productive.

Basically we need better ways to ensure that the probationary period really meets its objectives. We need faster and more relevant training, we need better assessment techniques that ensures that both employer and employee are going to meet each other's needs, and we need better ways to bring about a good match so that neither party is threatened or harmed.

Increased efforts to make persons transferable, improved methods of better providing information on realistic job needs to applicants, and constructive transfers within the organization are badly needed. Transfers are often used to give someone else our problem, rather than to establish a better match between person and position. The easy transference of persons from organization to organization would make for less pressure on an employee to stick with a job that is unproductive.

PROBATION, PRODUCTIVITY, AND THE NEW EMPLOYEE

If used constructively, the probationary period can be a positive experience for both parties to the employment agreement. If we use the period as a way of adjusting to each other as we structure the learning experiences appropriately, and if we build on the positive elements, we can do much to ensure a long-term productive relationship.

An important part of a successful probationary period is using ideas generated by the new employees. At least toward the end of the probationary period, the supervisor should conduct a final Creativity Conference in order to capture new employees' additional ideas. Whether the supervisor works with the new employees on a person-to-person basis, or deals with the ideas in a workgroup setting, the experience should be a positive one. The focus should be on making the suggestions work.

By the end of the probationary process:

1. All promises made for that period should be met (including raises if such promises were made or implied).

2. Neither party should be surprised by the results because good communication and feedback should be going on constantly.

3. The employee should have a clear idea of what his or her future with the organization will be, at least in the short run.

4. The organization should have a good idea of the performance expected based on proven accomplishment and individual commitment to mutual goals.

5. The employee should be well oriented and integrated into the organization.

If these objectives are successfully met, the new employee should have experienced a constructive, equitable, and successful probationary period.

STUDY QUESTIONS

1. In what ways is the probationary period mutual?

2. In what interesting ways do some employees tend to behave once the probationary period is over?

3. What constructive purposes should the probationary period serve?

4. In some organizations passing the probationary period involves meeting what two criteria?

5. The length of the probationary period often varies depending most often on what criteria?

6. Name ten basic issues that need to be resolved to establish a successful probationary period.

7. Name five things that make it difficult for some employees to establish equity with the organization when dealing with a two-way probationary period.

8. Name six things that should be achieved by the end of the probationary period for each new employee.

CHAPTER 11

INFORMAL GROUP INFLUENCES AND THE NEW EMPLOYEE

Some of the most powerful influences on new employees are those exerted by peers and by the informal organization that exists within the workgroup. Dealing effectively with that informal organization and with peer expectations and pressures can test the metal of any supervisor or manager. To ensure that those informal influences have a beneficial effect on new employees is critical in influencing future productivity. Individual performance cannot be fully separated from group performance in virtually all situations.

GROUP PRODUCTIVITY

One of the early research studies on productivity involved the Hawthorne Study, begun in the last 1920s, to determine the influence of working conditions on output. The first tests were conducted to determine the effect of increased lighting on the rate of output. In this effort the researchers were disappointed. The experiments did not show any direct relationship between illumination and productivity. The researchers discovered that employees were reacting to changes in light intensity in ways in which they assumed they were to react, i.e., when lighting was increased they produced more, and when reduced they produced less. The employees' reaction to variations in illumination was psychological rather than physiological. In one case, they replaced light bulbs with bulbs of the same wattage, but allowed the workers to assume that the lighting had increased. The workers commented favorably on the increased illumination and proceeded to produce more.

The researchers tried in subsequent experiments to eliminate these psychological effects on their research, and in the process revealed an even more critical human psychological phenomena—"The Informal Group." Up until then, management had assumed that they had a near perfect system which needed only to be "fine tuned."

In the Hawthorne Plant of Western Electric Company the work to be done had been carefully analyzed. Then it was organized, methodized, and timed with a stopwatch. The standard time established was used as a base for measuring how many units could be produced at a time. In the plant, such standard time was the level of acceptance. If you produced more than the number of units required you kept your job, and if you didn't make it you disappeared. Also if you produced more than a certain number you were paid an incentive. It was assumed that people were motivated to make as much money as they possibly could—and heaven knows that industrial workers in those days needed the money.

Following the illumination test, a long-term study was initiated to determine the effects of changes in working conditions such as rest periods, mid-morning lunches, and shorter working hours (there were no coffee breaks in those days). Six average working women were selected for the test. Their work was to assemble telephone relays. The experiments were paced over many months to ensure that the original psychological aspects of the employee attempting to meet management's expectations would disappear.

The tests went on for months. It was discovered that no matter what changes were made (even when working hours were reduced), total weekly group productivity continued to rise, and did so for nearly five years. Even when the rest breaks, the special lunches, and the reduced work week were eliminated, daily output continued to rise.

In searching for answers to this strange phenomena, statements from the women themselves were most important. Each operator knew that she was producing more in the test room than she had ever produced out in the plant. Yet each said that the increase had occurred without any conscious effort on her part. It seemed easier to produce at the faster rate in the test area than at the slower rate in the regular department from which she had come.

Each woman agreed on two points: (1) they liked to work in the test room ("it was fun"), and (2) the new supervisory relationship (where they were "informed of changes beforehand," where they were "asked for their opinions and suggestions," and where they were "treated with respect"), as opposed to the cold impersonal control in the plant, made it possible for them to work freely and without anxiety.

It is tragic that in the half-century since that study many supervisors have not yet learned those fundamental lessons about human dignity.

A number of lessons were learned at Hawthorne, many of which affected management thought for generations.

1. A primary motivator was the sense of importance of the work they were doing. These six employees knew that the research study they were involved in was important and would affect the lives of others.

2. Talking by the operators, which was discouraged and suppressed in the plant, was eventually allowed in the experiment and became the source of much useful data for the supervisor and the experimenters.

3. The reasons for each change in working conditions were explained before the changes were made. The women's views were consulted and, in some cases, they were allowed to veto what had been proposed. The group's sense of self-esteem was fantastic compared to comparable groups in the plant, and in return these women outproduced even their own expectations.

At this point, some managers might object to workers being able to veto management plans. If you have a similar reaction, ask yourself if your goal to maintain management prerogatives or to get the job done, i.e., get out the production. We are increasingly finding that as people become more free and more assertive, they want greater control over decisions affecting their lives. If employees behave responsibly and produce what is needed, is "management control" really necessary—at least in the old autocratic sense?

THE INFORMAL GROUP

Growing out of the Hawthorne studies came an even more challenging management phenomena—the discovery of the "Informal Group."

When I was a graduate student, I found an evening job inspecting steel tool bits at a division of Crucible Steel Company. These were small square or rectangular pieces that ranged in length from the size of a nurse's thermometer to that of a police officer's billy club. After we finished with them they were sold to machine shops to be fashioned into the final tools used on cutting lathes of various types.

The tool bits came to us magnetized by a machine that preceded our operation. We rolled the bits in a metallic dust and placed them on a metal board. We then checked the bits for cracks (which the dust revealed), chips, length, and straightness. After inspection we weighed both good and bad parts, put the weights on our production cards, and sent the tool bits through a demagnetizing device.

On my first day the foreman briefly showed me how to dust, inspect, and demagnetize the bits and to record my work. He didn't speak to me again for a month, except to say good evening.

I needed and wanted that job badly. It paid well, provided some opportunity for overtime earnings, was relatively clean, and the evening hours allowed me to go to school full time during the day. To say the least, I was motivated to succeed and I worked as hard and as fast as I could—even cutting short my breaks and lunch hour. Curiously, no one *ever* told me how much I was expected to produce. I was to learn the job standards *very indirectly* through the *Informal Group*.

Everyday our production records were recorded by office personnel, and only if there was a problem in the records did we have any discussion with them. The foreman checked the production records daily, but he never once gave me feedback on how well or how poorly I was doing. My coworkers also never told me what was expected, that is, they never said it directly. When I was new and my production was relatively low, several of my coworkers often added some of their output to mine. Thank God they apparently liked me.

When I began to average about 2,000 pounds of steel tool bits per shift, their help disappeared. However, I felt very insecure and kept striving to produce more. Gradually my friends began to suggest that we "knock off early and wash up" or "cool it down a bit." When my productivity continued to climb, the pressure to "cool it" increased. I found that if I averaged about 2,000 pounds an evening everything went along smoothly both from management and from my coworkers. I'm sure that I could have raised my average output 25 percent, but I had no incentive to do so from management and considerable disincentive from the informal group.

I didn't know it then specifically, but the group's power to withhold acceptance and to isolate an individual for noncompliance with group norms strikes at one of the most powerful motivators that a person encounters on the job—social needs. However, I felt this need subjectively and intuitively. Later, in that same position, I was to learn an even more powerful lesson in group dynamics.

A man in his late twenties was hired to do the same work we were doing. This man demonstrated in the first evening that he was a fast learner and a first-class producer. Within a week he was over the standard and his output continued to climb. He seemed determined to show everyone he was the best producer in the place, and, based on his output, I could hardly argue with him.

By the end of the second week the mild efforts to exert group pressure on this individual to slow down had turned somewhat mean. In that plant we brown-bagged since the cafeteria was not open nights. One evening our "Stakhanovite[1] worker" began to smell a rat. He opened his lunch and examined it more carefully than usual. When he separated the bread in his sandwich he found, neatly laid across the ham, a very flat and very dead mouse! Needless to say, before long our top producer asked for a transfer. When that was not readily forthcoming, he decided to leave the company.

Why did all of this occur? Because informal organizations are normal groupings of people who interact to meet their needs.

In an easy going environment, informal groups can be seen regularly eating lunch together, riding in carpools, forming clubs, or "playing cards with their buddies." In hostile, repressive, or threatening environments, informal groups of people band together for self-protection and to present a solid front to those who might injure them, just as animals will often form a ring against attackers and thereby seek safety. In creative, progressive, and supportive environments, the informal group will often merge with the formal organization and be supportive of organizational goals.

---

[1]From Alexei G. Stakhanov born 1905. A Russian miner who devised a system of high production. A worker especially in the U.S.S.R. whose production is consistently above average and who is therefore awarded recognition and special privileges. *Merriam Webster's Third International Dictionary*.

When I see people holding back ideas, restricting output, or fighting management as a group, I usually find that they have reasons for their actions. People are not stupid. If they sense that an increase in productivity will only lead to higher standards, and that they will not be rewarded for greater output but will be punished for failing to meet standards, they quite naturally take steps to protect themselves. This is what was going on in that steel mill, and I suspect it was also occurring in the main Hawthorne plant in 1928.

In the experimental area, however, something else was going on at Hawthorne. The group had started to evolve socially. The six women began to interact on a casual relaxed basis, and the company responded in a supportive fashion. The company even picked up on a joking suggestion made by one of the women to provide ice cream and cake when they were given their physical examinations (the examinations were a regular part of the experiment).

When one of the women was feeling mildly ill or justifiably tired, the others would "carry" her and compensate for her loss of output.

The group soon began to commit themselves to higher and higher standards—a continuous increase in production. Eventually they squeezed all of the improvement out of the job that they could, but this top output was far above the rest of the plant and far above their starting point—at least 25 percent within the first year and a half.

The group, within a relatively short period of time, had begun to work as a group and feel a togetherness. They were committed to high group norms and they were not about to slack off. They felt that they were a winning team.

Finally, in the workgroup there emerged an identifiable informal leader. This woman, who was not part of the original group but was brought in as a replacement for one of the women who had to leave, began to exert considerable positive influence on the group and on the achievement of its production goals.

THE NATURE OF THE INFORMAL GROUP

An informal group is any group of people who informally begin to interact to achieve their mutual purposes. They operate without charter or by-laws; they set standards of conduct and establish group norms; they have no set leadership patterns though one or more members may exert more influence on group activities than the others.

Examples of individual groups range from friends who visit each other socially on a regular basis, to that great tangled web known in the organization as the "grapevine." Informal groups cover such phenomena as the "old boy network," the school-tie syndrome, carpools, and the coffee klatsch.

Informal organizations are natural groupings of people which can be, as we saw with Hawthorne, powerful positive aids to productivity, or, as with my own personal example, foot-dragging methods of surviving in a negative environment. Since informal organizations are often formed to meet powerful (social, security, and even survival needs) efforts to wipe out the informal groups through isolation of members, restrictions on communications and punishment are not only futile but dangerous. Informal groups even exist in prisons (including maximum security units) and are virtually impossible to destroy no matter how repressive management is. Repressive management often fosters the growth of a more deeply-rooted hidden informal organization that, when forced to the wall, can turn violent.

Generally, however, informal groups can be as helpful as they are harmful. The informal group will often provide much of the training, orientation, and social integration of new employees. The informal group will often have a far greater impact on new employees than will the supervisor—if the supervisor does not take an active role in orienting and training the new person.

In work situations, the grapevine thrives on inadequate and inaccurate information. Supervisors often complain that in their organization "the word" often gets to the employees before it gets to them. The grapevine is often fast, but seldom accurate. It is nurtured by secretive people and encouraged by rigidly structured organizations. Bureaucracy is the lattice work and secrecy the sunlight on which the grapevine flourishes.

Ironically, informal organizations sometimes represent the only way to get things done effectively and efficiently. Almost any person who has been in an organization very long has developed a network of friends who provide information or help in times of trouble. We have probably carefully cultivated people who can give us access to needed equipment or who will rush a job through as a favor. I often hear the refrain, "If I always went through channels I'd never get anything done." A very successful executive once told me, "The trivial stuff I send through the chain of command—if it never comes back I'll never miss it—but the critical items I carry to my friends."

All of us can become more sensitive and aware of the informal groups operating around us. Such groups are so natural that chances are good we've been part of some informal groups without really being aware of it. In the job situation, four types of situations tend to bring people together, and this togetherness may lead to the creation of an informal group.

1. *Location.* Where drafting tables are grouped together, draftsmen tend to eat and talk together. Car pools are another example. Think of the possibilities for communication if a group of secretaries ride to work together.

2. *Occupation.* Accountants often attend professional meetings together. Selected members of an engineering group may play poker together one evening a week.

3. *Common Interests.* Members of the same bowling team often exchange at least a few words everyday. Have you ever had a subordinate who plays on the golf team with your boss? (Would that keep you awake nights?)

4. *Special Issues.* Women's rights or equal employment issues may bring people together.

All of the preceding goes to say that when new employees are hired, there is a vast variety of social interactions available. How much influence do we want to have on the possibility of establishing healthy and positive social relationships for the new employees? Can we assist them in finding a car pool, introduce them to people who share their interest in after hours activities, provide knowledge about professional associations, or indicate the existence of the credit union or a travel club?

Informal organizations are going to exist anyway and the new employees may eventually find them. It is better to use the positive ones than let the people simply drift into the negative ones.

THE OPERATION OF INFORMAL GROUPS

To survive, informal groups need five things. Groups will tend to evolve to full scope when these are present.

1. *Activities.* The job normally provides abundant opportunity for at least work activities.

2. *Interactions.* The chance to interact with others is common to most jobs. When interaction is impossible because of isolation, noise, or physical barriers, the jobs are often hard to fill unless the new person is using the isolation for some personal purpose such as studying.

3. *Sentiments.* When people have a chance to interact over a period of time and when they share common activities, feelings begin to develop both in relation to the other people and toward the activities. These sentiments may be volatile, but where they persist over a period of time they result in valued social payoffs of one kind or another. This is often where team building begins.

4. *Group Norms.* Eventually a cohesive group will develop group norms, i.e., what behavior is acceptable or unacceptable in that group. Sometimes this extends to dress codes, topics of conversation, or even how much work the group will consider fair. Often these norms are "understood" rather than made explicit. It may surprise some supervisors, but the group often has in its power the ability to set higher standards than the supervisor or the organization would ever dream of asking for.

5. *Informal Leadership.* In highly cohesive groups, one paramount leader often emerges. However, in a complex group doing complex or technical work various members might demonstrate leadership when the group turns to various specific tasks. In loosely knit groups various people may take leadership initiative from time to time.

Some of the things I have learned about dealing with informal groups over the years include:

1. The informal leader *can be a great help or hindrance* in getting the job done. It often depends on the behavior of the supervisor as to whether the effect is positive or negative.

2. *Opposing a strong informal leader* is like charging into a buzz saw—the group often chose that leader because they needed him or her.

3. Some informal groups come into being *for one purpose* and wither when that purpose is achieved, i.e., political groups are sometimes formed to fight a specific campaign and often die out after election day.

4. The informal group can be *a source of leadership talent.* An older brother of mine was a welder and a union member. He was unhappy about the existing union and organized a revolt among the members and threw out the existing union, replacing it with one more to their taste. The company wanted that type of leadership on their side and offered him the post of personnel manager (which he took).

5. Most important perhaps is the observation that when an organization practices *participative management* (not permissive management) and treats people like mature responsible adults they get the same treatment in return. In these instances (and they are rare), the primary informal group tends to blend with the formal group—their goals and objectives become compatible.

Every human being has a need for acceptance, belonging, and friendship. The question of who influences the new employee may become secondary where cliques and rivalry predominate. If we don't lay our cards on the table we can't expect other people to do so. If we provide a challenging supportive environment to the new employee, and to the old employees, we will tend to influence the informal group toward productive ends. Integrating the new employee into the workgroup is only part of the job. Knowing how the informal aspects of our workgroup are functioning might be vital to the success of the new employee. The signs are there if we will read them.

STUDY QUESTIONS

1. What three important lessons about workers were discovered during the Hawthorne Study?

2. What was the most significant discovery of the Hawthorne Study as it affects the new employee?

3. When and under what circumstances will the informal group tend to merge with the formal group and be supportive of organizational goals?

4. What is an informal group?

5. Why should we not try to suppress or destroy the informal group? How can we work with the informal group to attain positive ends?

6. On the job, what four types of situations tend to foster informal relationships?

7. List, in order of development, five things informal groups need in order to flourish.

CHAPTER 12

MOTIVATION BASICS

No one is apathetic except in pursuit of someone else's goals."
(Henry Ford)

How do we motivate new employees and keep on motivating them month after month, year after year? There is certainly no easy answer to that question, and in some cases we may fail. But there is much we have learned about motivation in recent decades, and much of what has been learned can give us positive guidelines for developing practical tactics for motivating people to be productive.

It has been said that there is no motivation except self-motivation, and to some degree that is real. It is also true that ultimately we can *only* be responsible for our own behavior. By "we" I mean both us and the new employee. The question then comes down to the nature of human kind. Is it natural to be motivated and productive or is the opposite true?

MASLOW AND THE NEW EMPLOYEE

Abraham Maslow developed a theory of motivation based on the then current research and presented his description of human motivation as a Hierarchy of Human Needs. My purpose here is not to teach Maslow, but to show how his scheme is especially relevant to understanding the behavior of the new employee.

Maslow assumed that human beings were motivated to meet their needs, and that a diagram of these needs could be structured in a pyramid from the most basic and most powerful and pressing needs at the bottom to the weakest and most complex and interdependent needs at the top. Maslow's work has been used by countless educators, social workers, and management personnel as a tool for understanding and explaining human behavior. His general theory, with the corollaries, exceptions, and variations he noted, has well stood the test of time and is useful today.

Maslow's pyramid diagram is given on the left side of Fig. 12.1. To the right of it is a diagram constructed to demonstrate a personal, job-related, response to the needs Maslow identifies.

Basic to Maslow's approach is the belief that a need, once satisfied, is no longer a motivator, and that if we satisfy lower-level needs (unless a person is behaving compulsively) that particular need will no longer push us toward action. Thus, at the basic level we have needs for food, clothing, shelter, sleep, sex, trace elements in the diet, etc. Once those needs are reasonably satisfied through food or sleep or shelter, etc., they no longer (for now at least) compel us to indulge further. We then move on to other, usually higher-order, needs.

The next order is the security or safety needs—ensuring that our survival needs get met on a continuing basis. These needs are basically to satisfy our anxieties and to ensure a reasonably predictable future. Once met, we tend to move up to the next level of social or acceptance needs.

In the social needs level we tend to try to meet our needs for acceptance, belonging, friendships, and love. These social needs are more difficult to meet, in one respect at least, since they are not things easily acquired by only our own actions. They are dependent upon the actions and feelings of others presenting us with a tenuous hold on meeting these needs (at best).

Before completing the hierarchy it is worthwhile to note that, to some degree at least, the new employee by securing a job and holding onto it can meet these three most powerful needs. The job itself usually provides the basics of

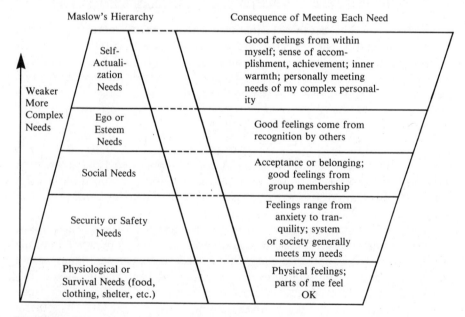

Fig. 12.1
Assumption—Needs Motivate

food, clothing, and shelter. By being a member of our society and through organizational fringe benefits, a person can become reasonably secure once the probationary period is passed. Pension plans, union membership, civil service status, unemployment insurance, sick leave, medical insurance, and police and fire protection are only a few of the ways an employee meets security needs. Most jobs also provide at least considerable opportunity to get many social needs met both during and after working hours. Also in many jobs employees can meet these needs by being only moderately productive once they are considered a permanent part of the work force. If we are going to motivate a person to be more than ordinarily productive we need to shoot for a higher rung on the hierarchy.

When we are attempting to motivate the new employee, we need to face two basic realities: (1) we can pressure the new employee by threatening these three basic needs (but such power to pressure is usually of limited scope and duration), and (2) the new employee, as with other people, might stagnate at any motivation level. Examples of efforts to pressure employees by threatening these basic needs came back to me.

"You like to eat, don't you!" The supervisor was a big old-fashioned "bull of the woods" type foreman. If it hadn't been for his size I think that the employee he was threatening would have laughed at him since the employee was well protected by a strong and militant union.

"What this country needs is another good depression!" This statement, made by the head of the security department of a major metropolitan newspaper, shocked me. "I remember the last one," I said, "what makes you think we need another?" "Because then," he said, "people would do what you tell them to do!" So much for his leadership style! Incidentally, the individual had retired from military service, had retired from the Philadelphia Police Force, and was working on his third pension—how is that for compulsive behavior?

The third supervisor put partitions between office workers "to cut down on the talking," and he earned a fantastic turnover rate—including himself (involuntarily) a year and a half later.

The basic conclusion I draw about these three lower-level needs are that:

1. These needs are powerful and will not be denied. You'll only get grief if you try.

2. Most jobs already meet these needs; therefore, in most cases, they can no longer be used as motivators.

3. The real key to productivity lies in the two higher-level motivators.

Esteem and Self-Actualization

At the top of Maslow's hierarchy is the need to enjoy self-respect and the respect of others, and to use our personal potential to the greatest extent possible—to achieve the best we can achieve.

While these are not the most pressing of needs, they are the most complex. These primarily psychological needs are also among the most recurring needs. They most nearly test our own complex inner self and require, at least in the self-actualization needs, that we know ourself. Our esteem and achievement needs also produce more than just satisfaction—they can bring us joy when they are fully met.

HERZBERG'S JOB SATISFIERS AND JOB DISSATISFIERS

Before looking at the top of the hierarchy in detail, however, let's look at some research on motivation conducted by Frederick Herzberg which has substantial meaning for motivating the new employee.

Herzberg asked two questions of a group of approximately two hundred engineers and accountants: "Think of a work-related incident that happened in your life that made you feel very negative about what happened and tell me why it made you feel negative." He also asked them for a work-related incident that made them feel good. He summarized his results and found surprisingly short lists of five positive factors and five negative factors.

Herzberg's Positive Job Satisfiers:

1. Achievement

2. Recognition

3. The Work Itself

4. Responsibility

5. Advancement

Herzberg's Negative Job Dissatisfiers:

1. Organization Policy and Administration

2. Technical Supervision

3. Salary Inequities

4. Interpersonal Supervision

5. Working Conditions

I've conducted a brief simplified version of the same exercise with over 8,000 supervisors, managers, and executives, and have found that their experiences correlated well with Herzberg's lists. (The order of importance tended to vary and some items, such as salary inequities, almost never occurred in government agencies or large firms because of wage and salary plans existing therein.)

Herzberg reached several conclusions about his results, among them are the following:

1. The lists are not directly comparable; they are not mirror images of one another. They are two distinct lists.

2. Improvement in the areas listed on the negative list do not provide positive motivation. They only tend to reduce the irritants in the organization—at best reduce them to ground zero.

3. The negative list tends to be organizationally-related (except for item 4) and is often viewed as the responsibility of those vague impersonal "they" people higher up in the organization.

4. The positive list is far more personal and involves individual motivation.

5. In the positive list *achievement* and *recognition* were by far the most frequently experienced motivators, but the good feelings experienced through the other three factors lasted longer.

I find that four additional factors are especially relevant to the supervisor of the new employee.

1. The two most frequently experienced positive motivators, achievement and recognition, correlate directly with the top items of Maslow's hierarchy.
   Self-Actualization—Achievement
   Esteem or Ego—Recognition

2. The supervisor (rather than the organization in general) administers the positive motivators.
   a. The supervisor decides how much *responsibility* will be given to an employee.
   b. The supervisor most often decides who will get what work assignments and thereby controls the degree of challenge and the variety of the work.
   c. The supervisor is the primary source of recognition on the job, and, if the research is accurate, the supervisor is the source of the most highly regarded compliments on expressions of appreciation.
   d. The supervisor, through structuring the work, through effective delegation, and by allowing freedom in decision making, determines whether or not the job contains opportunities "to show what you can do," i.e., experience the achievement motivation.
   e. The supervisor at least recommends people for advancement and largely determines whether or not they have been trained adequately to be ready for promotion.

3. Herzberg, in subsequent publications, made the clear point that "the work itself" (how it is organized, dispensed, structured, and evaluated) is the primary source of all of the positive motivators. (This business of work assignments will get considerable attention in subsequent chapters.)

4. Achievement and recognition give us some of our best feelings, but since their effect wears off rapidly they need frequent reinforcement.

When we come back to Maslow, it is now apparent that if we are going to motivate new employees and keep on motivating them, we must manage the work in ways which will provide opportunity for frequent and substantial achievement and from which we can draw accurate data for rewards and recognition. That is, as one supervisor said, "One hell of a challenge."

In other chapters we will discuss ways of dealing with work assignments which will help us meet this challenge. For now, however, I'd like to deal with the situation where a new employee turns out to be a disappointment to the supervisor. This is the individual who "talked a good game" when hired, and who maintained an adequate performance level beyond the probationary period, but who then seemed to turn sour. It is not uncommon for the supervisor, in his or her anger and disappointment, to label the employee as lazy or shiftless, and feel powerless to do anything about it.

"What are you going to do about a lazy person?" I'm frequently asked by supervisors and managers with whom I'm working.

"I don't know," I often reply, "because I've never met one."

My response is often reacted to with looks of amazement, disbelief, and sometimes pity that I could be such a fool.

The questioners, usually angry about "lazy people," react with anger or annoyance. "Just come on down to where I work and I'll show you some," they retort.

My usual approach at that point is to concede that I have seen many unmotivated people, as well as some who were ill, or discouraged, or beaten, but none that I could clearly label as lazy.

FIRST PRINCIPLES AND THE NEW EMPLOYEE

In response to their skeptical glances, I often offer two experiences. One involved a supervisor whom I disliked intensely. This man held his position primarily because his uncle was president of the firm. He spent most of the day staring off into space, tinkering with some device, or making sarcastic remarks about people. His supervisory role seemed limited to firing people and criticizing their performance without bothering to determine the facts of the case. When his uncle died and the company was sold, it was suggested that he look elsewhere, which he did. His supervisor then described him as the "laziest man who ever walked through the front door."

I held no good feelings for the individual, but I knew something about him that related to his motivation. It was true that he did almost no productive work and what he did do produced negative results, but when he went home at night he sometimes came alive. He had a deep interest in the theatre and displayed talents that could have made him an actor of considerable ability. It was tragic that acting (a profession his father had pursued to the consternation of his family) was not considered a legitimate occupation by his family. Instead, he dutifully became an engineer, a vocation which bored him endlessly.

The supervisor or personnel people might not easily rectify such career mismatches, but effective career counseling might begin to move the unmotivated employee in a more productive direction. That individual later showed some talent in the sales field—an occupation that was available within the firm and a job where an engineer could have been useful.

An even more common problem with unmotivated (not lazy) people is the reality that they are often working very hard—but not on the job (or at least not on the job for which you are paying them).

Ted was an easy-going amiable coworker of mine who produced "only enough to get by." Our supervisor was frustrated because Ted, bright and capable, did every job thoroughly, but "never did much." Ted didn't seem to want to get ahead or to accept responsibility. His boss eventually called him "lazy" to his face.

In the evening, however, Ted was a different person. He tended bar at the local American Legion hall two nights a week without compensation. He kept the organization's books, also for free. He was the organizer of the annual cook-out, and hosted many of the parties. When engaged in these activities he worked like a dog, and he seemed to enjoy the social prestige he was awarded. —Lazy? Hardly.

On the job one day Ted confided in me, "You'd have to be crazy to stick your neck out around here—there is always someone ready to chop it off." Punishing behavior on the part of management and the lack of social rewards on the job had deprived the organization of Ted's hard work and initiative. "It's all in eight," he used to say.

After a couple of examples like this, supervisors and managers in my seminars with whom I'm working are beginning to suspect that I'm playing word games with them, but I'm not! To switch the wording from *lazy* to *unmotivated* opens up a whole world of possibilities. The use of the word *lazy* to classify a person is a way of dumping responsibility onto that person and of avoiding our own responsibility. If a person is inherently lazy there is nothing that we as supervisors or staff specialists can do about the person—or even need to do. "They are just that way." To instead label the person as *unmotivated* at least leaves open the possibility that we might be able to do something about the situation.

A case in point: A woman working for the Agency for International Development often came in late for work. At break time, morning and afternoon, she would put her head down on the desk and sleep for fifteen minutes, to be awakened at the end of the break by a friend and coworker. At lunch she would eat a bag lunch hurriedly and again sleep during the remainder of the lunch period. She often stayed after hours to make up for coming in late.

The supervisor referred to her as lazy and took steps to have her fired. Under questioning, he said he thought she was moonlighting on another job. Besides the fact that he had never checked out the moonlighting charge, he failed to see the inconsistency between her being "lazy" and holding two jobs.

Before the discharge process had gone too far a personnel specialist suggested that the woman have a physical examination. Fortunately the doctor was sharp on diagnosing rare ailments, for he discovered that the woman had a form of narcolepsy—a sleeping sickness apparently picked up in a previous overseas assignment. The woman was subject to attacks of compulsive sleeping.

Another example I ran into in classifying people as lazy involved a supervisor's generalization about a whole class of workers. The term "lazy Latins" was used to describe one person of Latin American descent. From a business trip I had taken to Latin America I knew that the label "lazy Latins" was factually false. My Latin counterparts worked as hard as I did, but they preferred to do it at times other than the heat of the day, which made much sense. They started earlier than I normally did and worked later into the evening, but took a long noon-day break.

The term "lazy Latin," however, was more invidious than this example. It conjured up a mental image of a peasant sleeping under his sombrero in the mid-day sun. What I verified on that trip was that many "peasants" were sick and simply lacked the energy to do sustained work. Even in the United States, there are rural people, without adequate shoes, infested with hookworm, and weakened by dietary deficiencies to the point that they cannot match others in energy output.

The preceding examples lead me to consider what I call *first principles* of motivation. Before concluding anything about people who are (factually) not producing, I need to ask the following questions:

1. Is there a mismatch between the person and the job, and if so, what can I do about it?

2. Is the person motivated by off-the-job activities, and if so, what might I do to simulate similar motivators on the job?

3. Is the person physically or emotionally able to meet the job requirements and to go beyond them as would a motivated person?

4. Am I applying a class stereotype to an individual when the person's performance doesn't meet my expectations?

A variety of possible answers to principles one and two will be explored in this and in subsequent chapters. Item three is often far more complex and may require expert opinion and the involvement of outside professional help in the resolution of the problem. Item four involves items as diverse as poor nutrition and conflicting cultural values.

What does all this have to do with new employees? Companies do not normally hire "lazy people"—at least not knowingly. Yet every organization seems to wind up with a fair sprinkling of people labeled as such. How does this come about?

Important decisions about long-term relationships are often cast in the context of a few brief interviews. During those interviews the applicants are often at their best. Organization personnel *may be* at their worst. Interviewing is often a chore because interviewers are generally overworked and reluctant to spend a lot of time with any one person since many are to be interviewed. Also the nature and scope of the work the person will be doing may not be clearly conveyed. How much influence will the new employee have? What decisions will be delegated? Before answering those questions, interviewers want to "wait and see" how much initiative the interviewee will take. He or she may be "waiting to see" also.

The answer to the question about the first principle's application to the new employee involve at least the following items.

1. Strive to create as realistic a picture as possible about the nature of the work and its motivators (or lack of them), and transfer this picture to the prospective employees.

2. Seek out clues as to what a person is really aspiring to in the organization, how the person likes to operate, and what support and permissions the person will require.

3. If new employees become unmotivated on the job, avoid classifying them. Seek creative productive solutions.

4. Actively involve the new employees in the problem—only they know, deep down, why they aren't motivated.

5. Look for causes that neither party might have suspected (such as physical causes) and develop creative ways to resolve such causes.

THE ORGANIZATIONAL ENVIRONMENT

Years ago I came across a list of five ways people deal with conflict and frustration in an organization. As well as I can remember, the list included:

1. *Leaving the field.* People may simply quit and go elsewhere to seek a more supportive environment.

2. *Giving up.* People may simply stop beating their head against the wall and retire on the job. They will generally do what they have to do, but will frequently say, "What's the use around here?"

3. *Detour behavior.* Some people don't give up, but focus their creative energies on getting their way despite the organization. They may use experiences gained in the organization as a stepping stone to go elsewhere.

4. *Aggression.* The possibilities of fighting, sharp-shooting, and "taking it out on others" certainly is nonproductive to either party.

5. *Problem-solving behavior.* Tragically this seems to be the least common way to deal with conflict and frustration in the organization. We might ask ourselves why this is so, and are we a part of the problem?

People can best approach a problem in the organization when they are feeling good about themselves and about others. Is a lack of motivation impeding the problem-solving process?

When I observe any of the first four types of behavior, I do not merely accept it as "that's the way some people are." I didn't hire them that way, why are they behaving that way now? I accept that they have *reasons for their behavior.* Their behavior makes a kind of sense to them—at least emotional sense—and I want to know more about how things add up in their context. I try to discover: (1) why they are feeling and behaving the way they are, and (2) what could we mutually do to solve the problem.

More often than not this brings the person into the problem-solving mode, and improved results prevail. Such a problem-solving effort, when applied early to troubles of the new employee, may be especially important in starting the person off toward a productive future.

STUDY QUESTIONS

1. What three conclusions might you draw about the hierarchy of needs?

2. What five conclusions did Herzberg draw from his research results?

3. Name five ways in which the supervisor "administers" the list of positive motivators.

4. Why does the author claim "I have never met a lazy person?"

5. Name the four "first principles" of motivation.

6. In what five ways can the "first principles" be applied to the new employee?

7. Name five ways people meet conflict and frustration in an organization.

CHAPTER 13

DELEGATION—THE KEY TO COMPETENCE

When I discuss leadership styles with supervisors and managers, I often lead into the subject by asking them to think of the best leader they ever worked for, and to write down one thing that that person did or said which showed leadership. The emphasis here is on identifying specific behaviors, not traits. After allowing a few minutes for completion of the task, I ask the seminar participants to share their incidents without identifying the person. From one-third to one-half of every group says something to the effect that he or she "told me what they wanted and let me do it my way."

This freedom to do it "my own way" was one of the most frequently used and most powerful motivators experienced by group members. It was remembered often years after the incident and caused people to have good memories of their relationships. When I've explored this good feeling with some individuals, they reported feelings like: "It made me feel like I was being treated as an adult," "It showed respect for my experience and good judgment," and "It gave me a chance to show what I could do." Delegation—the willingness to let people do it their way is the pathway to the *achievement* motivator and the primary source of well-earned recognition within the organization. For new employees especially, the willingness to trust them to do it their own way —with all that that statement implies is the harbingering of whether or not new employees are successful in the job and sufficiently motivated to want to be productive. Delegation is a vital ingredient in job success, in motivating new employees, and in keeping life interesting and challenging.

WHAT IS DELEGATION?

I have a simple technique for sorting well trained from untrained or badly trained supervisors and managers. I ask them to explain the meaning of delegation, "in a management context."

Untrained or poorly trained supervisors usually respond by saying some version of "passing out work assignments." Where do supervisors learn such nonsense? Usually from *their* boss who treats delegation as just that—passing out work assignments—often just dumping them on the subordinate. Passing out work assignments is just that—passing out work assignments, nothing more, nothing less, but that has nothing to do with delegation.

Semi-trained supervisors sometimes respond "passing out authority and responsibility" because no one has ever bothered to clarify the meaning of delegation and they have never looked it up in the dictionary. I have even seen the phrase "delegating authority and responsibility" in management textbooks, indicating that the author didn't understand one of the basic principles of organization. Well trained supervisors respond by saying something like "turning over your authority to someone else."

Delegation, as described in *Websters Third New International Dictionary—Unabridged,* is: "The act of investing with *authority* to act for another" and "One or more persons appointed or chosen to represent others." To delegate is "to entrust to another—transfer, assign, commit," while a delegate is "a person sent and *empowered* to act for another." Thus, delegation implies the act of giving up or giving away *power* or *authority*. When you truly delegate, your power resides in another person. Delegation deals with power, not work. You can assign work and/or you can delegate authority, but they are not the same.

Some people assign work and then excessively check up on the person doing it. They tell the person not only what to do but how to do it, and they insist that the worker check back with them before making any decisions. They have assigned work, but they have not delegated authority.

In a similar sense, you cannot delegate responsibility. If a person is put in charge of an operation or workgroup, he or she cannot pass on that responsibility. Subordinates can be held responsible to the person in charge, but they cannot be made responsible to the person's supervisor. In short, you are responsible for whatever happens in your organizational unit, and that personal responsibility cannot be passed on to others. If we could avoid responsibility by offering our subordinates as sacrificial "goats" to our supervisors, we in effect would create an irresponsible organization. Thus we have the ancient principle: "Delegation of Authority—Assignment of Responsibility." We can hold subordinates responsible to us, but we must accept responsibility for a subordinate's actions.

IMPLICATIONS OF DELEGATION OF AUTHORITY

What are the implications for new employees of this principle of delegation? Quite frankly it often means the difference between job success and failure. It can determine how new employees feel about the job, the supervisor, and their personal future. It can often be the key to personal job-related growth and development. If new employees enter the organization as supervisors or managers, success or failure in the art of delegation can determine their competence.

Delegation is like handing someone—often someone you are not yet sure of—a loaded gun. That person now has power—power to get you in trouble if you are the one who delegated your authority. If Joe or Josie Thumpwaddle messes things up, you are the one who gets in trouble, not they. You may later come back to Joe or Josie and extract retribution, but for now you are "it." Your boss may become justifiably impatient if you try to pass the buck. It is your job to manage things so that they turn out right. No amount of alibiing will remove your responsibility.

This is why delegation is so scary to many supervisors and why they avoid it like the plague. Supervisors often prefer getting mediocre results from unmotivated subordinates rather than risking getting into trouble. In a punishing environment true delegation often implies risks that supervisors are unwilling to take. They see few potential rewards and considerable opportunities for loss. "Why should I bother?" they often ask. Frequently no one can give them a good answer. The effect on new employees is that they often get turned off by dull routine assignments and statements like "don't rock the boat" when they push for greater use of their abilities.

WHY WE FAIL TO DELEGATE

The three primary reasons behind a failure to delegate are:

1. The people with power do not understand their job or the implications of their behavior.

2. People like the feeling of power and do not see any need to share it.

3. People fear getting in trouble or are afraid of not doing a good job.

Frequently people in charge (particularly if they are new supervisors) fail to realize that the core of their position is to get the objectives of the organization done through others. Their job is not to control people. Control is just *one* means to an end. Whatever control is exercised by the supervisor or the subordinate is not particularly important as long as the job is accomplished and the desired results achieved.

Supervisory Job Knowledge

How do employees normally get promoted from worker to supervisor in the first place? Despite a lot of cynical remarks about family and friends, most people first become supervisors not because of any demonstrated ability to lead others, but because they have usually outperformed most other people when doing the work. They may not be the best performers, but they have usually been quite good—conscientious, hard-working, effective, and they usually have demonstrated some social or communications skills that led management to conclude that they would be good candidates for supervision.

When people enter supervision, they often feel more comfortable in doing the work themselves than in supervising others. After all, they so far have built their reputation on doing the work well, the work has been the source of their good feelings about themselves, and finally, they have been rewarded with promotion for their attention to detail and their proficiency in performing the work. When they become a supervisor, they often continue to do some of the work and to nitpick their subordinates, for they "know the best way."

Another variety of this type of person is the one who says, "It is easier to do it myself than to explain." While that may sometimes be true with unique tasks, the supervisor often applies it to many repetitive tasks and therefore is frequently *doing* rather than *managing*. "Doing" usually indicates that the supervisor does not communicate well or is not an effective trainer—an important ability for a successful supervisor.

Reluctance to Surrender Prestige and Power

In organizations which do not manage by measurable objectives and where "going through the motions" gets rewarded, the need to delegate, and thereby produce results, is not a pressing matter. In those environments, the supervisor is indulged by not having to seriously motivate people and can therefor stroke his or her ego and rule the roost. This is why, I think, so many supervisors who are not by tradition or training true autocrats do not relinquish authority and do not see the need to. They are more often "checker-uppers" and "so-so" performers who produce "enough to get by."

Fear The third category is a highly complex one. Fear of failure, fear of being criticized, fear of not doing what is right are all doubts and fears of managers at one time or another. Despite rhetoric to the contrary, these fears are the hardest with which to deal. A supervisor often feels that their job is on the line when they delegate—and that's scary. Long after many supervisors have recognized and accepted intellectually the principle of delegation and its implications, those gnawing fears eat away at their self-confidence and impair their willingness to let go of their authority.

This fear comes in many shapes, including the shadow of the organization hanging over them. Many supervisors complain that their boss won't let them supervise. "The boss wants to know what's going on at all times and expects me to have instant answers. If I let people do it their own way it means they can make decisions without consulting me and this upsets my boss." Those laments are justified in many cases. They simply reflect the reality that you cannot give away something you do not possess. You cannot delegate decision making to others if you are prohibited from making the decision to delegate. The more restrictive the upper levels of management become and the more punishing the environment, the less initiative the new employee or any other employee is able to show.

THE EFFECTS ON NEW EMPLOYEES

In a practical sense, failure to delegate involves telling employees not only what needs to be done but prescribing the exact method by which it will be done. I am not talking here about training, which is the process of showing employees one acceptable method of doing the job, yet recognizing that there may be many other acceptable and possibly even preferable methods of getting the job done. Instead, I am aiming at the attitude that "there is a right way, a wrong way, and my way, and you'd damned well better do it *my* way!"

When a single approach is prescribed and no other methods are tolerated (or at least not encouraged), there is a barely hidden message that the employee is not to think, not to speculate, not to innovate, not to risk. The message is, "We only want nice compliant people around here who will do what they are told. We have not hired your mind, only your hands or your skills."

Whether we insist on standard operating procedures (without challenge), on the one right way, on our way, we are dehumanizing the subordinate. We are saying, in effect, that the employee is less than human—a robot assigned to us for control and guidance. We make such subordinates extensions of our own hands and personalities—they are not fully developed human beings in their own right.

New employees anxious to be successful in a new environment and recognizing that they have much to learn often go along easily with such direction at first. But as competence, job knowledge, and self-confidence grow, the employees may become impatient with the "Father/Mother knows best" syndrome.

This dissatisfaction of the new employees may grow gradually and be interpreted as boredom or melancholy, and its source may not be recognized, for there is no joy in pure routine. If new employees are not allowed to get involved, to take responsibility, to make decisions, then life becomes pretty dull.

Only by taking an active part in what is going on, by participating, by taking the risks inherent in decision making, can new employees show what they can do. Only if they stretch themselves can they experience the joy and satisfaction of achievement. Only in this way can they earn the praise and recognition most people want. Only by effective delegation of authority can new employees, in a positive way, achieve Herzberg's two top positive job satisfiers—achievement and recognition. In Maslow's hierarchy, delegation best offers the hope for meeting esteem and self-fulfillment needs.

ORGANIZATIONAL IMPLICATIONS OF THE FAILURE TO DELEGATE

Some of the common results of failure to delegate authority effectively are:

1. The supervisor becomes overworked checking details, the inbasket overflows, he or she begins to keep late hours, etc.

2. Gradually there is a loss of control of the work.

3. Subordinates fail to develop, thereby placing an even heavier load on more experienced people.

4. Subordinates become frustrated and bored.

5. Interpersonal relationships begin to decline in quality.

6. The supervisor does less planning and spends more time "fighting fires."

7. The supervisor sets limits on her or his own growth and in effect becomes incompetent.

8. The lack of trained subordinates hurts the growth and future of the organization.

I often refer to delegation of authority as the *Key to Competence*—both for the supervisor and for the employee. For the supervisor it can mean salvation from the Peter Principle.[1] For the employee (particularly the new employee) it is the pathway to personal development, to recognition and achievement, and to future opportunities and advancement.

Dr. Lawrence J. Peter and Raymond Hull described a phenomenon that often occurs in organizations, and labeled it the "Peter Principle." The major premise is that "In a hierarchy every employee tends to rise to his [or her] level of incompetence." We can all probably cite individual examples of where that principle worked out fully and resolutely. However that principle need not prevail and, in some cases, it does not. In the ranks of management the principle often foreshadows reality because of a tendency of supervisors and managers not to delegate or to delegate ineffectively. If people are promoted, but they do not delegate well, they soon lack the time and energy to check on all the details with which their subordinates are dealing. They thereby limit their *span of control*—"the maximum number of people that they can supervise directly or effectively." They may be able to get away with supervising a small group but if they are promoted to the next level and insist on managing all the details of all their new subordinates—that is, not allowing their subordinates to exercise their own judgment and authority in running their own work group—the managers soon become incompetent. No one has the time and energy to handle the details of a great number of other persons' jobs. The lack of skill in delega-

---

[1] Lawrence J. Peter and Raymond Hull, *The Peter Principle* (New York: William Morrow, 1969).

tion and the reluctance to delegate accounts for much of the incompetence observable in management. At the same time the employees, new and old, languish. Nothing makes a new employee old as certainly as the supervisor's reluctance to delegate.

DELEGATING TO NEW EMPLOYEES

Peter and Hull offer two fascinating corollaries drawn from their basic principle that apply with a vengeance to new employees: "In time every post tends to be occupied by an employee who is incompetent to carry out its duties," and "Work is accomplished by those employees who have not yet reached their level of incompetence." A chilling prospect.

Though the Peter Principle may deal in extremes, there is enough reality in it to scare the hell out of most serious-minded people. If upper-level positions become cluttered with incompetents, what hope does the new employee have? In all too many cases I'm afraid that answer is not much. It is not too difficult for an observant person to go into an organization and sniff out the tone of the organization—to see whether people are achieving or not, to ascertain if they are satisfied and happy, to perceive whether they have hope for the future. Where these positive feelings are not present, effective delegation is usually also missing.

However, if an organization, and the people in it, accept that real delegation of authority is necessary to get the organization's goals accomplished, why is real delegation of authority so scarce and what can we do about it? To encourage real delegation and to offer new employees a chance to participate, several things need to be achieved:

1. The environment has to be supportive rather than punishing or new employees will learn that risk-taking is foolish.

2. The delegations must match abilities with a little stretching of the employees to provide challenge.

3. Subordinates must be adequately trained so that they accept increased responsibilities from a solid footing of knowledge, skills, and proven accomplishments.

4. The assignments need to be structured so that they build a pattern of success—not a sink or swim situation.

5. The checkpoints for monitoring the assigned project or task should be mutually agreed upon and appropriate to the risk involved.

6. New employees should not be unreasonably limited in seeking help from others and from using their own initiative in solving problems.

7. The supervisor needs to be available for consultation and guidance.

8. The supervisor should review the work and provide thorough feedback (information—not criticism) on the results being obtained.

9. The supervisor needs to avoid overreacting to mistakes and should be placid enough to realize that mistakes occur as part of an employee's growth and development.

10. The supervisor should overcome the notion that all good ideas must come from herself or himself, and recognize that subordinates will be more committed to carrying out their own ideas than they ever will be in carrying out the supervisor's ideas.

11. The supervisor should refrain from always being the expert and showing how much he or she knows. "Well, I would have done it a little different" or "I'll show you a better way" tears the guts out of any sense of achievement the subordinates might have felt.

12. All the jobs in a work unit, including virtually all of those performed by the supervisor, must be considered fair game for delegation—at least *eventually*.

PLANNING DELEGATION

The key to successful planned employee development efforts is the careful analysis of all the tasks being performed by the group which new employees can reasonably be expected to eventually learn and master. We should err on the generous side in preparing that list of tasks and consider almost everything as possible, even if it is years in the future.

In later chapters we will discuss the technique of analyzing tasks for training, for delegation, and for restructuring work for motivation and employee development. For now, we will restrict ourselves to two topics: planning delegation and controlling delegation as a means of developing new employees.

In planning delegation, we might ask ourselves the following questions:

1. Will the assignment challenge the individual?

2. Has the assigned task been explained in detail so that it is clear?

3. Approximately how long should the task take?

4. Is the individual prepared (trained sufficiently) to succeed?

5. How much work and authority can I give the person on this assignment?

6. Have the effects of the tasks and its importance been explained?

7. Can we agree on mutually acceptable check points?

8. Does the individual clearly know the level of performance expected in carrying out this task, and have those standards been carefully checked out using playback techniques?

9. Have I listened carefully to any doubts expressed by the individual, and have we mutually worked through those doubts to a resolution that makes the employee comfortable? Have I made sure their concerns have not been discounted or brushed aside?

10. Can we mutually solve problems as they arise so that both of us succeed?

11. Will objective feedback on the results of the project be given to the subordinate?

12. Will the employee be in a better position psychologically to accept the next assignment after this one has been completed?

In controlling delegations, we need to follow these general guidelines:

1. Establish performance measures before the assignment has been given.

2. Do not dump work on the subordinate. Prepare the individual for the assignment.

3. Check work adequately, but do not overdo it or insist on knowing everything—use milestones or checkpoints.

4. Allow the person freedom to innovate.

5. Worry more about what gets done rather than how it gets done—as long as the work meets the performance standards for quality and quantity (and no intolerable negative side effects occur).

6. Set clear-cut objectives and measure results against the objectives.

7. Respond appropriately to problems so that the person will feel free and comfortable in discussing problems.

8. Watch for trends that may in time defeat the objectives.

The foregoing ways of managing assignments prepare people for mature responsible participation in the productive process of the organization. If we are successful in delegating authority and manage well enough to achieve beneficial results, the future of new employees will be brighter and more rewarding than normal. The foregoing is only a detailed prescription for applying the golden rule in a work situation. Effective delegation can meet new employees' needs for recognition and achievement and they will, if effectively motivated, return to the organization its just due. People learn to make decisions by making decisions. Share credit generously and there is no limit to what can be accomplished.

STUDY QUESTIONS

1. Define delegation—both in the dictionary sense and in a management sense.

2. Why does delegation only deal with authority and not with responsibility? Why can't a supervisor or manager delegate responsibility?

3. Why do supervisors tend to find real delegation of authority scary and often avoid it if they can?

4. List three primary reasons behind a failure to delegate.

5. List five ways in which fear interferes with a supervisor's ability to delegate.

6. List at least five organizational implications of a failure to delegate. Use some of your own ideas in developing the list.

7. List at least ten things that can be done to encourage effective delegation in an organization.

8. List ten questions you might ask yourself in planning delegation.

9. List at least five ways to control delegations effectively.

CHAPTER 14

THE CREATIVITY CONFERENCE

The only place where you can sit down and rest is immediately in front of an undertaker's establishment. For the moment you are satisfied, the concrete has begun to set in your head.

(Charles Kettering)

The vital issue concerning economic payoffs from new employees is *how to ensure maximum contribution by new employees while they are still new to the organization.* How can we garner useful ideas that new employees have about your operation which are based on prior experience or current insights? The ideal time is when an organization is new to employees—before they get set in their ways, before they know all of the accepted practices. During this all too brief period, all is fresh and new to recent hirees. At this time, better than at all other times, new employees can see things with unclouded eyes. We need this freshness to refresh ourselves; we need this excitement of discovery to clear our own vision.

It is at this point, unfortunately, that we often make new employees old before their time by suffocating their curiosity, their enthusiasm, their fresh insights, their new perspectives, and their new ideas. A fully developed creativity conference is an antidote to this poisonous behavior.

When all of the members of a workgroup become involved in a conference to solve organizational problems, and especially to seek ways to implement the thoughts and suggestions of the new employee, we are carrying the creativity conference idea to its logical conclusion and ultimate payoff. However, before such a conference can be successful, training and employee development efforts may be necessary. We may also need to adjust our normal way of thinking about new employees.

It has long been an article of faith that the training and orientation period is largely an expense to the organization because it takes new employees time to become really productive. How long this period lasts and consequently the ultimate loss depends on the complexity of the job, the prior experience of the new people, and the speed with which they master the new job. It is my contention that in many instances this "loss" need not occur. In many cases, new employees could easily turn a profit during their learning period if their experience, insight, and ideas were turned into assets. One new employee I've known earned his salary for the next three years with one suggestion that was made during his first week on the job.

The belief that training costs money, and because of low productivity from the new employee at first, this investment can only be recouped over a long period of employment, is very old and very false. In many cases the foregoing may be very descriptive of what has happened, but often it need not have happened. In *many* instances, new employees could pay for their training period if their ideas were accepted and used.

CONTRIBUTIONS BY NEW EMPLOYEES

The primary obstacle to accepting the notion that new employees have much to contribute may lie in our own intellectual lethargy. For many supervisors and managers to acknowledge that a new employee has a good idea might mean that something would have to be done with those ideas. Consequently we have a variety of ways of getting rid of those ideas, or at least of dismissing them out of hand. Besides the usual, "We've tried that before," "Don't rock the boat," "It won't work here," "It costs too much," and "I'd never get it approved" (and dozens more), we discount the whole idea that new employees could possibly come up with a workable idea *in our environment*. Besides the defense mechanisms that are triggered because we regard such suggestions as criticism of our past performance, we honestly believe that many suggestions new employees might develop would not be practical because they don't yet know the "big picture."

However, if we were positively oriented toward receiving and accepting suggestions from new hires, such suggestions could form the basis for discussing the big picture as it relates to that idea, and thus such conversation could become part of the new employees' orientation and training. If we focused on how to make their suggestions work rather than concentrating on its flaws, the process could shorten the training program, motivate the employees, and perhaps return savings to the organization.

"What can the new employee possibly contribute to our operation?" "It takes years to learn some of the jobs we do." "The new employee knows nothing about what we do or why we do it." "They get confused by the complexity and need to be told every step to take." "You have to walk before you can run." The assumptions made in these types of statements often do not fit the case, but even if they did, it would not mean that new employees have nothing to offer.

New employees may have considerable experience in other jobs, other organizations, or other activities (such as parent, homemaker, or club member), some of which could apply to the new organization. One of the most valuable uses of prior experience is to transfer it to a new situation and apply it artfully to solving problems in a different environment. I've had many new employees say to me, "Over at XYZ Company we used to do this this way and it was a lot easier." Since I've never considered it necessary to assume that I or my group had all the brains in the world, I was interested in using what XYZ had that could improve my operation. I'm sure that in some cases we were inadvertently exporting some of our technological know-how to XYZ company in return. But more importantly, ideas and know-how are the prime ingredients of productivity, and I find that the new employees, irrespective of their background, can often make significant contributions.

The Effective Use of Human Resources

New employees often become effective workers or producers long before management discovers the fact. Often they learn how to get the job done despite the organization—at least get the job done as they see it.

At Litton Industries, I had groups of experienced, sharp, ex-shop people who scientifically methodized and timed operations and then trained people to do the job using the prescribed "best" methods. No matter how hard we tried, inevitably within a few weeks employees could get the job done faster and were using the extra time to their own advantage. As often as not, some of the people who learned fastest were the new employees.

I've witnessed the same thing with maintenance personnel who were able to meet the standards rapidly, and then used the extra time for playing cards or drinking coffee for long periods of time. Technical writers, program planners, and research engineers all have their ways of speeding their work, and seldom do they share their techniques with others. This hoarding of techniques, I suspect, is primarily defensive and a guard against arbitrary decisions of management. However, some of it is not visible simply because no one asked for or even implied that there might be an interest in the ideas of employees.

If management, and particularly first-line supervisors, were to be more candid about sharing problems of the organization with new employees—not in a complaining way but in a participatory fashion—they might be pleasantly surprised at how many ideas employees, particularly new employees, are able to generate.

In many organizations, in private industry as well as government, individual ingenuity is often diverted into pranks or spent on trivia. Barroom type games played on the job, such as "Name the capitals of every state," or questionnaires using anonymous reply cards are often efforts to overcome boredom. Such activities, though usually nonproductive, do show some imagination and demonstrate a desire to be involved in something more complex than the work. This striving for something different could be harnessed toward the examination of problems in the organization and the relief thereof. The new employees then at least have a choice between boredom and applying themselves to challenges.

All this brings us back to the reality that the people closest to the job are best suited to improving it. New employees have no investment in current methods and are therefore free to explore new ways of doing things. They are thinking more actively about the job and how it is done than they ever will be again, after they have become experienced people. New employees are probably learning faster than anyone else in the department (for the rest are probably doing things they've done before), and they are struggling to apply everything they can to succeed in the job. These advantages offered by new employees should be exploited, for both they and the organization will gain from such use of human resources.

It is often said that efforts aimed at improving methods and procedures are most productive when dealing with production, clerical, or maintenance workers than with professional and managerial positions. That is true, however, it is these very clerical or maintenance functions that impact most effectively and harmfully on professional and managerial personnel when something goes wrong. When the copying machine goes out, when the word processing center fails to function, when a light bulb goes out, when supplies don't arrive from the stockroom, professional tempers flare. I have often observed professional employees suggest alternative methods because they have seen such methods work in another organization. The new professional or managerial person often brings with them a lot of know-how from previous training or experiences.

How do we glean all of these ideas and suggestions from new employees? A primary method suggested was through the use of the creativity conference. However, for the creativity conference to be effective it is helpful to start way back at the first day of employment.

PREPARATION FOR THE CREATIVITY CONFERENCE

It was suggested earlier in this book that the supervisor begin an early dialogue with a new employee in which the new person is asked to identify problems and/or make suggestions as to ways in which the operation might be improved. It was also suggested that if a suggestion was found to be immediately feasible (as opposed to something that required some study, affected others adversely, or incurred unplanned for expenses) that the supervisor implement the idea at once and give full credit to the new employee. Further, when a complex or more far-reaching idea is presented it was suggested that the supervisor record the idea, describing it fully but in no way evaluating the suggestion. These more difficult to implement ideas are those left for the creativity conference.

There is one thing more that the supervisor can do in preparation for the creativity conference. He or she can *demonstrate* interest in new ideas by teaching the employee some simple analytical tools for simplifying work and improving methods. Then the supervisor can focus on helping to make the employee's ideas work rather than shooting them down or delaying implementation.

For over forty years there has been a variety of work simplification techniques that are easy to learn and can be applied to almost any work with surprisingly good results. At times they appear almost too simple, yet they force us to apply a systematic questioning attitude to almost everything we do. As a result, new ways are constantly being found to do work easier and better. Surprisingly, I find very few younger supervisors and virtually no employees that have been trained to apply these easy analytical tools. A great number of supervisors, unless they work in factories, never even consider it their responsibility to reduce costs and simplify work. Perhaps this is why productivity problems exist and why employees are so dissatisfied with the way their organization is run.

Work simplification is built on the premise of "Work smarter—not harder." By working harder most people cannot increase their output by more than 10 to 15 percent (though we all probably know some notable exception to this rule). However, by working smarter we may be able to eliminate a whole operation or create a new product or service.

Work simplification has been described as the "organized use of common sense to find easier and better ways of doing work." Its methodology is basically questioning everything we do. There is a five-step method of work simplification that simply states:

1. Pick a specific task to improve.

2. Get the facts relevant to that task. (Answer the questions, "What? Where? When? Who? How? Why?")

3. Challenge every detail.

4. Develop the preferred solution(s).

5. Implement the improvement(s).

When the details of the work are identified we should ask the four basic questions about each of these details:

1. Can the step or action be eliminated?

2. Can the step or action be combined with another operation (to eliminate duplication or backtracking)?

3. Can the details (or steps) be rearranged to give a more efficient or less lengthy sequence of operations?

4. Can the operation or any of its details be further simplified in any way?

Amazing results can occur as a result of asking these very basic and simple questions.

I once was chatting with an employment specialist at a transistor division of General Instrument Company. He was complaining because he had the following employment request: "Find a woman 5'6" or taller." In the ethnic milieu in which the company was hiring, women that tall were scarce (why the position had to be filled by a woman was not even discussed). He also complained that there had been a great deal of turnover on that job, and even if he found a suitable employee she probably wouldn't stay long. I asked him why the woman had to be 5'6" or taller. He stared at me for an instant and then said, "I don't know. Let's go find out."

We found the job to be on what they called the cascade. This was a series of trays on a stepped platform where water from a faucet flowed into the top tray to the one below it, and so on, in a cascade, which washed a small quantity of special transistors. The operator's job was to move these transistors either up or down the cascade (I don't remember which). Looking at the operation from a fresh point of view one thing was obvious. The stepped platform rested on a table that was thirty inches high. By substituting a twenty-four-inch table, which was found unused in a nearby room, and by running a six-inch hose from the faucet, the operator's height requirement was now reduced to five feet. If two wooden pallets, which were also nearby, were used, and the hose lengthened, the operator could have been 4'2" tall.

This again demonstrates the addage that "Some simply remarkable things are remarkably simple." But why did it take that magical "Why?" to unlock that absurd problem. The people running that department were not stupid. I suspect that the answer lay in passive workers who were not invited to think, and who were even punished when they did make a suggestion, and in busy supervisors who never *took time to save time.*

The late Arthur D. Little said long ago there are four marks of a creative (problem-solving) mind:

1. *The simplicity to wonder.* The true problem solver wonders about things many of us take for granted.

2. *The ability to question.* The kind of questioning that encourages answers leaves the other person feeling OK.

3. *The power to generalize.* When we get the facts or reasons behind the obvious thing, we need to determine if there is some law or principle working that would apply in other instances.

4. *The capacity to apply.* The payoff is in applying or using what we have learned.

One of the great problems facing our society is that all too often these four behaviors are not encouraged and are often blatantly discouraged. Many people are passive and tend to do what they are told, and they are actually punished if they prove too curious. Hence thousands of small, or sometimes significant, opportunities to improve operations or reduce costs are missed. The best way to cure this passivity is not merely to state, "I'd like to hear your ideas," but to demonstrate that we have a personal stake or commitment to simplifying and improving the way we do things in the organization.

There are many tools and techniques of methods analysis and work simplification which are beyond the scope of this work on new employees. However, I remember the thrill and enthusiasm that passed through my small workgroup at Litton Industries years ago when all of my employees were given a company-sponsored course in work simplification. Within weeks, our work flow was reorganized from within and therefore enthusiastically supported by my subordinates who did the analysis and developed the suggestions. They came up with dozens of new ideas which we tried and implemented. The payoff to me was that budget funds that were available began to cover more of my goals for the department because of the savings generated. More work got done and the quality of output was better. The employees reported less fatigue and the backlog of work began to melt away. The net effect on the workgroup was not only great enthusiasm, but the measurable improvement in output was equal to about a 15-percent increase in the budget.

The work in our office tended to increasingly focus on the creative and professional tasks, for the clerical, redundant items were simplified in some cases toward the point of extinction. The long-term effects were probably even more significant. Two people were eventually upgraded from semi-skilled to professional. The effects did not stop there. The primary result was that we had a group of people that throughout their lives were better able to return benefits from their creativity and imagination to their organizations because of this human resource development effort.

How much you need to teach new employees depends somewhat on the nature of the organization and the work that the employees are likely to be exposed to (not just the work they are doing now). Tools of work simplification such as flow process charting, work sampling, motion analysis, or task analysis are applicable someplace in almost any organization. In this training process it is always safer to provide too much rather than too little, for part of the creative process is to see new opportunities in old situations.

Unfortunately, many organizations do not provide incentives for work simplification or cost reduction. Government organizations, for example, where the number of people you supervise determines your grade, provides a disincentive for improving operations and thereby reducing people power in the organization. On the other hand, in these same organizations grade levels of subordinates is also included in determining position level, and if lower-level personnel can eliminate routine tasks and be trained for higher-level tasks, improvements in the supervisor's grade level are possible. Regrettably, large "empires" often do pay off in power, in prestige, and often in the paycheck.

Equally sad is the reality that if budgeted funds are saved in one area, bureaucratic rigidity often prevents them from being applied in another area. Therefore, more interesting, more challenging, and more cost effective work often does not get done. Supervisors have often said to me, "Why should I bother changing things? I've got the person available—I may as well keep him or her busy." Busy doing unneeded but time-consuming work. Again, it often comes down to "I'm alright Jack—I've got mine!"

Nevertheless, both supervisors and employees generally would rather be doing something productive and worthwhile if they believed it possible. This is where some simple questions come in handy.

1. What? Why?—leads to elimination.

2. Where? When? Who?—leads to rearrangement and combination.

3. How?—leads to simplification.

How to Identify Problems for the Creativity Conference

The focus should be on looking at problems in a new light. We need to ask ourselves questions about our daily activities as we go about performing our job. What work-related events made me mad today? What took too much time? Did I encounter a bottleneck? What caused too much chasing around? What needs improvement most? What jobs use (or waste) a great deal of materials, energy, or time?

Part of the art of reducing costs and improving methods involves elevating our level of consciousness about what we do and how we do it. Habit is a great provider, but it keeps us doing things the same way. Personally, our greatest resources are our time, our energy, and our intellect. We need to use the latter to conserve the two former resources, for time and energy are our most limited resources.

From teaching work simplification principles and practices to supervisors and managers in a variety of organizations, I have often seen a short-term payback of five to ten times the cost of the training recouped in a few weeks by the organization. The long-term effects sometimes have meant the survival of the organization. One example will show the value of this type of training. A young, new employee and I conducted a work sampling study of support staff activities in a 450-bed hospital in the Northeast.

We noticed "dietary aides" lined up to receive patients' food trays as they were prepared by dieticians in several diet kitchens scattered throughout the hospital. When we began to question this idle time, one of the trainees suggested that temperature-controlled carts were available for a modest investment. Trays could then be prepared in the main kitchen, placed on carts to be rolled through the corridors, and trays taken off at each room so as to eliminate the waiting. In the long run, this would have been a marginally profitable routine.

However, the question was then raised as to what would be done with the "to be abandoned" diet kitchens. Upon arrival in that hospital I noted that overcrowding of facilities was so severe that two patients were on beds in an alcove (partitioned off with a curtain) waiting for a room to become available. More questions led to the suggestion that the diet kitchens be converted to patient rooms.

The net result of that idea was that after state permission was granted to reduce the room size by twelve square feet, the hospital added seventeen beds without laying a single brick. Even at the prices of hospital rooms in those days, this change increased hospital income by $430,700 per year, improved service to the community enormously, and greatly increased the value of the hospital's physical plant.

The principal point here is that new employees have a fresh perspective to offer. They are not tied to past routines and, if properly trained and encouraged, they could act as a catalyst to the workgroup in reexamining past practices and developing mutually beneficial improvements. It is often new employees who are given the dog work to do and, if trained early in work simplification techniques, they would be highly motivated to improve or eliminate such odious work.

THE CREATIVITY CONFERENCE

Some organizations have instituted the creativity conference (or problem-solving conference) on a monthly or biweekly basis, involving all employees in a workgroup. Here they focus, one at a time, on problems any member of the group chooses to bring up that is in any way impeding operations or creating difficulties for an individual. This is not a gripe session, but a focus on group problem solving in creative and effective ways.

The creativity conference is based on three tenets:

1. Everyone has a responsibility for identifying problems and reporting them to the group.
2. No problem (nor the person who brought it up) can be discounted (made less of or diminished) by any member of the group—especially by the group leader.
3. Each group member has a responsibility for contributing personal experience, knowledge, and ideas in a positive vein towards solving the problem.

A modified version of the six-step method of problem solving is used:

1. Define the problem in terms of needs rather than solutions.
2. Develop relevent facts. Inventory human and physical resources available for solving the problem.

3. Generate possible solutions by using brainstorming techniques, if applicable.

4. Evaluate solution(s) and pick best solution(s).

5. Implement solution(s).

6. Monitor, follow up, and modify if necessary.

There are three primary requisites for group behavior during the creativity conference that are especially critical when new employees are involved:

1. The definition of the problem must be relatively open-ended. Often we state a problem in single-dimension terms which only allows for us to discuss a variety of ways to achieve an answer that is implied in the statement of the problem. "How can we add another outside telephone line?" implies a solution (a new telephone line). "How can we respond to customer complaints more quickly?" is closer to a statement of a basic need which might be able to be met in several ways.

2. If brainstorming or similar techniques for generating a host of possible solutions to a problem is used, the idea generation phase and the evaluation phase must be kept rigidly separate. No critical statements, or even derisive laughter can be allowed during the idea generation phase. Criticism in any form during the period when ideas are developed is taboo for it discourages input, blocks creative thinking, and prevents the building of one idea on another. The supervisor has responsibility to see that no one uses negative, turnoff responses on anyone else.

3. "Spectrum policy" should be applied to ideas by everyone in the group. Spectrum policy[1] is based on the belief that ideas (except the simplest ones perhaps) are not simply good or bad. Any suggestion made by an employee has at least the germ of a good idea in it. Empirical research indicates that people contribute ideas because they see *some* connection between their idea and a solution to the problem. Ideas can be described as a spectrum having useful and nonuseful (negative) aspects to it. Unfortunately, our competitive habits and critical training have caused us to focus on the negative parts of the idea. Consequently, we often hear, "It won't work" or "That's a good idea, but . . .," and then we proceed to tear it apart.

---

[1]George M. Prince, *The Practice of Creativity* (New York: Collier Books, Macmillan Publishing Company, 1976).

Spectrum policy suggests that each of us practice the habit of: (1) focusing on the positive aspects of the idea first, and (2) focusing on not just identifying the faults but in making suggestions that will cure the faults—item by item. Thus, you get to avoid the fatal flaws but also keep the creative process going. However, with new employees the application of these three positive approaches means a group that will value the new employees' opinion, work to make their ideas work, and provide a wholesome environment for all employees to develop and grow without fear.

Finally, if the ideas of a new employee are accepted and strengthened, he or she should be part of the implementation team if such is needed. The primary concern here is that the new employees experience the joy of having their ideas become reality.

The primary magic of the creativity conference is not only the originality of the solutions generated by the group, but the creative ways that are developed to justify a change (cost and other savings), to plan its implementation, and to sell or carry out the improvements.

STUDY QUESTIONS

1. What are some ways of discounting ideas the new employee might have about how to do things better?

2. Think of some examples of the new employee making a contribution to the organization—even things learned in a nonsimilar job elsewhere.

3. What factors might make the new employee a good source for ideas to improve the work?

4. What is the key slogan of work simplification, and why is it important?

5. What are the five steps in the work simplification method?

6. What are the four basic questions of work simplification?

7. List the four marks of the creative (problem-solving) mind.

8. What are the three basic tenets of the creativity conference?

9. What are the three primary requisites for group behavior during the creativity conference? Why are they especially critical when the new employee is involved?

10. Describe the basic principles underlying spectrum policy.

CHAPTER 15

DISCOVERING THE INDIVIDUAL'S POTENTIAL

My boss and I were engaged in a creative problem-solving session, trying to meet each other's needs in a work-related incident. A client wanted us to begin a training program on Monday, but we didn't have the training materials ready because they had just notified us that day—Thursday. Many of the items only I could prepare and I had been looking forward to a long-planned weekend with my daughter in the Boston area. I agreed to take some material with me and work on it over the weekend, but I still needed to get overhead slides prepared for Monday's presentation. My boss, the head of the firm, suggested that I dictate the material over the telephone and it would be prepared in the office. That sounded good, but I knew that our secretary/typist was going to be away on the weekend and mentioned the fact. He said, "That's OK, I'll type it."

"You can type?" I responded with surprise, for not once in our ten-year association did I get any notion that he could type.

"Oh hell, yes," he responded, "I taught typing for ten years at a local business college." Ten years and I had not an inkling.

I turned that experience around and began to wonder about how little I knew about my subordinates and their unrevealed talents and abilities. And what about how little I knew about my coworkers or even my neighbors for that matter?

If it is true that we know so little about the people we have known for a long time, how much more likely is it that new employees will have facets of their personality, or background, or skills that we know little about? Could it be that because of uncertainty or their reluctance to come on too strong they are holding back information that could be of value to us?

Joseph Luft and Harry Ingham have offered a concept called the Johari Window[1] that has helped me and many others to put this business of how

---

[1] Joseph Luft, *Group Processes,* 2nd ed. (Palo Alto, Calif.: National Press Book, 1970).

much we know about other people into perspective. With some apologies to the creators for my own interpretation and use, the window demonstrates some of the reasons we assume we know much about other people, particularly subordinates, when in fact we know little.

The open or obvious area

Things I know about me
(what each person knows
about herself or himself)

	This contains obvious physical characteristics and general knowledge items	
Things others know about me (including what the supervisor knows)	This contains obvious physical characteristics and general knowledge items	

In the upper left quadrant we have the things that others generally know about me and that I know about me. These are the obvious things like height, approximate weight, hair color, skin color, etc., plus those things (in a particular environment) which have become common knowledge. This is the kind of data that is on a resume, those things that I tend to advertise, and the items that are part of my public record in an organization or community. Unfortunately, this may only reveal a small part of myself and would only make a portion of me available to my supervisor.

The Hidden area

In the lower left quadrant there is an area where the things I know about myself meet the things others don't know about me. This area includes not only things I might feel embarrassed or ashamed of, or which might be used to my disadvantage if they were known, but all the things that I was never asked about. It could also include some of my dreams and aspirations that others might deride. It might include all of the problems that might burden others, things that are "personal," perhaps my politics and religion. It might include much I don't see as relevant to my job or things I am good at but don't like to "brag" about.

These things are hidden from others for many reasons, but one of the big reasons is we are not sure if other people would handle the information in appropriate ways. Because there is not a high level of trust in all situations, we

	Things I know about me (what each person knows about herself or himself)	
Things others know about me (including what the supervisor knows)	Obvious and general knowledge	
Things others don't know about me (including the supervisor)	Hidden—the area of potential for real sharing	

hesitate to share. We may also carry some cultural messages around in our head about "things that are nobody else's business" or "You don't wash your dirty linen in public."

Do we need to know what is in that quadrant for other people? We are only hiring people to do a job. If they do it, what do we care about those other things?

Other than finding out that people are probably a lot more interesting than we originally thought, there may be no value as long as nothing ever changes. If the organization is never to grow or offer more opportunity; if the job will always be the same and no problems will ever arise; if no one ever retires, dies, or gets sick; there is no need to know more about other people than those things related directly to their job.

One of the best things to ever come out of the Human Resource Development field are the skills and interests records being kept on many employees by an increasing number of organizations. When new opportunities arise or conditions change, people can be matched to needs if enough is known about them. However, we still have the need for employees, especially new employees, to share with us many of those little-known things about themselves which might in time be of value in the work situation.

A caring, trusting environment where information is used appropriately and for mutual benefit is essential to create this willingness to share. However, once it has been shared, confidences must be kept and data used constructively.

One of the most powerful tools for building confidence and learning about people is to simply listen—listen for feelings as well as facts. A good listener will often learn more about a fellow employee in an hour than an interrogator will learn in a life time. Good listening builds trust and confidence.

The Blind Area

	Things I know about me (what each person knows about herself or himself)	Things I don't know about me
Things others know about me (including what the supervisor knows)	Obvious and general knowledge	Blind area of *meaningful feedback*
	Hidden	

In the upper right quadrant of the Johari Window we find things others know about me and things *I don't* know about me. Strange as it may seem, these are the things that may have the most to do with our careers. This realm includes our subconscious mannerisms, our ticks, our habits—the things we do frequently but aren't aware of. It also may include our impact on others, how they see us, how they feel about us, what flaws or problems they detect in us. This is the side of us that is blind.

Does this part of us make a difference? Yes, primarily because if we were aware of these subconscious habits, the way we were impacting on others, flaws in our *behaviors,* we could do things to correct them if they were serious enough.

Unfortunately, all too often no one will tell us if we have bad breath. "Oh! I couldn't tell him that," or "It's not for me to say, but. . . ." By-in-large those statements are monumental "put downs." They say in effect that I am not able to handle the information they have. In short, they are saying that I am inadequate or will respond inappropriately. Usually they haven't even tried to find out how I would respond, and those statements are their excuses for not trying.

On the other hand, people *do* respond inappropriately when they are given feedback on how they appear to others or how others are affected by them. Curiously, when feedback is given it often is given in a way, judgmentally, that virtually guarantees rejection and hurt feelings.

I personally do not believe that there is any such thing as "constructive criticism." The dictionary tells us that criticism involves "making judgments, evaluating, making unfavorable remarks or judgments, finding fault." Criticism is just that. Calling our evaluative and judgmental remarks "constructive criticism" is sugar-coating a bad pill. What people need is *information,* not evaluation.

Feedback is most effective when it is proffered genuinely as help. Help, however, can only be defined by the *receiver* (that is, only the person who has the problem can truly decide what is helpful to them). "I'm only trying to help" is often a subconscious negative psychological game when evaluation is proffered as help, and as such is forced on a person who neither wants it or needs it.

Information is descriptive rather than evaluative, and it is specific rather than general. Feedback given about something that *can't* be changed is also not helpful. (I said *can't* rather than *won't*.)

Why is this feedback so important to new employees? Because no one needs information more and no one is likely to be more sensitive to criticism than the new employee (who needs to succeed so badly).

One of the most helpful things in my life was an all-day interview by a psychologist from Rohrer, Hibler & Replogle. They were interviewing me for an executive position with an aircraft firm, and the job was of far greater scope than anything I had ever done before.

After a battery of tests, a prolonged oral interview, and several other exercises, he gave it to me straight from the shoulder, "You could handle the job in time, but at this moment you are not ready for it." He then spent our final hour giving me detailed feedback on strengths and weaknesses. Not once did he evaluate. The information was factual and descriptive. I came away feeling I had just left a man I could trust.

He had also unlocked my understanding of what I was doing that was getting in the way of my career advancement. He helped me to rethink my career goals. If I had gotten the job, I believe that his help and information would have been instrumental in making a success of it.

An arrangement between people where real sharing and meaningful feedback operate in both directions allows all of us to enlarge the areas of knowledge about ourselves and each other. It is the basis of a healthy and productive relationship.

The Unknown Area

	Things I know about me (what each person knows about herself or himself)	Things I don't know about me
Things others know about me (including what the supervisor knows)	Obvious and general knowledge	Blind area of meaningful feedback
Things others don't know about me (including the supervisor)	Hidden—the area of potential for real sharing	Unknown— My undeveloped potential

The final quadrant is the Realm of the Unknown. This includes those things that others don't know about me and those things that I don't know about me. This area can include ailments that are not yet manifest, future events, and external or mutually subconscious things that affect our relationship. But the most critical part of this area for new employees, and for all of us, is that this area describes our undeveloped potential.

This undeveloped potential includes all of the things we have never tried, yet might succeed at—at least passably—if we were to try them. It includes all the things we've dreamed of (and many things that we haven't yet dreamed of) but never had the time, the money, or the opportunity to try. Our undeveloped potential includes all of the things of life we've avoided out of fear or distaste. It also includes the items we've never had any interest in, though at which we might be good if we developed the interest. It includes a myriad of things that we've never heard of or that have not yet been invented.

How many of you are doing things successfully that your grandfathers or grandmothers would never have dreamed of? The chances are good that the bulk of your associates are engaged in occupations, or hobbies, or sports that were unthought of a century ago. I often ask seminar participants, "What would the astronauts most likely have been (occupation) if they had been born five hundred years earlier?" A sprinkling of people usually respond: explorers, adventurers, pirates, sailors, etc. Often a lone individual may mutter: farmers.

There seems to be a persistent romantic notion in people that certain adventuresome people would have been exceptional no matter what. This notion is generally a lot of crap. The chances are almost perfect that the astronauts would have been farmers—probably working someone else's land.

The reason for the foregoing ungracious statement (it is not nice to abuse heroes) is that five hundred years ago farming was nearly the only thing going for most people. The great bulk of the people at that time tilled the soil from sun up to sun down, had no education, and were locked in by physical, financial, and cultural barriers that kept their eyes pointed to the ground. Is it unlikely that the astronauts (exceptional as they may be) are any brighter, any more physically capable, or any more conceptually able than their grandparents or great-grandparents, ad infinitum. The primary difference between them and their great-great-great-grandparents is that they had opportunity. Trace your own family history and consider these facts. The astronauts had free public education, they lived in a highly complex technological society, and they had a heritage of freedom. Countless generations had been involved in creating a society in which, at last, their individual talents could be used. Trace your own family history if you doubt that reality. You may have a princess or hero or two scattered through your family background, but the chances are good that the bulk of your ancestors (until the last hundred years) were farmers. So much for romanticism.

The primary thing that the astronauts had over their ancestors is opportunity. Society, and perhaps some individuals, gave them a chance to show what they could do and they did it. Can we do any less for new employees? This is why training, delegation of authority, a free flow of information in the organization, and a fair shake on job opportunities is so critical. We can no longer afford to waste the undeveloped potential of so many of our people.

In the last diagram of the Johari Window, there are some dotted lines up near the top and along the left margin. I suspect that those lines delineated the undeveloped potential of earlier peoples including our, and the astronauts' ancestors. If it is true, as some claim, that we are only using a small portion (5 to 10 percent is the estimate) of our inate intelligence, perhaps those dotted lines could outline the realm of our own undeveloped potential.

Today we are undergoing a quiet social revolution of our undeveloped potential. It has long been said that a leisure class is necessary for the development of the arts and invention. We have that situation. A large mass of people have more leisure than ever before. People are retiring early, not to sit idly while the world passes them by, but so that they can join the mainstream and perhaps for the first time in their lives do what they want to do. The great growth in education in recent decades is in adult education, in noncredit courses where people are experiencing a great number of learning opportunities just because of individual curiosity or a hunger to develop potential that is only vaguely visible. At Prince George's Community College in Maryland I saw busload after busload of senior citizens arrive for one-day workshops and seminars on a whole plethora of subjects. One eighty-six-year-old man was taking a course on leadership—now there is an optimist. However, that man also knows the value of the time he has left, and he wants to use it to the fullest. Lifetime learning has arrived with a flourish.

Yet, while all of this is going on, millions languish in unchallenging jobs yearning for the day when they can retire and do what they always wanted to do. Talent and ability in great quantities is going to waste because so many do not know how to release it or even to recognize its existence. A great question facing our society is how to identify our unused resources, how to assess them, and how to develop plans and mechanisms for capitalizing on this undeveloped potential.

WHY WE HAVE TROUBLE ASSESSING POTENTIAL

Part of our problem is involved in a cultural lag. We know what to do, but individuals are reluctant to give up outmoded ways of thinking and behaving. We all too often assume that "what is will be." All too many people still too often think of people as static resources, not developable creatures. Even some people in the human resource field, when interviewing a prospective employee, think primarily in terms of the job to be done—the slot to be filled. Some skilled interviewers discover much more about a person and may record or re-member this or that piece of background that is not job-related but may have relevance elsewhere in the organization, and they may even use that data. But all too often, the supervisor is so preoccupied with getting someone to do a set of tasks that all else is subordinate.

In trying to find out what else a person has done, or likes to do, or would like to try doing, we run into a wall of realities that frustrate the free flow of data, feelings, and ideas.

It is not uncommon for an employee to shape a resume to fit a job open-ing and to ignore or actually hide other experiences or abilities that could be useful to the organization at other times and in other circumstances but which might lead to them being considered "over-qualified" or a "dilettante." When I was in graduate school my fellow workers at a steelmill went out on strike. Since I needed work and had no long-term commitment to my job, I ap-plied at many local firms. After being told I was over-qualified—almost to the point of starvation—I told one firm that had need for a stock handler that I had been in the Army since high school and had been doing clerical functions. Therefore I was eligible for hire and got the job. I knew that the organization was too small and the job too insignificant to bother checking. Later when I made a suggestion to the supervisor on a methods improvement, he retorted," "What the hell does a stock handler know about running this place?"

Since people's skills and experience are often assessed only in terms of the immediate job to be done, is it any surprise that a lot of useful data gets lost in the system? When people have been doing a job for a while the supervisor often assumes they know all the important things about those individuals, and seldom do they look deeper.

New situations require new answers and create new opportunities. How-ever, it may be that talents and abilities not previously brought forth can be critical. This lack of in-depth knowledge about people often leads to an orga-nization laying off one type of worker while hiring another type without ever knowing that appropriate human resources were being disposed of. At Litton Industries I saw the opposite happen. A lay-off of factory workers coincided with some growth in engineering. Two people were found in the shop that had clerical and other skills that could be used in my department. They turned out to be excellent employees. Because of similar efforts with other people, the lay-off was far less severe than anticipated.

The key to using human resources effectively is the realization that with our increasingly complex technology, with our growing approach to life-time learning, and with our media-oriented enhanced levels of social sophistication, people are far more complex and versatile than ever before. Matching people to jobs is no longer the rather simple process it has been in the past. People have more to offer than ever before and the trend toward developing all of a person's abilities is accelerating. We need better ways to assess the levels of skills and the degree of human potential than ever before.

Tragically, supervisors, managers, and personnel specialists often allow their minds to go to sleep. Credentials are substituted for abilities. Job applicants hide facts or discount experience because it doesn't seem job relevant. We don't hire people for their potential (potential is hard to assess), we hire them for a slot. We make decisions on the basis of irrelevant paper and pencil tests. We promote people on the basis of our "comfort quotient" with subordinates rather than on ability. We work harder than we need because we fail to utilize other's abilities effectively. We fail to recognize that individuals are developing informally all the time.

Where does all this leave new employees? Often with a rather drab and unfulfilled future. What can we do about it? We can offer the best training available. We can provide information about the task to be done. We can provide support and help. But finally, the ultimate truth will only be revealed when we do something incredibly simple—give each person a chance to show what he or she can do.

The American dream has been built around this being a land of opportunity, and we have seen some remarkable results of the driving force of that simple idea. What we need to do now is ensure that the power of opportunity is extended to all new employees.

STUDY QUESTIONS

1. What are the four dimensions or inputs for the Johari Window, i.e., "Things I know about," etc.?

2. Identify the four sections of the Johari Window as they relate to each of us.

3. What is one estimate of the proportion of the Johari Window that represents our undeveloped potential?

4. What is the primary key to potential inherent in the "undeveloped potential" portion of the Johari Window?

5. List three things that can be done to shrink the area of new employees' undeveloped potential.

CHAPTER 16

TASK ANALYSIS
THE "OPEN SESAME" FOR TRAINING AND DEVELOPING NEW EMPLOYEES

Most supervisors do not do a very good job of training and developing new employees because they have no comprehensive plan nor any detailed plan. Things tend to happen as the supervisor thinks of them, or when a new employee becomes insistent, or when work pressures build up to the point where the supervisor can ignore them no longer. None of these situations are favorable. Because the supervisor is busy, new employees are often assigned dull routine tasks which keep them off the boss' back until he or she gets time to think of something else. Seldom is there a step-by-step plan for increasing responsibility, and even more rarely is there a plan that involves variety and challenge.

Years ago I was involved in a study of the training program for apprentices in three maintenance trades, electrician, millwright, and machine repairman, at Ford Motor Company. Each apprentice was receiving 2,000 hours of work experience in a variety of departments, with each employee being carefully scheduled from department to department to ensure that the person was exposed to all types of equipment and machinery. That part of the program worked fine, but as a corollary, each apprentice was to be given a variety of tasks or taught to use and operate or repair the various types of equipment peculiar to each department. The foremen (and they were all men at that time), however, had demanding production schedules to meet, and the most effective way to meet those schedules was to teach the apprentice to operate one piece of equipment or do one simple task and then let them practice only that task over and over. It kept the apprentice off their back, and the young person learned one skill well enough to become highly productive. One apprentice spent 300 working hours turning spindles—a task he learned in three hours. Another changed light bulbs in "the tunnel" at the River Range plant for six months. Meanwhile, obviously their training languished. Tragically, when their apprenticeship was over, these new journeymen were expected to know how to do the tasks that were listed on their training sheets—what a set-up for failure—of those new employees. Lacking a detailed training plan may be setting up the new employees to fail, almost as thoroughly as did those foremen at Ford.

TASK ANALYSIS AND PLANNING FOR TRAINING

Before we can effectively train and develop new employees (or any other employees), we have to identify what training they will need. Every supervisor has three types of tasks under their control: (1) those tasks relating to the specific position a new employee has been hired for, (2) those tasks performed by other employees, and (3) tasks that are currently performed by the supervisor. All of these need to be analyzed before setting plans for training, delegation of authority, or restructuring work for job enrichment or personal growth.

When an enterprise is new, one person, usually the founder, tends to do all of the tasks personally. As the enterprise succeeds and grows, certain tasks (usually the easiest to learn and less complex tasks) are spun off and given to new employees. Sometimes a specialist is employed to handle a group of specialized tasks such as bookkeeping/accounting or advertising. The relationship may be part-time or full-time. If success continues, more and more people are brought aboard, and tasks of various types are spun off from jobs and given to others. This splintering of jobs into tasks, some of which are passed to others, continues as long as the organization continues to grow. Government agencies and institutions tend to follow the same pattern of splitting off tasks, though they may do so in very formal ways. Planning for human resource development involves this splintering process used in a planned manner.

Planning is "the arrangement of the factors involved in a situation so as to achieve desired results." The significant "factors" involved in a work situation are the *tasks* involved in doing that work.

Most supervisors know or are aware of the tasks performed in their unit, though they may not be able to perform them (for example, typing and shorthand). However, planning for human resource development involves: (1) identifying or listing those tasks, (2) determining the knowledge, skills, abilities, and decisions (KSAD's) required to perform those tasks, and (3) transferring to or developing within new employees those knowledge, skills, abilities, and decisions required to successfully perform the tasks.

When supervisors or managers have broken each job down into its manageable components, *tasks,* they are ready to train employees and delegate authority on a planned basis. This level of analysis is also sufficient for supervisors and employees to look at each component for ways to simplify the work and reduce the cost of doing it.

Task analysis originally developed as a tool for work simplification and methods improvement. Decades ago, task analysis was described as "a method of dividing work into manageable units which are small enough to be studied for possible elimination, combination, rearrangement and simplification.'' That use is valid today. Often the supervisor and the new employee looking at tasks afresh may see opportunities for simplifying the work and reducing costs.

However, from a training and development standpoint, the important pay-off is that at this level we can begin to see the KSAD requirements of the task, and therefore can begin to plan our training and development efforts in detail. If we care to go so far, the identification and specification of the KSAD requirements can make possible detailed job-related performance objectives which provide directional/content guidance and adequacy tests for training. It is not our objective here to strive for the latter goal, but rather to focus on effective job-related training which most supervisors and staff personnel can accomplish.

TASK ANALYSIS—THE LEVELS OF WORK

The greatest problem in conducting a task analysis study is to ensure that we reach a proper level of detail so that the KSAD's become visible without being mired down in minutiae. There is a general hierarchy of work:

Job
Duties
Tasks
Elements
Motions

This basic structure, common to all jobs, makes it possible to develop and apply a standardized method of studying work. We need that standardized method if we are to create effective and cost-efficient training, if we are to delegate authority on a planned and constructive basis, and if we are to re-structure work for maximum motivation, personal development, and lowest performance cost. The hierarchy is detailed below.

Job The duties and tasks performed by one individual constitutes her or his job. Several individuals can hold essentially the same job if they perform the same tasks and duties. In organizations people often hold the same job *title* even though they do not perform the same tasks. For our purposes here it doesn't matter a great deal, but some purists in the task analysis field (for their own good reasons) require that incumbents with the same job perform identical duties and tasks.

A secretarial job will be used to illustrate the nature of this type of detailed analysis.

Duty Each job is composed of one or more duties. A duty is a large segment of the work done by one individual, often a major subdivision of the work content of his or her job. A duty is usually recognized as being one of the employee's principal job responsibilities. A duty occupies a significant portion of the employee's time, occurs with reasonable frequency in the work cycle, and involves operations which use closely related skills, knowledge, abilities, and decisions.

A partial list of secretarial duties might include:

- Take dictation

- Type letters and reports

- Transcribe minutes of meetings

- Check travel vouchers

- Answer phone and relay messages

- Make travel reservations

- Process incoming mail

- Requisition supplies

- File

- Perform miscellaneous errands for the supervisor, etc.

A duty is performed to achieve some major job objective by using some method, and achieved according to some standard with respect to speed, accuracy, quality, or quantity. The performance standard may have been developed by the employee through trial and error or by experience, or it may have been provided by the supervisor in the form of oral, written, or graphic instructions. Duties are frequently characterized by the consequence of error or by the significance of the decisions made by the incumbent. (Personnel departments often use the term *Job Description* to identify a written work analysis of a job and its *duties*. Job descriptions are normally *too* generalized to be useful in specifying the behavioral objectives required for effective training and development.)

Task A task is a unit of work activity which forms a significant and consistent part of a duty. Tasks are not homogenous units of behavior; they are logically differentiated segments of work activity. If we were to divide one of the duties of a secretary into tasks, it might read as follows:

Duty: Process incoming mail

Task 1: Sort mail by addressee

Task 2: Distribute mail to individuals' in-baskets

Task 3: Open supervisor's mail

Task 4: Answer routine inquiries

Task 5: Date, stamp "critical" mail

Each duty can be broken down into a series of logical steps or activities. A task, then, has the same relationship to a duty that a duty has to a job. Each duty is made up of one or more tasks. Each task occupies a reasonable portion of the work time spent in performing a duty. It occurs with reasonable frequency in a work cycle of the duty, it meets some standard, and it involves closely related KSAD's.

Element Sometimes tasks are further detailed into their component parts called elements. If this is done, the KSAD's generally become even more closely related to each other. Often the element level is the work unit that deals with the details of how the methods, procedures, and techniques involved in the task are carried out. For the purpose of this discussion, it is at the element level that the great opportunities for work simplification, improved methods, and cost reduction are realized. In our secretarial example, we can illustrate this level as follows:

Duty: Process incoming mail
Task: Distribute mail to individuals' in-baskets
Element 1: Sort mail by delivery sequence
Element 2: Deliver to in-baskets

Elements are the smallest components into which it is practical to subdivide any work operation without analyzing separate motions, movements, or the mental processes involved in the operation. An element is a meaningful and useful grouping of these basic work units, but it is *a matter of judgment* as to when it is helpful to break a task down into its elements. Work is often best assigned at the task level (after adequate training) so that the specific methods of achieving the objectives can be worked out by the employee.

Motions It is not useful for our purposes to break task elements into their individual motions. In the secretarial situation, to do so would look like this:

left hand	*right hand*
reach 8″ for letter	grasp letter opener
grasp letter	hold
move 8″ to center	hold
position letter	move letter opener to flap
etc., adnauseam	

Motion analysis can be very useful for analyzing and measuring highly repetitive work in offices or manufacturing, but it is far too detailed for our purposes. Recently this approach has been used in detailed analysis of work slated to be performed in word processing centers because the results could be used to economically justify the acquisition of new equipment.

USING TASK ANALYSIS FOR TRAINING
AND DEVELOPING NEW EMPLOYEES

Visualize a situation where the work in an office has expanded to the point where the single secretary present could no longer handle the work. Temporary help had been used for a while, but now it was decided by the supervisor and the secretary that the workload justified the addition of another person. A clerk was hired.

In deciding what the new employee would do, several decisions became fairly obvious. The new person lacked shorthand and typing skills, so for at least the time being, duties involving those skills can be set aside. However, it leaves such broad categories as:

- Answer phone and relay messages

- Process incoming mail

- Requisition supplies

- File

- Perform miscellaneous errands for the supervisor

- Make travel arrangements

- Check travel vouchers (prepared by salesmen)

In many offices the press of work leads to the new employee being given filing to do until they go crazy.

However, since the clerk has certain basic skills, reading, writing, and arithmetic, and we have a detailed task list, tasks can be sequenced easily and graded for levels of increasing complexity. A plan can be structured to give the new employee opportunities to learn, to become more familiar with the organization, and to experience a variety of behaviors—at least a temporary respite from boredom.

- One hour of filing chronological correspondence

- One- half hour of sorting and distributing mail

- One- half hour of requisitioning supplies

- One hour of checking travel vouchers

- Two hours of general filing

- One hour of answering the phone (during the secretary's lunch)

- and so on

With a list of tasks to be performed, a planned approach to training and orienting the new employee can be achieved. Such simple planning will avoid the happenstance that so often occurs, and each day the new employee can grow in confidence and competence.

TASK LISTS AND TRAINING

When we reach the task level of work analysis, training needs also begin to make themselves apparent. Under the secretarial duty of processing incoming mail, we have a good example of training needs. To sort mail by addressee and to open supervisor's mail only, requires the ability to read—a skill the new employee possessed before she or he was hired.

The task of distributing mail to an individual's in-basket requires only that the new employee learn where each employee sits. This training can be accomplished in a few minutes with some later reinforcement. Even in this simple task, training can be systematized by making a rough chart of the desk locations. This might take only a few minutes and might achieve two objectives: (1) orient the new employee as to who the other employees are (an important item when other workers are frequently in the field and only rarely at their desk, or when several people share a common desk), and (2) the new employee need not ask the secretary even once for the location. Where name tags are on the desks, this procedure would not be necessary for mail delivery, but could help the new employee to associate names with faces, hence, speeding the orientation process.

Similarly with other tasks, date stamping "critical" mail would take some knowledge of what is critical and what is routine. The secretary may withhold that task for a while, but if the clerk is eventually to perform that "critical" function, a means of discriminating critical from routine would have to be developed so that the clerk could acquire the knowledge required. Once that barrier is passed, the clerk could be trained to answer routine inquiries. If typing were required, the new employee could often gain that skill gradually while other structured learning experiences were being accomplished.

If the new employee knew that modest typing skills were required for performing some of the more interesting work, he or she could (and probably would) make efforts to prepare to do that work.

STRUCTURED COMPETENCE

Over the years I've taught a great many people who had very limited education and virtually no work experience to perform some rather remarkable tasks. This was because any job can be broken down into its component parts, and the knowledge, skills, abilities, and decisions required to perform those tasks can be transferred to or developed within the individual, one step at a time. Gradually we can develop "trains" of learning experiences that lead to understanding and high performance—the integration of the KSAD's.

David Booker, President of Booker Associates, Reston, Virginia, provided an example of how this can be done with very unsophisticated employees.

If you were to tell a new, inexperienced clerk that you were going to train her or him to be a bookkeeper (a *job*), you would probably get a skeptical glance. If you were to start by saying, "Today I'm going to teach you to journalize cash disbursements (a *duty*)," the new employee would probably conclude that you were crazy. You could then get out the journal book and tell the employee that you are going to teach her or him to perform two *tasks:*

1a. Record in (this) multiple-columnar journal cash payments, using checkbook stubs as a source of information.

1b. Total the amount columns in the journal using a ten-key adding machine and prove the totals.

At this point some of the mystery of journalizing cash disbursements would begin to disappear. When we come to the elements or steps, virtually all of the mystery disappears.

Task 1a:

1. From each check stub record the following information on one line in the journal in the appropriate column.

    a. Date of check

    b. Name of payee

    c. Check number

    d. Amount of check in "Cash Credit" column

    e. Amount of check in proper account column as shown on the check stub

2. Leave one blank line at bottom of journal page for totals.

After a few hours of going through this procedure, the new employee would have the steps firmly in mind and would then be ready to learn the equally simple procedure of learning to run the adding machine and proving the totals. At the end of the day the new clerk might not know everything about running an adding machine, but it is a start. That evening the new employee could report to family and friends, "Today I learned to journalize cash disbursements and to prove the totals using an adding machine. I'm becoming a bookkeeper." This example may seem like small potatoes to some, but to the new, unskilled employee, it can open up a whole new world of possible competence.

The same detailed approach has been applied to virtually any job, including running computers, repairing typewriters, writing progress reports, preparing salads, diagnosing physical ailments, checking trees for bud bursts, and operating sewage disposal plants.

How much time and effort you want to spend in detailing task elements depends on the degree of investment you wish to make in new employees, and the likely returns you will get from the efficiency of training, increased motivation, and overall employee error reduction.

HOW TO PREPARE A TASK ANALYSIS

The simplest way to develop a task analysis is to write down the things you do or that a subordinate has to do. This can usually be done in forty-five minutes or less, but it is not likely to be complete. You may have to check the activities of yourself or the other person for several days to make sure you've gotten everything. You may even then forget things that occur only occasionally.

Another approach is to write down (or have the subordinate write down) everything done for several days or even a few weeks. The details can be compiled into a task list. The list can be supplemented by other rare tasks as they occur to you. This approach works well for ourselves, but in order for the subordinate to provide us with an honest list we must assure the employee that the list will only be used for purposes of training and developing a new employee. If the employee suspects that the list will be used for work measurement, reorganization, evaluation, or other purposes perceived by the employee to be harmful to him or her, the worker is likely to be less than candid. This method of preparing a task list only takes a few minutes out of every hour but it requires conscientious effort.

The third method is to get a small group of supervisors (who have similar jobs) or workgroup members together and go through a two-step process:

1. Have each participant write down a list of all the tasks he or she performs.

2. Have the group build a common list, while each participant adds items to his or her own list which the group members suggest. These items should be tasks the individual actually performs, but which he or she had forgotten to list.

This group method is often fast (an hour or so) and effective. I've done this with individuals, then had them develop a common list while working in small groups, and then pool all the items in a large group. (I ask each person to add tasks to the individual lists which they hear mentioned in the group—tasks which they also perform. The ultimate length of each person's list surprises them. I've had supervisors jokingly say, "I never realized that I perform seventy-four individual tasks," (not an uncommon number) "I'm going to ask for a raise."

I find that most people have about six to twelve principal duties, and twenty to fifty specific tasks that they perform in carrying out those duties. Supervisors and office managers tend to have more, and technical specialists often have fewer.

The greatest problem in training people to do a task analysis is to get them to deal with the appropriate level of specificity. Personnel people who deal with job descriptions tend to be too vague, and technicians often get too detailed.

The proper level of task analysis is that at which we begin to perceive clearly and in detail what needs to be done and we begin to formulate how it might be done. Task analysis is a tool and needs to be suited to the job to be done. Other examples of task analysis will be given later in this book, so that eventually it should become fairly obvious when we have a suitable level of analysis.

USES OF A TASK ANALYSIS

What can task analysis do for us?

1. It enables us to simplify our work.

2. It allows us to delegate authority effectively.

3. It helps us identify the knowledge, skills, abilities, and decisions necessary to perform the task.

4. It permits us to assemble work assignments of progressive levels of responsibility and learning requirements.

5. It may be used to create efficient and progressive training programs.

6. It enables us to create building blocks for progressively restructuring jobs for job enrichment and greater challenge.

7. It permits us to document economic gains from work restructuring and methods improvement.

8. It may be used to plan the training and development efforts for new employees.

Subsequent chapters will demonstrate how task analysis is used to achieve the primary goal of this book—to develop a productive human resource with new employees.

Task analysis is a simple concept, but it requires some work to complete properly. However, it is the magic word needed to open the door to greater productivity that many supervisors and managers want to pass through, but don't know how. It can be used to analyze the work a group has to do, and then arrange the task building blocks into effective systems for integrating new employees into the workgroup. It also orients the new individuals to the organization and trains them to be productive members of their workgroup.

Task analysis is a technique that needs to be mastered by everyone interested in methods of developing human resources. Personally it can offer each of us a tool for planning our own work, for managing our time more effectively, and for focusing on the essential items among the many things we are asked to do. For new employees it offers a path to a productive and rewarding future.

STUDY QUESTIONS

1. Every supervisor has three types of tasks under their control. List these.

2. Define KSAD's and give an example of the idea behind each letter in the acronym.

3. List four important uses of task analysis.

4. List the five components of the general hierarchy of work.

5. Distinguish clearly between duty levels of work and the task and task element levels of work.

6. Take a job with which you are very familiar. List the general duties, then the tasks inherent in one of the duties, and then determine if one of the tasks can be further broken down into task elements. List those task elements.

7. Why do we generally avoid dividing a task or task element into basic "motions"?

8. How can task lists be used to vary job assignments and training for new employees?

9. How is task analysis the key to structured competence?

10. List eight valuable uses of task analysis.

11. How can task analysis be used to successfully train and develop new employees?

CHAPTER 17

RESTRUCTURING WORK FOR PERSONAL GROWTH AND JOB ENRICHMENT

There are many ways to restructure work assignments so that they encourage personal growth, motivate employees, and provide job enrichment. The variety of approaches and the results obtained are often only limited by the imagination and hard work of the person (supervisor or staff specialist) who is reordering the work. There are comprehensive approaches which break a job down into all of its myriad components, identify the KSAD's in great detail, and reorder the learning components so that new employees with minimal skill and education can be taken from very simple tasks to performing very complex technical and professional work.[1] Here, however, I'll deal only with a rather simplified approach which can be used on a task-by-task basis by the supervisor in achieving a variety of growth goals that suit the organization, the supervisor, and the new employee.[2]

PASSING OUT WORK ASSIGNMENTS

Generally there are two ways of passing out work assignments: (1) simple assignment of tasks, or (2) spinning off tasks.

---

[1]See David Booker's excellent case history in "How to Structure Job Tasks for Training the Disadvantaged," in the National Civil Service League's Reference File No. 7 *Public Employment and the Disadvantaged,* 1970. This work was republished along with works by this author in "Training and Testing the Disadvantaged," a Manpower Press Publication of the National Civil Service League, 5530 Wisconsin Ave., N.W., Washington, D.C. 20015.

[2]For those who are interested in building career ladders and developing formal training programs for upgrading employees, see:

   A Handbook for Job Restructuring (U.S. Department of Labor, Manpower Administration, 1970). For sale by the Superintendent of Documents, U.S. Government Printing Office, Washington, D.C. 20402. See also: *Training and Development Handbook (A.S.T.D.)* Robert L. Craig, ed. (New York: McGraw-Hill, 1976), especially section 15.

Simple Assignments

If new employees are replacing other workers, or if they are simply an addition to the workgroup who will do pretty much what everyone else is doing, then tasks are generally assigned on an as-needed basis. The supervisor assigns the tasks, gives the new employees the necessary training, demonstration, or instructions, and allows the new people to proceed in doing the work.

If the new employees are experienced in the trade or occupation for which they were hired, the instructions are often curtailed and revolve around only what is necessary to accomplish the task *in your particular organization*. If the people are inexperienced, the task assigned is generally simple requiring only rudimentary skills and knowledge (such as cleaning up or obviously simple routine work). However, the instruction usually need not be very complex because of the simple nature of the work. In either case, of all of the tasks that need to be done in a workgroup, new employees are generally given the easiest, most routine, and frequently dullest assignments. There is seldom any challenge for new employees while "they are getting their feet on the ground."

Spinoff Assignments

When an organization is growing or changing its mission, and new people are being added, there is a tendency to collect the simpler tasks from subordinates, those which require less experience, and form those into an entry-level job. This approach, in effect, creates a new job (at a lower level) and generally changes (and frequently upgrades) all of the other jobs in the group. This approach can be most clearly seen when an executive hires an administrative assistant and begins parcelling out the more routine tasks that, up to this point, the manager has been doing personally or has been hiring specialists to do. Another example is the small business person who often does the work, bills the customers, and even keeps the books. As the business grows it is common to hire a part-time bookkeeper or typist, and then eventually create a full-time job for a new person. This spinning off enables the owner to focus on the most specialized and often most valuable tasks. This is also how line people eventually spin off specialized jobs that can be done by a staff specialist.

Both ways of passing out work assignments can be appropriate, depending upon the situation, but it *can* go too far. In both examples, the new employees tend to get the dregs of the job, and sometimes this diet of dregs goes on far too long.

Whether the new employees are experienced or inexperienced, when the first approach—simple assignment—is used, the employees with longer tenure tend to get the best, most interesting, and sometimes the easiest work. This type of assignment is usually perceived as an appropriate reward for faithful service, but it may have little to do with long-term productivity.

If a new employee is a highly qualified specialist, such as an accountant, the spinoff approach at least means tasks are assigned in the person's own speciality—even though usually many tasks are at a low level because the specialist must cover the whole range of tasks related to a particular type of job.[3] If a new employee is relatively inexperienced, the spinoff approach frequently means that the new employee gets all of the "dirty" jobs and little of the gravy.

If we are going to make new employees productive, motivated, and challenged, we need to attack some basic assumptions we often make about how work assignments are passed out. We need to look at the work of the unit as a whole and design assignments that are flexible, that achieve optimum motivation for *all* employees, and that meet the organization's long-term needs for a versatile well-trained work force.

QUESTIONABLE ASSUMPTIONS ABOUT WORK ASSIGNMENTS

Play it safe—give important tasks to most experienced person Supervisors often tend to play it safe by giving an assignment to a person who has done that task well before. As a consequence, that person may get the same kind of assignments over and over again. This can lead to monotony and boredom on the part of the overexperienced employee who might just enjoy a change of pace, even to a task requiring less skill and knowledge. Such a person might feel, "Here comes the same old thing again." At the same time, such supervisory habits may be denying the young person a challenge, variety, and a chance to show what he or she can do. If variety is the spice of life, passing assignments around may not be as resisted by long-term employees as the supervisor sometimes assumes.

Subordinates must not do supervisors' work Another assumption is that there is supervisors' work and subordinates' work. This had better not be the case if the organization is to remain healthy. If the supervisor is struck down by illness, disaster, or just other pressing business, it is not uncommon for the work to be delegated upward; that is, the supervisor's boss does the supervisor's work (at least the critical part of it) thereby letting his or her own work suffer. Such a process indicates an unhealthy organization. If the supervisor does not have several people able and ready to take over in the event that the plague strikes, that supervisor's segment of the organization is a hostage to fate. The basic principle should be that there is no work of the supervisor that a subordinate could not take over and do if the subordinate is adequately trained.

---

[3]This last item may cause trouble in on-the-job productivity because, after hiring, if the new employee is enough of a high-level specialist to encompass a whole job spectrum, the person may feel frustrated doing lower-level work "beneath their professional skills." Often the only way that hiring a specialist can be justified is to give him or her the whole job when the job constitutes a full-time position. This personal feeling of "being above the work," however, tempts the specialist to push for hiring a lower-level person to do the menial tasks, so that when this happens the professional is now underemployed. This is a prime factor in overstaffing in many government agencies and even in small firms.

Some supervisors fight a last ditch battle over some situations where laws or regulations require that only a given supervisor can sign a particular document. This is seldom true and, even if it were true, it is no excuse to not train somebody (or several people) in the approval process in case they are called upon to be "acting supervisor." Another point of contention is that one employee could not rate or evaluate another. Aside from even that questionable claim there is no excuse for not training one or more persons in the rating process in case they had to conduct an appraisal if the supervisor became incapacitated.

The principal point is that even the tasks the supervisor normally performs should not be sacred when considering training and experience for new employees, or any other employee for that matter. I know the notion that subordinates, especially new ones, could and perhaps should be brought to the point where they could perform at least some supervisory tasks, scares the hell out of a lot of management personnel. However, to create a barrier between the supervisor and his or her subordinates when it comes to performing certain tasks not only makes the organization vulnerable, but it limits the growth potential of the supervisor because there are no trained people to replace the supervisor if he or she were to be considered for advancement.

Workers can't supervise themselves The notion that only the supervisor or a deputy can pass out work assignments is coming under close examination in many organizations, and has been found to be false in many instances. Workers in some Swedish automotive plants no longer work on assembly lines where engineers carefully measure and balance the work and control methods. The employees work as a group and make most of the decisions, as to who will do what and for how long, collectively and on a day-by-day basis. The supervisor functions in a support role. In this type of system, new employees have a hand in influencing the group and in making the decisions that affect them.

In a similar fashion I have seen printing press crews in the United States hold meetings before beginning their shift to get information on how the press is running, how the group members feel about various assignments that day, and then decide among themselves who will do what, when. This system works; the workgroup views themselves as a team and takes responsibility for high productivity, good quality output, and low absenteeism. This group approach is not a dream, it is a working reality. Perhaps when we stop treating people as children, they begin to act as adults. These people on the press felt as though the press was theirs and they "owned their job." The new employees in this situation, from the start, owned a piece of the action.

Nobody wants the "dog" jobs The assumption that there are good jobs and bad jobs or good tasks and bad tasks needs to be examined more closely. There are clearly some tasks that are dirty, dangerous, monotonous, and possibly even degrading, as there are tasks that are varied, easy, and which produce visible results. However, the question arises as to "good for whom?" The person to hold the job has to be taken into account when qualitative issues of work are concerned.

I was once with an oceanographic research firm where several secretaries were grouped together, each serving two or three engineers and project managers. These secretaries performed a great variety of work and often used common project files. Though their other tasks got done well, these secretaries never seemed to get time to catch up on their filing. After several unsuccessful efforts to resolve a problem which got worse day-by-day because of organizational growth problems, we decided to hire a young woman with clerical skills but of rather limited (but adequate) intelligence. This woman was put in charge of the files and, though she made few decisions about the way they were organized, she took possession of them and made them her empire. She owned her job and took a fierce pride in making sure that everything was correct. Thereafter, service was fantastic. Everything got filed the day it was generated or received, and she felt fulfilled in every sense of the word.

In a similar vein, I have known renowned chemists who periodically enjoyed washing bottles because it gave them something worthwhile to do while they were thinking. If we are going to enrich work for a person, we need to know that person pretty well, and most often we must get their views on what they would consider to be rewarding. With new employees it is particularly important to listen carefully and observe closely the verbal and nonverbal signals being sent when work assignments are discussed, for new people may not feel comfortable in expressing their feelings about work assignments because of their vulnerable position.

RESTRUCTURING WORK

In this book, we are not talking about restructuring jobs or redesigning jobs. We are restricting ourselves to *restructuring work assignments* for beneficial purposes. *Restructuring jobs* is a complex act, for jobs have a high proprietary content that task assignments do not necessarily possess. Jobs usually have owners, and messing with a person's perceived property can be dangerous. Jobs are affected by such factors as union contracts, wage scales, operating practices, work schedules, the equipment used (i.e., lathe operator, etc.), the supervisor's practices, and even customer relations. Jobs also have great impact on an organization's efficiency and effectiveness and on an employee's self-image and status. We are talking about something far more simple—the discretionary power that a supervisor has when it comes to passing out work assignments and the degree of freedom that goes to the employee along with those assignments.

Therefore, what follows is not a technical, comprehensive type of job redesign that leads to new job descriptions. Instead, it is a practical, one step at a time approach to enriching work for new (and old) employees that can be done with little or no administrative activity.

Virtually every supervisor has *some* degree of discretionary authority when it comes to passing out work assignments. Even when I worked on an assembly line—perhaps the most controlled environment imaginable—my supervisor had the authority to assign me to clean up work, to maintenance and repair work, and to "filling-in" when one part of the line became unbalanced and the work began stacking up. The options were few, but they were there. Most supervisors have far greater freedom than that.

External constraints such as crises, deadlines, unpredicted delays, shortages of materials, and heavy-handed punishing management practices may make it difficult to alter procedures and perhaps even try out a new person on new tasks, but there are still opportunities if we seek them. Basically I have found three rather simple and direct ways of assigning work for personal growth, for job enrichment, and quite frankly for spinning off assignments. These methods free me to do more planning and more creative work, yet the assignments can still be a rewarding experience for new employees.

The Work Assignment Matrix

If I have several employees and a complete task list of the things the group does, it is fairly simple to list the tasks along the left side of the matrix and the people by name across the top. See Fig. 17.1.

When a task comes up for accomplishment I can look at the chart and (with a small group) determine who has done the task lately, who has mastered the task (M), who would most likely be challenged by the task (C), who needs training to do that task (T), who could learn and develop by doing the task (D). The blank spaces would indicate areas where the person has had no previous experience and the options have not yet been explored with the person.

To some degree this represents a training and development plan that has its own utility in developing a cross-trained (and hopefully cooperative) group.

	Mary	Joe	Felix	Marty	Jane	Twila	Key:
Task A	M	T		M		D	M = Mastered
Task B	C		M		T	D	C = Challenge
Task C	M		T	M	M	M	T = Training needed
Task D	C	M			T	T	D = Development opportunities
Task E	T	D	T	M	M	M	Blank spaces =
etc.							No experience yet

Fig. 17.1
Work Assignment Matrix

If the tasks of the group are highly varied and numerous, this approach can be complicated and perhaps time consuming, but if the task list were already created for other organizational or supervisory purposes, its use here might not be time consuming. However, when the workgroup is composed of diverse specialists and perhaps a secretary (each person tends to have a collection of tasks peculiar to them), cross training can be difficult. Each specialist may also have a very proprietary interest in her or his tasks and may resist sharing them with others. This is particularly likely in a punishing or threatening environment, as when job analysts are always ready to pounce on opportunities to downgrade jobs.

However, a workgroup where each person is a highly trained specialist is not too common, and even where such exists it is false to *assume* that people will resist sharing some of their tasks with others. First of all, if the sharing is widespread there can be a gain for every loss. People better understand the nature of their coworkers' jobs and how those jobs relate to their own, and their own jobs usually continue to get done (at least to some extent) when they are away sick or on vacation.

How many times have you been faced with a situation where one person fails to show up at work on a certain day and you discovered that no one in the office knows where anything is or how to run a critical piece of equipment? Situations are not unknown where it was necessary to disturb a very sick person at home in order to keep the organization functioning. How often have proposals or projects been held up because only one person knew how to make a PERT-Planning chart or only one person could type?

The Supervisor's Daily "To-Do" List

Most successful supervisors and managers plan the things they want to accomplish each day. Sometimes long-term items on their lists are there because what the supervisor wants to do that day is to plan when and how these larger items will be accomplished. Those long-term items are in the process of being broken down into bite-size chunks for future accomplishment. What we are concerned with is the myriad of things that need to be done that day and any bites of the larger projects that can be included on that day's work.

When the daily "to do" list is assembled and prioritized (an important aspect of effective planning), some items can be identified and assigned to others that will free the supervisor and perhaps provide meaningful growth assignments for others. The trick with the daily "to do" list is not merely to push unwanted assignments onto others, but to use it as an instrument for enriching the work of others. After all, a properly structured daily "to do" list usually has a lot of short discrete assignments which will provide employees with a sense of closure and a sense of accomplishment. Ask yourself: What on today's "to do" list could be given to a new employee which, along with a little instruction, would provide new and rewarding experiences for the individual?

The Building Block Approach

A list of tasks and task elements organized into similar items can be likened to piles of building materials out of which can be fashioned anything from a hovel to a cathedral. Each item has its own special characteristics and dimensions—the KSAD's. Each item also has some characteristics in common with others, be they *skills* such as reading, or *abilities* such as motor control (as when creating art work), or *knowledge* as in knowing mathematical formuli. Visualize a variety of kinds of stone, tiles (of different hues and sizes), and a variety of wood products. I once watched an artist create an original mosaic using similar materials to produce a stunning product. I wonder if the inner beauty of an effective, competent supervisory achiever might not be a task of similar proportions. Using work and all its elements, might we not create as beautiful a product in a competent, achieving human being? Perhaps the art of management is just that, except that we are not dealing with inanimate material. We can shape a portrait of a human being—the new employee can bring it to life.

I am not much of an artist, but I believe that I have, on occasion, used task assignments creatively, and then watched the employee make my vision a living reality. I have seen other managers do the same thing, often with superior results. This can be a very satisfying type of work, and very productive for the organization and for the new employee. Since the employee can help, no supervisor need face the task alone.

In using the building block approach, I will often think of a problem area where I could use some help and then write down what I'd like to achieve in that area. From there I list the tasks that would have to be performed to accomplish that objective. Next, I write down the KSAD's required for each task, or at least for as much of the task as I might be able to convey in the near future. Then I look at the employees that are available and ask certain questions (not among my questions is "Who has done this task well before?") such as:

1. Who has *not* done this task before?

2. Who can learn from this task?

3. Who might be able to grow from this experience?

4. Who might feel challenged by this assignment?

5. Who might need this piece of work to lend variety to their life?

6. Who might be able to contribute creative ideas toward accomplishing this task?

After asking myself these questions I try to approach each person that I believe might play a role in task achievement, and then see if my perceptions are accurate. It is important that the employees feel freely committed to the task if they are going to contribute originality to its accomplishment. After that, it is primarily a matter of training the person(s) and defining the objectives and delegating authority sufficient to get the job done.

While I acknowledge that deadlines, crises, and other considerations may at times rule out the full realization of such goals, I find that even under pressure some opportunities exist to structure task assignments creatively. Often the only way to get a complex job done under crisis conditions is to involve the employees in creatively planning the assignment.

THE HUMAN ASPECT OF WORK RESTRUCTURING

When employees are presented with something new in the way of assigned tasks, they may feel threatened or worried and therefore resist the change. New employees, however, seldom having any set patterns as yet, tend to be adaptable. Even if they do have strongly ingrained habits because of lengthy prior experience in a similar job, they usually expect to make some changes. Therefore, it might be easier to pass out new and challenging work more easily to new employees than to more long-term employees. You also may get the greatest innovations from those minds used to other experiences than your work normally offers.

When I have seen supervisors try enriching a job or restructuring work to make life more interesting and rewarding, it is not unusual to hear, "That's not in my job description." Indeed it may not be, except in the ubiquitous "other duties as assigned" category. Other employees may call the union representative or file a grievance. Obviously in such cases there has not been much employee participation in decision making up to that point. But aside from that, the supervisor who thinks she or he is *doing something for the employee* often feels hurt and possibly angry when she or he is thus rebuffed. The employees, on the other hand, sometimes perceive the supervisor's behavior as an attempt to *do something to them,* and so feel justified in rejecting the offer. Unfortunately most supervisors see such attitudes and expressions as hostile and fail to use such feedback as *data* for problem solving.

In an oppressive or punishing work environment or where employee relations are bad, being suspicious of management's intent may be quite justified. The most effective response that a supervisor has may be to acknowledge the hostility (do not evaluate it or take a negative reaction to it) and listen to what the other person has to say. At some point (and they may talk for a long time) you may be able to provide the person with information about your intentions, but it must be recognized that the worker may be the person best able to work out that hostility.

The employee may have a fear of being exploited, and if your conscience is clear in that regard, there is no need to buy into negative feelings about that person who is "laying it on straight." Feeling offended or overreacting to his or her negative response seldom does any good. It is better to let the employee ventilate, and then ask what she or he would like to do about this "choice as-signment." If you are told to shove it—don't walk away mad—listen. The most important thing is not to give up on the employee—keep offering. But make sure that those employees are not punished if they fail. Instead, make sure you work to see that they succeed.

If we apply these techniques fairly and evenly, new employees are likely to get their fair share of the interesting assignments and will grow and develop ac-cordingly. Such fair treatment will pay substantial dividends from the new em-ployees in the years to come.

STUDY QUESTIONS

1. List the two primary methods of passing out work assignments and de-scribe each.

2. Identify four questionable assumptions about work assignments and describe each in some detail.

3. How does restructuring *work* differ from restructuring *jobs* or *rede-signing jobs?* Why are these distinctions important?

4. List three rather simple methods or techniques of assigning work for personal growth, for job enrichment, and for freeing the supervisor for planning and more creative work.

5. List four (of the six) questions to be asked about each employee, when considering work assignments, that would help to ensure employee growth and development.

6. How can you ensure that the new employee has an increased oppor-tunity for growth and development when sharing work assignments?

CHAPTER 18

ON-THE-JOB TRAINING

On-the-job training often means no training. In a surprising number of occasions, the supervisor introduces new employees to the workgroup, gives them a few things to get them started, and then drifts away to do other things. The new employees are left to drift or flounder until the other employees come to their rescue, or the beginners figure out ways to busy themselves.

This lack of training is often most apparent when new employees represent the greatest investment to the organization. Highly skilled and experienced workers, professionally trained people, and management trainees (or interns) are the most likely to be considered to be able to fend for themselves. Ironically this may be true, but not in the way management assumes.

The higher the level of the employee, or more professional the person, the greater the current cost of employing the person. Therefore, the more long term the payoff is expected to be on that person. However, professional or managerial personnel often find it easier to look busy, to engage themselves in nonproductive pursuits (hobbies), and to absent themselves from the workplace on one pretext or another. It is often harder to measure results in these complex occupations, and whether the employee produces much may not be noted for some time. Only when the employee begins to miss project target dates, when flaws develop in the designs, or when customer complaints reach a high level does the manager realize that a problem exists. By then, the supervisor has absolved herself or himself of all responsibility because the training period was so long ago—"It must be something else!"

Hourly employees, unskilled laborers, and semi-skilled workers, on the other hand, often have the best thought-out and planned training. Part of this is because the work is often relatively easy to analyze, it is frequently repetitious, and the results are probably clearly visible in a relatively short period of time. Also, people with lesser skills are often assumed to be less interested in the organization and in the results they achieve (though this has not been proven) and therefore need to be more closely controlled. Hourly employees seldom have the freedom to move about a facility or to take irregular breaks unless their tasks relate to moving about (as with housekeeping or maintenance). Even then, such workers are often controlled by measured work standards, time clocks, and sharp-eyed overseers.

DETERMINING TRAINING NEEDS

Because some employees already know how to do the work (they are well trained or well educated), or offer considerable experience in the occupational field, it is often assumed that their training needs are minimal. In one respect that is true, as far as performing the job-related tasks is concerned, but new employee training involves much more than just the performance of tasks.

Every organization has its own policies and procedures, its own job standards, its own unique environment, its own specialized products or projects, and its own culture to impart. Every supervisor has her or his own quirks and preferences. They each have unique standards and they have their work-related needs to feel comfortable with the progress being made. Supervisors need well-trained people so that they do not need to compensate for substandard performance by sacrificing their own needs.

All new employees need to understand where the work they are doing fits in with other projects and programs. They need to know the importance of each task and what the implications are of possible errors. They need to know how they and their work will interface with other people, other departments, and other programs. Most of all, they need to know the value of the contribution they are expected to make to the organization. The value of on-the-job training that meets these diverse needs is important, no matter what the level of existing job knowledge and skill is for the new employees.

How much training? A long time ago, someone replied as follows: Job requirements minus the existing job knowledge and skills equals training needs. This is a pretty good formula, but it extends far beyond mere performance of tasks. Indeed, it includes all of the learning experiences of a new employee that are required to make that individual productive.

Determining what people already know is frequently a problem. We assume much from the credentials they offer, and these assumptions may not be realistic. A well-trained engineering graduate may be unfamiliar with the kinds of reference materials available at an employing firm. A research scientist may not really know how to structure a good project report (or how the Air Force wants their reports prepared). A young person with a certificate from an auto mechanic school may not have experience working on expensive or foreign cars, etc. Some organizations respond to such problems by structuring programs to train new employees completely and in everything related to a job, regardless of prior experience or background. Such efforts waste time and money, but worse—they cause boredom and loss of interest. Self-paced, self-instructional materials have been developed to overcome such problems, and in some cases they do an excellent job, but often peripheral yet important material cannot be economically included. In the last resort, much of the training needs will have to be determined by the supervisor and the peripheral training provided by the supervisor or staff specialist (such as with organizational orientation programs).

Determining what people already know and can already do is difficult unless we get down to dealing with specific tasks and what is needed to be able to perform those tasks. An equally difficult problem to deal with is that new employees may feel insecure; probing and questioning about what they know may therefore conjure up in their mind the fear of a test or being under pressure. The anxiety so generated may defeat the efforts to determine training needs of the individuals.

It is far more effective to simply:

1. List the important or significant tasks to be done in the near future and share the list with the new employees, explaining priorities that you consider important.

2. Identify those tasks that you consider to have significant learning potential for the new employees and see if they share that belief. Listen very carefully to the responses. Focus on the specifics of why each person feels as they do—the "because's" are the meat of the discussion. Feelings are a form of data and should be used as such—they should not be discounted or dismissed.

3. Negotiate a series of assignments that will meet the needs of both parties. Remember the focus at the moment is on training, not merely getting the work out. Perhaps not all parts of everyday can be devoted to training. The supervisor has a legitimate need to get the work out, and that includes some dull routine jobs, but the employees also have needs for challenge, satisfaction, and a chance to show what they can do.

The items new employees "jump at" are most likely those that they perceive as being the most valuable, the most achievable, or the least risky. The supervisor should pay special attention to those tasks that are avoided, and listen carefully for the verbal and nonverbal clues as to the problem items. Those items last on employees' lists will frequently reveal the most serious training needs. However, I've never found it useful to force the issue during the early days of the relationship. One of the principles of learning and remembering is that *learning takes place one step at a time* and it should *lead from the familiar to the unfamiliar*. Thus, if I can focus on another principle—*establishing achievable goals*—I can move from the things a person feels comfortable with to those more difficult assignments (difficult to the trainee, that is) which can be given out as the person builds a pattern of success with its accompanying growth in self-confidence.

I have found that while this process is going on, the new employees are feeding the supervisor information on training needs as they perceive them. Not that the needs are often expressed as such, but as the employees talk about the problems they expect to encounter or are encountering in carrying out the next assignment, they are revealing their deficiencies. This is a way of involving new employees in identifying training needs and in developing plans to meet these needs.

Sometimes you may get a bonus payoff—an employee may suddenly realize a generalized need that has not previously been noted, such as, "I guess what I really need is some advanced training in calculus" or "I need to check out the government specs on this topic." Upon recognizing such overall needs, the person usually also perceives the prescription for meeting those needs. This self-discovery is far more valuable and far more likely to get the employee involved in self-development than any amount of pontificating by the supervisor.

CONDITIONS FOR EFFECTIVE ON-THE-JOB TRAINING

Tasks chosen for training new employees should be reasonably small at first and grow in dimensions. As success is achieved, the employees develop more skill and knowledge. If an electromechanical design engineer is hired, it is usually best to assign a component of a device to be designed rather than a whole system. I am not saying that the person couldn't eventually (or possibly even now) handle a whole system, but a whole system would not as well meet some of the basic criteria for effective on-the-job training. Assignment of a small piece of a system could be used to adequately check a person's skill and knowledge, allow the person to experience success, provide quick feedback from the supervisor, and be used to communicate the organization's standards and requirements quickly and effectively.

A small assignment (or a series of short assignments) ensures that constant and critical interaction between trainer and trainee that is vital to effective feedback and early corrective action. Short assignments also meet the criteria for some additional principles of learning and remembering.

1. *Interest and attention are critical.* It is easier to keep the interest level high when the attention span is not overly stretched. Starting new things often keeps us on our toes.

2. *Identify and/or establish a pattern.* In operations requiring months to complete, patterns often emerge slowly and often too subtly to be perceived. Behavior patterns are easier to identify and use when they are repeated fairly often, especially for new employees.

3. *Appropriate repetition aids learning.* When tasks are short and occur frequently, a variety of behaviors involved in starting a project or

assignment, carrying it out, and ending it appropriately are reinforced. The feedback on standards and procedures is rapid and tends to reinforce the learning.

4. *Spaced learning can aid in learning more and retaining learning.* This principle seems to argue with #3 above when we apply it to short-term tasks or projects, but that is not necessarily so. A judgment must be used to determine the appropriate space between learning something and repeating it. Some operations need to be repeated constantly and often, as when learning to drive a car. In other situations we may need time to internalize the learning, mentally massage it, and make it part of our awareness system—and we need some time to accomplish these aspects of internalization. Much research supports the notion that early repetition should occur shortly after learning, but also that fairly frequent reinforcement imprints the message or behavior deeper on our brain.

5. *A context is needed for learning.* This is a framework for the new learning—a cosmology of sorts which allows us to fit the pieces into the larger picture. Part of the process of successful training is to enhance an individual's ability to relate one's own activities with those of the larger organization. Only by being able to place new learning in its proper context can people tell if a mismatch exists between their activities and those of the organization. Otherwise, the person is consigned to the darkness of doing things blindly—a most unproductive and demotivating position.

6. *Use as many senses as possible.* It has been claimed that people tend to retain 10 percent of what they hear, 20 percent of what they read, 30 percent of what they see, and 70 percent of what they do. Combining several senses in carrying out a task generally produces the best results. The greater the variety of senses involved (appropriately), the more likely learning is to occur.

FACTORS AFFECTING THE LEARNING PROCESS

Training starts with the first contact by the person who will do the instructing (whether the relationship relates to a professional and novice or supervisor and subordinate), and the learning process goes on constantly from that moment. Some of the training will be unconscious (such as imparting attitudes, concerns, styles, etc.), some of the learning will be equally unconscious, and some is likely to be negative. Mistakes and failures in learning can often be traced to lack of knowledge, skills, proper habits, and constructive attitudes. These four deficiencies can often be overcome through good training. Since learning is an internal, personal thing, however, a trainer cannot assume (as many do) that because he or she has taught, the trainee has learned. Below are four items that are recognized by trainers as having an influence on the success of training.

1. *Assuming the ability to learn.* Some excellent studies in the behavioral sciences indicate that the relationship between the teacher and the learner is so critical that, for the most part, students perform according to the instructor's expectations. Low expectations on the part of the trainer produce poor results; higher (but not unrealistic) expectations produce good results. Research results demonstrate that these expectations are particularly powerful with new or young employees.

2. *Emotional involvement.* The emotional condition of the learner is of great importance. Anxiety reduces learning. An overall feeling of inferiority, a temporary humiliation, depression, anger, a feeling of being rejected, and many other emotional situations diminish learning. The reverse is true: a feeling of well-being, and of being respected by others, stimulates the mind and increases willingness to participate and is excellent preparation for learning.

    Most people want to have the sense of accomplishment that comes from work, or they want the job to be easy, or they seek material rewards for work. When the learner can relate learning to the satisfaction of his or her personal needs, that person is likely to do a good job.

    We do not learn efficiently when resistance is present. Prejudice against, resentment toward, or hate of a subject, an activity, or a person interferes with, or entirely obstructs, the learning process. Learning is often furthered by the individual's being an accepted member of a congenial social group.

3. *The more vivid the experience, the more it is likely to be remembered.* We learn best when we play an active part in what is being learned. Though we may learn things from fear and shock, they may not be the things intended. A fear-and-shock approach is a dangerous training plan (if used outside of really hazardous situations), and is most likely to achieve conscious forgetting and create unconscious negative reactions to similar situations. Our basic human defense mechanisms cause us to react that way.

4. *Acceptance of responsibility.* We learn (and hear) only what we are ready to learn (and hear). We learn most efficiently the content which we perceive to be related to our own purposes and interests. We learn best and retain content longest when we believe in what we are learning. A large measure of the instructor's work is to relate the things to be learned to the learner in a relationship which is meaningful to the receiver. "Desire to learn" is a key phrase in the prescription for success.

Trainers have long recognized that four basic conditions are needed for effective learning:

1. *Motivation*. We recognize that people's motivations are varied and complex. Even when one concentrates on a single individual, the task of harmonizing her or his goals with the knowledge, skills, attitudes, and habits to be learned is difficult. Assumptions are dangerous. Diagnosis, through individual and small group discussions (if training several new employees) and concentration on the means of achieving (insofar as possible) each individual's hopes and desires offer promise in training, but we must recognize that only the learner can ultimately tell us what motivates her or him.

2. *Appropriate Stimulus*. Instruction that uses the most direct, realistic, and visually apparent methods, equipment, and situations produces best results with trainees who need to feel that what they are doing is "for real." Pure classroom lectures, inappropriate examples, and "make work" often lead to student disinterest and frustration. The more precisely the training simulates the work it represents, the more successful the trainees are likely to be in transferring learned skills to subsequent work situations.

3. *Response*. A chance to practice and show what he or she can do is important to the success of any trainee. Nothing builds pride, sense of accomplishment, and productive work patterns in the new employee faster.

4. *Confirmation*. Frequent indication of how well the trainee is doing is important for her or his future progress. If the emphasis is placed on what is done right (instead of what answers are wrong, as usually has occurred in prior school experience), the confirmation becomes a type of reinforcement and reward. However, more than a response which indicates that the trainee's behavior is correct or incorrect is often needed. Feedback to the trainee should give some indication of *how* actual performance deviated from the correct performance. Then a discussion of what can lead to further improvement should be held, with the new employee taking an active part in the conversation and keeping primary responsibility for subsequent improved performances.

PLANNING EFFECTIVE TRAINING

The successful trainer follows the rule: "Plan your training and train according to your plan." Also, the effective planner should thoroughly develop answers to questions such as these:

1. What is the job to be done?

2. What tasks are involved?

3. What knowledge, skills, attitudes, and habits need to be developed by the trainee?

4. What real abilities and background are needed by the trainee before he or she can learn the required tasks?

5. What is the best way to perform the job?

6. What steps are required for training on this job?

7. What is the best order for and method by which to teach these steps?

8. What is the best way to prepare the trainees for the training?

JOB INSTRUCTION TRAINING

World War II provided requirements for training great numbers of people to perform work that was entirely new to them; they had to be trained rapidly and well. The four-step Job Instruction Training (JIT) plan, described here, was used successfully for training millions of people. This method proved so sound that it was still recommended in the 1976 *Training and Development Handbook*[1] published by the American Society for Training and Development.

No matter what type of training is contemplated, we should start systematically with a written breakdown of the job—a task list—so that we avoid oversights, needless repetition, and hit-or-miss learning. We might then highlight important key steps in the operation and indicate the "what" and the "how" of each of these. We should then identify the knowledge, skills, abilities, and decisions required for successful completion of all acceptable items.

Whether the task to be learned is simple or complex, short or long, involves many types of learning or only a few, we need to focus on ways to make new employees successful.

The training methods used—whether we use flow charts, algorithms, decision trees, cassette tapes, films, simulators, or just conversational feedback—should emphasize moving from the learning to the doing as soon as possible. We need to estimate when certain learning objectives will be achieved and perhaps prepare a time table. If a work place is involved, we should be sure it is properly arranged, for a bad habit once learned is hard to correct. You also teach a person about the trainer when you train them. If the trainer is the supervisor, the standards which the trainer practices, versus what he or she preaches, will be assumed as the norm. It is also important to have the right materials, tools, and equipment ready for the training of new employees—for they want to be productive, not just busy.

Finally, it must be decided who will train the trainee on the job. The supervisor may or may not be the best person. An editor, if the job is one

---

[1] *Training and Development Handbook* (New York: McGraw-Hill, 1976), Section 32.

which requires writing, may be better. The senior cashier might have far more experience to impart than the person's immediate supervisor. Who does the training may depend on how many trainees there are, the availability of training space or equipment, how much should be done in the classroom versus out on the job, etc. But we must not overlook the reality that the supervisor (the most logical choice for trainer) may be rusty, may have personality problems, or may not currently be involved with the details of the job. A senior associate might make the best trainer.

In the addendum to this chapter, some material on the JIT method is presented. This method tends to focus on training people to perform physical tasks, but the four main steps are valid for almost all jobs, and the steps include a number of good ideas that are helpful in training people for all kinds of jobs.

FINAL POINTS ON TRAINING

Anyone who trains is a trainer, and trainers should be humble enough to recognize that training is only the take-off point. When the trainee graduates, the real test begins. Routine work can be given to a trained employee on the spur of the moment. New work can be assigned on a planned basis. Effective training not only pays for itself—the organization couldn't perform effectively without it. Yet only when the trainee produces or serves effectively is there any return to the organization. The most influential (and perhaps benevolent) influences on our lives might be those who trained us well. The trainee (not the trainer) is the one who must eventually do the job that pays off. This in no way detracts from the value of the trainer, but good training has to produce effective people or there is no payoff. The trainee deserves ultimate credit for performing. We must respect the trainee's positive contribution to the process.

A primary consideration in respecting the trainee's primacy in the training process is to accept the reality that there is no "one best way" of doing something. Though I may not want to argue with a person instructing me in methods of disarming a nuclear device, there is always more than one way to skin any cat.

Trainees should be trained in the best way we know, but we should recognize that at best it is only one acceptable method among many. They should be taught a method that gets the job done and meets all of the requirements for quality, quantity, safety, time, etc., but we must recognize that the employee might always come up with a better way.

Even if you *were* able to create or define a perfect method, next year it will probably be out of date as new tools, material, techniques, or people come along. It may take longer than that, but eventually someone will refine it. New employees are a primary source of fresh insights and new ideas. They bring new perspectives and creative interests in the job, and perhaps considerable prior training, experience, and exposure to other people's creative insights. We need to tap that creative potential not only in the training process but on the job afterwards.

If the person is passive and compliant a single method will probably be followed with adequate results. If the person is more inclined to explore other possibilities and take risks (within acceptable limits) the freedom to innovate is a powerful motivator. For effective job-related training, we need to encourage people to think for themselves—not by saying they should, but by demonstrating our acceptance of variation. We need to:

1. Explain the big picture.

2. Show relevance of the task being learned to the overall product or service.

3. Detail consequences of errors.

4. Teach the best method known (among the many possible methods that would get the job done).

5. Explain pitfalls or possible errors.

6. Demonstrate alternative methods that produce acceptable results (not the same results but acceptable results). Focus on results, not method.

7. Invite suggestions from trainees.

8. Try out any methods suggested by trainees if they will not produce unacceptable results or negative side effects.

9. Explain why some alternative methods may have been tried but rejected. This explanation should not necessarily close the door to new methods, but deepen understanding and provide food for thought. A new employee might later develop a variation that would make a rejected approach acceptable.

10. Suggest that the new employees (trainees) keep an open mind about possibilities for improvement.

In all of my years of training I have seldom seen this open-ended approach tried. The search for uniformity of results (which can still be produced through better methods), fear of the untried, and a desire for (assumed) efficiency often denies us the productivity many new employees are capable of producing.

Some trainers I have suggested this open-ended approach to are surprised. They seem to believe that:

1. If one best(?) method can be developed, it should be taught and variations could be distracting.

2. They assume they already have the best method.

3. The cost of variation could be expensive and lengthen training time. However, economic gains always represent a matter of investment versus return on investment and many people tend to minimize risk rather than maximize opportunities.

4. The payoffs are nebulous and occur after training, whereas costs and time are being expended *now*.

5. They never thought of it. Some trainers aren't used to teaching people to think—only to perform.

Considering the above, is it any surprise that new employees frequently conclude that their job is to do the tasks the way they have been told and to take no responsibility for developing better ways of doing things? Often if employees develop a new and better method, the organization will be the last to hear of it. While the employees constantly develop easier and better ways to do the job, the results are often reaped by the individual employees. Sometimes they'll share a better method with another employee, but not often with the supervisor. Only by creating a free and open society where the employees believe that innovation is genuinely welcome can we hope to have real participation by new employees in developing more productive methods.

WHAT THE INSTRUCTOR LEARNS

There is an old saying, "By your students you'll be taught." We really understand a job when we can teach it to someone else. In addition to knowing and understanding the job, the trainer reaps some of the richest possible rewards. Not only does the trainer have the satisfaction of helping people become productive, but he or she learns a great deal about human nature, and can spark appreciation. Effective training for new employees hopefully will set them off on a highly successful and productive career.

STUDY QUESTIONS

1. Why does training higher-level and more professional new employees often represent a greater challenge and opportunity than the training of lower-level employees?

2. List three simple and direct ways to ascertain a new employee's training needs through job assignments.

3. List six conditions for effective on-the-job training.

4. Identify four factors that affect the learning process and explain each.

5. List the four basic conditions that are needed for effective learning.

6. What are the four basic steps in the JIT method of job instruction?

ADDENDUM

FOUR-STEP METHOD OF JOB INSTRUCTION

1. Preparation—to prepare trainee's mind to receive new information and ideas:
   a. State the objective.
   b. Stress the importance appropriately.
   c. Tell where the job fits into the overall picture.
   d. Find out the employee's previous experience related to this task.
   e. Make the employee feel at ease.
   f. Make use of the person's existing background.
   g. Tell where the trainee fits into the overall picture.
   h. Introduce the trainee to tools, materials, equipment, and new words.

2. Presentation—set the pattern in trainee's mind:
   a. Tell and show the trainee the job:
      1. Present one point at a time.
      2. Do so slowly and clearly.
      3. Relate the job to the trainee's past experience. (Association of ideas arouses interest.)
   b. Ask trainee to "use your hands and your mind":
      1. Have trainee tell you what to do, one point at a time.
      2. Have trainee tell you the key points and ask questions.
      3. If, as you are doing the job as he or she tells you, the trainee makes an error, correct the error (as errors occur) and review the correct procedure.

3. Performance—help the trainee form correct habits:
   a. Have trainee *do* and *explain* the job while under supervision:
      1. Have trainee do the job, one point at a time, telling you in advance what he or she is going to do before she or he does it.
      2. Have trainee tell *how* and *why*.
      3. Let trainee ask questions, but help her or him *recall* what was told.
      4. Anticipate possible errors.
   b. Have trainee do job again, this time without telling about the operation. Ask "what" and "how" questions.
   c. Have trainee repeat the whole job until he or she has learned it.

4. Check and follow up—see if trainee has formed proper habits:
   a. Have the trainee do the job "on his or her own":
      1. Tell trainee what and how much to do.
      2. Tell trainee where to go for assistance and advice.
   b. Inspect job critically:
      1. Observe the trainee at early and frequent intervals.
      2. Taper off observation gradually.
      3. Encourage progressive learning.
      4. Use praise as appropriate.

WHAT THE INSTRUCTOR SHOULD REMEMBER (REVIEW)

1. No two people learn at the same rate. One learner's experience and background in a particular subject may vary from a few weeks to many years in scope from that of another learner. The trainer who recognizes these and other individual differences, and plans the instructing accordingly, will help each new trainee approach maximum learning within her or his own capabilities.

2. Mistakes and failures in learning can often be traced to the trainees' lack of knowledge, skills, proper habits, and constructive attitudes. These four deficiencies may be overcome by good training, but the trainer must not assume that because he or she has taught, the trainee has learned.

3. People do not like to do work that lacks meaning; they deserve to know why the job is necessary.

4. People fear exposure and ridicule. Don't ask questions which force trainees "into a corner."

5. Nonverbal forms of communication give indications of trainees' readiness to proceed with instruction.

6. Nervousness may indicate concern for success and indicate a positive trait, but it blocks learning. Plan methods of reducing such tension.

7. What trainees already know about the job (or information which relates to it) can be used as a foundation for "new material." Learn how much the trainees know—don't assume they know and don't force exposure of lack of knowledge.

8. Trainees are action-oriented, so prepare to get to the "doing" as quickly as possible.

9. Cooperation is earned. Develop ways for trainees to gain confidence in your ability and willingness to help them.

10. Job "language" is very often unique. Consciously avoid special jargon or nomenclature unless it can be explained then and there. Invite the trainees to share in this mysterious job language, for such knowledge creates the feeling of having been initiated and builds identification with the organization.

CHAPTER 19

RESULTS-ORIENTED TRAINING

A primary problem in ensuring that new employees receive the type of training they need at the time it is needed to guarantee effective job performance, is that new trainees usually appear at the supervisor's desk one at a time. Since the supervisor is the primary source of on-the-job information, this naturally casts her or him in the role of primary trainer. In reality though, except for the types of specific job orientation and training particular to an organizational unit, much responsibility for new employee training often devolves on staff specialists or trainers, or perhaps a variety of supervisors if the new employees are in some type of intern program or apprenticeship program.

Besides all of the administrative and scheduling problems involved in training new employees (or upgraded employees) from a variety of organizational units, there is the very tough problem of making such training relevant to the specific tasks that the trainees will perform when on the job. All too often we hear the complaint, "They taught me a lot of things, but most of it I never use on the job." Whether we are training clerical workers or management trainees, there is always the problem of providing learning experiences that will be job-related when the trainees (even though they may hold the same job title) will be doing quite dissimilar tasks within the organization when they get back on the job.

"NICE TO KNOW" VS. "NEED TO KNOW"

Whether the anticipated training or education program is designed for cost effectiveness or not, there are certain habits of training program designers that do not push toward tangible results. A primary flaw is the tendency to determine how much training (in terms of time) will be supported by the organization (be it one day or four years) and then to try to fill up that time.

The man whose primary assignment was to set up and manage the Henry Ford Trade School and its related apprenticeship programs once told me an interesting story about how they went about it "in the old days" (approximately 1916 to 1917).

> We wanted to give the young men a combination of on-the-job ex-
> perience under the guidance of experienced journeymen and to provide
> them with supplemental education (which eventually became the junior
> college program we have now). The first thing we did was to take the
> fifteen-week semester (because that was the way schooling was orga-
> nized then) and see what we could fill in the time with. Later the need
> to get our apprentices draft exemptions (because we were a vital de-
> fense industry), led us to establish a four-year (twelve-semester) pro-
> gram. This combination of education and on-the-job training expe-
> rience was needed in order to get Department of Labor approval of our
> program. This approval was critical to our gaining draft exemption
> status for our apprenticeship program.

Thus, even in establishing this excellent program, productivity objectives were complicated by other considerations, and the result was that they took "to filling the time." Unfortunately, even to this day, over a half-century later, people who design programs are still involved in "filling the time." Why else would Congress mandate and the Civil Service Commission (Office of Personnel Management) enforce the "eighty hours of supervisory training" requirement now current in the federal government? To some extent, this fill-ing the time will always be one way of designing programs, but there are bet-ter, results-oriented ways. At least if we focus on results, the end product of even "filling the time" will not be a mere grab-bag.

After having analyzed several hundred training programs for a variety of government and private organizations, it is not difficult to conclude that in-structional programs often: (1) include irrelevant content, (2) omit content re-quired by trainees to perform the job, (3) misplace emphasis, (4) produce undertrained or overtrained "graduates," and (5) consume more time than needed.

A good deal of the problem of training which proves to be nonjob-related seems to stem from the difficulty of clearly distinguishing between *training* and *education*. These two words are often used interchangeably, and in any given program of instruction we might not be able to separate them. However, a clear-cut definition and distinction could be helpful in developing results-oriented training so that job-related training can be both efficient and effec-tive.

In my view (with some support from *Merriam-Webster's International Dictionary*), *education* (1) is general in nature (a broad process), (2) aims at de-veloping understanding, and (3) has an objective of preparing learners for complex decisions or interpretation of new relationships. *Training* (1) is specific in nature (task oriented), (2) aims at developing performance abilities, and (3) has an objective of preparing learners to apply knowledge and/or skills to performing specific tasks.

From this set of definitions it can be seen that an early elementary school teacher is both a trainer (reading, writing, and arithmetic are basic performance-oriented skills) and an educator (history, literature, and geography aim at increasing knowledge and understanding). As we progress in schools, training (performance orientation) often becomes secondary, as education (understanding) becomes primary, until we reach the age when adolescent students have to get ready for continued education and/or the working world. At that time (high school) the curriculum often splits, as it may also do in college or trade school routes.

This distinction between education and training is of more than academic importance when it comes to preparing new employees for job success. The lack of distinction between training and education when designing training programs has often led to: (1) the inclusion of content that is irrelevant to job performance (and that is easily perceived by trainees once they start working), (2) overlong training programs, (3) unnecessary expense, and (4) postponement of a sense of job achievement and satisfaction.

I have no objection to organizations educating employees, and in most cases encourage it vigorously, but one type of human development should not interfere with the other. The values and objectives of education are dealt with in another chapter. Specifically, here we concentrate on training, and the issue of new employees becomes paramount. If we are going to encourage the development of productive new employees, the new people need to experience the satisfaction that comes from doing even a small part of the job satisfactorily. Similarly, this positive satisfaction ought to be reinforced as soon as possible. Overlong training programs offering "currently irrelevant" information, the "nice to know" sort of thing, often puts off these satisfactions unnecessarily. Especially while employees are new to the organization, we need task-related training which gives the employees a sense of achievement and enables them to gain recognition for a job well done. That feeling of competence is vital in building long-term productivity.

This issue of overlong training programs, often containing theoretical material, which postpones job satisfaction is particularly relevant to young, often impatient employees, and especially those who come from disadvantaged backgrounds. Disadvantaged people in particular have often failed in the regular school system which stresses very long-term payoffs and much theoretical material. These individuals need psychological payoffs now!

A large part of separating the necessary from the nice, in the short term, is dependent on focusing on the tasks to be done and separating out as much educational content as possible and holding it for later development efforts. While recognizing that education which focuses on understanding cannot always be separated from training which emphasizes doing, we often have to make choices in training program content. In the early stages of employment the emphasis should usually be on training.

To summarize these distinctions we can visualize:

1. *Education* is general and long-term, which is hard to measure but which provides the basis for broad judgments.

2. *Training* is specific and short-term, aimed at behavior change which is observable and which concentrates on performance.

If we keep these points in mind it is easy to see why effective training for new employees focuses around an analysis of the tasks which will be performed on the job.

TASK-ORIENTED TRAINING

The following are characteristics of task analysis:

1. It identifies the duties, tasks, and task elements of job content.

2. It provides the specific details necessary for identifying the knowledge, skills, abilities, and decisions (KSAD's) necessary for results-oriented training.

3. It permits the preparation of specific job-related performance objectives which provide:

   a. guidelines in preparing training content

   b. tests for adequacy of performance—the measurement factor.

Basically, a solid detailed analysis of the tasks that new employees will be expected to perform now and in the future can be used to:

- avoid wasting the time of both trainer and trainees by teaching only what is relevant ("need to know")

- prepare clear-cut training objectives

- conserve training resources (especially time)

- ensure that trainees meet job requirements

- motivate the trainees based on the increased likelihood of job success

- identify the types of decisions the trainees must make on the job initially and as they grow in the position

- identify areas where increased education is needed for career growth and greater responsibility

- single out critical points in the work cycle where safety is critical or the cost of error is high so that extra explanation and training can reduce risks.

For those of you who fear that the time and costs of preparing a detailed task analysis and the identification of KSAD's be far too great to ever justify the effort, consider the following:

1. The effort involved in task analysis should be costed against several supervisory responsibilities, not just training. These responsibilities include: delegation of authority, effective work planning, motivation of employees through personal development and job challenge, cost reduction and work simplification, and perhaps most important of all, planning for organizational continuity by having people ready to fill all organizational positions adequately at any time.[1]

2. The overall time and effort to conduct a task analysis need not be great. I have seen supervisors sit down with their workgroup and within three hours come up with task lists that covered every job in the group, including the supervisor's.[2]

3. The creation of the task lists encourages the whole workgroup to be more work-oriented with the inevitable result that people take a fresh look at what they are doing and how they are doing things, and hence develop improved methods.

4. The identification of the KSAD's for each task breeds realism and tends to eliminate phoney credentialism, unreal job specifications, and grade-level padding. It soon becomes apparent that cross training is less of a challenge than previously assumed, and that tasks can be passed around to better balance the workload and to cover critical jobs during emergencies.

5. The knowledge gained from this task analysis activity remains available and can be updated from time to time as the mission of the organization changes or new technology is introduced, thereby allowing the organization to adapt to change less painfully. More important, it means that employees who are new, now or in the future, can be trained more rapidly and more effectively because the basic information on KSAD's is available.

6. With the tasks identified and KSAD's specified, training can be more personalized. New employees can more easily grasp the overall task, envision where that task fits in the general scheme of duties, and learn

---

[1] I strongly believe that the supervisor and his or her group, rather than staff specialists, should prepare the task analysis. This allays suspicions that staff people will use the results to downgrade jobs or engage in other nefarious behavior. Staff people can teach line people to prepare task analysis, but it should not become the staff person's project.

[2] Generally, however, a little additional time is necessary because some seldom performed tasks may be forgotten. Within the next week the lists are usually completed, and cumulatively no more than another hour has been spent.

the behaviors (KSAD's) that will be necessary to perform that task. Therefore, trainees' prior knowledge and skill can be used effectively and things the trainees already know need not be covered.

7. The growth pattern for individuals can become clearer and more attainable. With the full knowledge of the tasks to be done and the requirements for performing those tasks standing out in the open, new employees can take a more active role in self-development. Often the thing that discourages employees from self-development efforts is the prospect of only very long-term payoffs (in the sense of accomplishment). But with the job broken down into bite-size chunks, fulfillment can be gained at every step of the way. The sense of mastery can be reinforced and patterns of progress become clear.

8. The KSAD's can easily be adjusted as technology changes, and *massive* retraining programs seldom become necessary. Retraining can occur in smaller increments and often closer to the job. Unproductive organizational shifts can also often be avoided.[3] For new employees, this can reduce confusion.

9. The specification of KSAD's for each task can be developed gradually. Since tasks are identified as discrete units, so can the KSAD's required to perform those tasks be developed as discrete units. By focusing first on the simpler tasks, the transfer of knowledge and skills to the new employee can often be organized so that a steady and continuing learning process can be instituted. The specification of the KSAD's required for even a complex task seldom takes over an hour, and more often it is closer to ten minutes. The mastery of the KSAD's for any *given* task may take from an hour to a week or more, but the detailed specification of knowledge and skills can easily be sequenced logically. Then the supervisor or trainer can go on to the next task.

10. The task analysis/KSAD approach can pay off in better training, more productive employees, organizational rejuvenation, and lower overall training cost. The task analysis/KSAD approach represents an investment in people—particularly in new employees. This investment can be made slowly and reasonably. The data can be stored for future use, and be adjusted as events require.

CONDUCTING A TASK ANALYSIS AND PREPARING KSAD STATEMENTS

Imagine that you are a supervisor who is responsible for training a new employee for the job of "building equipment maintenance repairman" (or repairperson if you prefer)—a person employed to service equipment in an apart-

---

[3]It is tragic that many organizations set up word processing centers without the above task analysis and KSAD approach already in place because it could have saved much grief and eliminated many costly inefficiencies. This technology was badly needed, but the method of implementation was often ghastly.

ment project. Putting yourself in such a fantasy should not be too difficult since most people are at least somewhat familiar with heating and air conditioning equipment, washers and dryers, and faucets and pipes. The scale of the equipment might be larger than you are used to, and your practical experience might be limited, but assume that you are an experienced maintenance supervisor who is training a new employee from scratch.

Task Analysis Example

The new person's job description might involve, among other things, these duties:

1. Apply monthly preventive maintenance routines to all blowers and fans in heating and air conditioning units according to Service Manual HP20F.

2. Inspect filters of all heating and air conditioning units monthly and at times of conversion (from heat to cooling and vice versa), and replace as required.

A task statement for duty 1 might include:

a. Disable power supply—Diagram #1 Manual HP20F.

b. "Lock Out" equipment—Page #3 Manual HP20F.

c. Remove guards and cover plates.

d. Identify lubrication points from Diagram #26 in Manual HP20F.

e. Select oil of proper SAE rating for the coming season, according to chart #7 in Manual HP20F.

f. Apply oil to lubrication points according to illustration 9 in Manual.

It is at this point that a knowledge of power supplies and "Locking Out" procedures, as well as skill in interpreting diagrams, come into play. For some new employees (from severely disadvantaged or foreign backgrounds, perhaps) the basic prerequisite ability to read English may also be a factor.

Often, if you, the supervisor, were to simply demonstrate the procedure once and supply the manual to the employee, the training would be in effect over. However, it would be appropriate to have the employee perform the operation, to monitor the employee's performance at later times, and to provide feedback as required. But essentially the employee, with manual in hand, could probably get the job done. This procedure, however, might not be efficient or effective since it allows for a variety of inefficient methods and there may be a need to transfer the knowledge from the manual to the employee's head so that the job is done more quickly.

In some cases, you may want to go one step further in the task analysis and actually identify task elements. A task element statement for a part of task "c" above might be: "Remove cover plate on blower 'd.' "

(1) Remove four screws with Allen wrench.
(2) Grasp plate by tabs.
(3) Rotate to right until released.
(4) Pull plate straight out.

Simple as element (1) might be ("remove four screws with Allen wrench"), it is the first level for this task at which identifiable *skill* appears. This may be going too far in the analysis, but it does identify the skill and knowledge required to get the job done. Further refinement of this task would involve motion-type analysis and that much detail is seldom needed.

KSAD Statements

KSAD statements are the raw materials from which training programs can be constructed. Sometimes, however, people feel that KSAD statements are too detailed, which may be true at times. The real issue is: How much detail is necessary to avoid hit-or-miss training? How much time and momentum can be lost in training if the new employee does not have a clear idea of what is to be done and how to do it? Only the person who will conduct the training can actually decide (with some information provided by the trainee on what that person already knows or can do).

Examples of this uncertainty are legion. A surprising number of people do not know what an Allen wrench looks like, or which end to use. In a similar way, the duty, "apply preventive maintenance to all blowers and fans" does not in itself indicate that the trainee must show knowledge and discretion in selecting a lubricant proper for the equipment and the season. Only when we reach the KSAD level will the need for such know-how become visible. In regard to this last item, I remember the time a new service station attendant was about to put automatic transmission fluid in my oil system because no one had told him the difference. The young man was not stupid (as his boss insisted on calling him), only untrained.

For preparing detailed KSAD statements the following definitions might be helpful.

Knowledge (K) defines the specific information a person must know or have available in order to satisfactorily perform a segment of a task. For example, a draftsman trainee would need to know the markings and conventions particular to a given industry which are used in scale line drawings, in preparing a drafting layout.

Skills (S) refer to the physical dexterity and motor controls a trainee must possess or have developed to satisfactorily complete the various activities related to a particular task segment. For example, a technician preparing an animated display may be required to "lay out" panel board sections, operate light wood-working machine tools to a satisfactory tolerance, use a paint airgun, and position, wire, and adjust electrically-operated animation units and sound tape units.

Abilities (A) defines physical and mental attributes which are prerequisite to performing a task segment. Examples of abilities in this sense are the ability to see (unaided) an object of a given size three hundred yards away, to possess an acceptable depth perception (for piloting a plane), to be able to distinguish certain colors, or the ability to estimate the size of a room without being able to measure it. Obviously some of these abilities are inherent or natural, while others are learnable (but usually only over a long period of time).[4]

Decisons (D) refer to the discretionary demands of the job, usually in having to learn and make discriminations and decisions regarding job data. The inspector, the editor, the grader all make choices of this type. A variety of classification and coding tasks are on-the-job examples of this type of work. Such decisions may be major, like deciding to open the flood gates on a weakened dam when the stream below the dam is already over its banks, or relatively minor, such as when to throw out overripe produce in a grocery store. But such opportunities to make decisions constitute a great deal of the motivating force of the job and its intrinsic worth to new employees, as well as to others.

PERFORMANCE OBJECTIVES FOR TRAINING

To ensure that training is results-oriented we need clear performance objectives for training. Whether these objectives are written, or explicit only in the mind of the trainer, without such clarity, the training may drift from the goal of producing useful work.

Up to this point, the use of task analysis and KSAD's applies to the creation of effective cost-efficient training whether the new employees are learning under the guidance of their supervisor, from another experienced worker, in a classroom situation, or by training devices or simulations. Now special attention needs to be given to the difficult task of developing performance objectives for training under any circumstances.

A performance objective is a statement which clearly communicates an instructional intent, but more important, it is stated in terms of a learning expe-

---

[4]Task statements frequently use the term *ability* as the capacity to perform some complex task element without splitting hairs over whether a knowledge or skill is required, e.g., "The ability to operate mechanical counters." The key factor in deciding to call something an ability or use a more precise term depends on whether performance requirements can be clearly identified. However, the catch-all nature of "abilities" should not be used as an easy "out" to avoid detailing learnable skills and knowledge.

rience. A performance objective for training describes a proposed change in the behavior of a trainee. A behavior change in this context may mean nothing more than the ability to type fifty words per minute with no more than a 2-percent error rate by the end of the training program. For precise training, the objective must clearly describe:

1. What the trainees must be able to do at the conclusion of the training—the terminal behavior.

2. The conditions under which they must be able to perform.

3. The standard or criterion of acceptable performance
   a. during the development of the skill or knowledge
   b. at the end of the training experience.

The terminal behavior requirement involves the ability to demonstrate that the trainees have achieved the required behavior through the *application* of their learning.

The second part of an objective identifies what the employees will be given to do the job (reference materials, job aids, tools and equipment); what will be denied (budget funds, etc.); what assistance they will have (if any); what supervision will be provided; and the physical environment in which they will perform (climate, space, light, etc.).

The criterion of acceptable performance describes *how well* the trainees must be able to perform—the minimum performance requirements for a task or task element. The criterion statement must cover applicable details of quality of the work product or service produced (accuracy, completeness, clarity, tolerances, etc.); the quantity or volume of work units to be produced; and the time allowed to complete each task or element (or combination of the quality, quantity, and time standards).

Such a detailed statement of performance objectives for training might seem far too time consuming and costly to prepare, and in some cases this is true. For rarely occurring tasks and for situations where only one trainee is being developed at a time, the expense might be hard to justify. The preparation of detailed performance objectives is most suitable for developing a classroom-type training program for many trainees or when preparing programmed instructional material that will be used again and again over a long period of time. However, when return on investment appears to be small, a trainer may be tempted to "wing it" and do the job verbally from the top of her or his head. This may be acceptable with noncritical tasks, but there are benefits from actually writing out the performance objective, and the gains may be worth the investment, especially with new employees.

First, not all tasks require the detailed statements that others do. Where training is critical or will produce long-term benefits, the investment made by thinking through the objectives carefully may be warranted. This sorting of critical tasks from the others will get rid of many small items and focus the investment.

Second, much low productivity among employees at all levels, can be traced directly to never having the standards of performance communicated clearly to the employees in the first place. Similarly, sloppy, unclear training objectives tend to breed sloppy work. If the supervisor or other trainer is casual about what is to be achieved, is it any surprise that a new employee gives a casual response?

Third, the performance objective tends to become a contract between the trainee and the organization (through the trainer). This contract needs to be clear-cut and explicit so that each party knows clearly when it is being carried out. "If I can learn to do these things and can demonstrate proficiency in doing them under the prescribed conditions my performance is therefore satisfactory." This type of honest, open contract tends to get rid of the subjective, often one-sided, evaluation that is so common in informal training programs.

Fourth, the employees, particularly new employees, have a right to know objectively how well they are doing—not just so that they can improve performance when needed, but to feel good about their competency when they can demonstrate it. A lack of clear-cut training objectives might be a "set-up" for failure of new employees.

Fifth, a useful performance objective of some sort should probably be set for every significant task under a supervisor's purview. How else can employees be guided toward desired outcomes? How else can their performance be evaluated objectively? How else can the organization goals be met effectively? Solid performance objectives are just another way of implementing a Management By Objectives (MBO) program at the worker level. The translation of a measurable organizational objective into a training objective should be a small step.

In writing a performance objective for training, two things should be kept in mind:

1. A useful objective must be a literal picture of the performance expected, which will be interpreted in the same way by all the people involved in the training.

2. The statement must be a clear expression of an objective, action-framed picture of the behavior to be demonstrated.

Generally, the method of meeting this goal is to begin with the word *To,* followed by an active verb such as, *To calculate.* Another approach is to state: "Following the training, the trainee must *repair* a seventeen-jewel wristwatch." An important part of both approaches is to use behavioral verbs instead of vague passive terms. Group I lists *examples* of usable behavioral terms, as opposed to Group II which contains vague and passive terms.

Group I	**Group II**
Following training the	The training objectives
trainee must ----	are to ----
adjust ----	provide a working knowledge of ----
repair ----	provide a general knowledge of ----
classify ----	know about ----
install ----	understand ----
construct ----	develop an appreciation for ----
select ----	be familiar with ----
assemble ----	orient ----
organize ----	qualify for ----
calculate ----	
modify ----	

The use of the more specific, action-oriented behavioral terms will generally keep us on the right track. If those words don't fit your training objectives, your objectives just might not be clear in your own mind. Try to see how specific you can get about outcomes for your training.

Examples

A very simple example of identifying tasks, stating KSAD's, and writing behavioral training objectives for an "entry-level" job is given below.

Urban Planning Data Collection Aide

Task 01:

> *Count* people, cars, trucks, etc., passing a specific location in a specified time period and record the tallies on Data Collection sheets.

KSAD's for Task 01:

- Ability to operate hand-held mechanical counting devices possessed by employer
- Knowledge of how to set and reset alarm-type wristwatch for specific timing periods[5]
- Decide on method of locating self in relation to subjects to permit accurate counting

---

[5]It may seem surprising, but when teaching disadvantaged employees to do this task some could not tell time and others had never held a wristwatch in their hands. Yet within three months some of these individuals were conducting complex traffic surveys because they had been able to learn one step at a time.

Behavioral Objectives for Task 01:

- Given a specific intersection, highway, or other location, count the subjects (people, cars, trucks, etc.) selected for the study which pass the spot in specified time periods indicated on the survey sheet within ± 2 percent accuracy.
- Operate a hand-held Rockham counter model XK2
- Record tally figures in premarked locations on survey sheets
- Set and reset alarm-type wristwatch according to verbal instructions or the times indicated on survey sheets.

This may seem awfully detailed for the simplicity of the job, but these trainees were starting from real scratch as severely disadvantaged trainees. Today some are full-fledged city planners. They got their start, their productive work habits, and their effective training from the task analysis approach, from specific KSAD statements, and from meaningful behavioral training objectives. Today they are well-trained, long-term employees who everyday return full measure for the effort spent on training them well. More new employees could benefit from such careful and considerate planned training.

STUDY QUESTIONS

1. Name five ways in which training programs often miss the point.

2. Distinguish between training and education.

3. List some of the negative results experienced from an inability to distinguish between training and education.

4. List five benefits derived from task-related training.

5. Identify ten ways in which task analysis and the specification of KSAD's can be justified in an organization.

6. Describe in detail the main characteristics of the knowledge, skills, abilities, and decisions used in task-related training as developed in this book.

7. Identify three criteria for effective performance objectives for training.

8. List five benefits gained from actually writing out performance objectives.

CHAPTER 20

CAREER COUNSELING FOR SUPPLEMENTAL TRAINING AND EDUCATION

Before new employees become old employees the potential of their relationship to the organization should be assessed in terms of "Where can I go from here?" Whether the employees expect or hope to go anywhere can only be determined by talking with the employees, and assumptions about their goals and objectives should not be made too early. This subject should be explored quite early and quite thoroughly so that the employees do not merely drift into situations, but come to expect to participate in making decisions about their own future. To be effective, this process should be mutual, for new employees need information on where the organization is going and what its needs are likely to be. All too often in the past, organizations have assumed that a well-trained and educated work force would be available to draw upon as needed. Until recently, few organizations have adequately planned for meeting their human resource needs, or even assessing their long-term needs.

THE EMPLOYEES' PROBLEM

Some people tend to be passive and just wait to see what happens. Such passive individuals often expect to be considered for promotion, for upgrading, for raises, and for other jobs as they occur just because they have been loyally sitting on their duff longer than their coworkers. The idea of preparing for opportunities may never occur to them, and for good reasons (good reasons at least to themselves). They haven't perceived a payoff for such efforts.

A significant proportion of our population (perhaps as high as 30 percent) feel rather powerless to have much influence on their own future. Early life experiences have often convinced them of this (emotional or feeling) reality, and no amount of arguing is likely to change them. They communicate these expectations verbally and nonverbally, consciously and subconsciously, and often wind up in situations which tend to become self-fulfilling prophecies. If anything good comes their way, it is ascribed to luck and seldom alters their perceptions. They also tend to blame others, act out and feel the victim role, and watch life pass them by. For some who are deeply into these passive behaviors (and their accompanying negative feelings), only a great shock or therapy might resolve their problem. Others can be influenced and shown that planning ahead, assertiveness (rather than aggressiveness), and taking responsibility for their life can lead to improvement in their life and work.

Certain practices in management might also reinforce this feeling of helplessness. Arbitrary authoritarian bosses, unpredictable explosive supervisors, and a management which doesn't explain reasons for its actions (thereby making them seem a part of a threatening unpredictable world) often lead to the feeling of powerlessness in some people. Playing favorites, rewriting job specifications to fit a given candidate, and surrendering to the seniority syndrome (even when seniority is not a conclusive factor as might be the case when a union contract applies) can reinforce the feeling that "things just happen." One antidote to this feeling of helplessness and hopelessness is to aid employees in realistically planning for the future and, insofar as possible, helping them implement this plan. This effort will of necessity be a long-term effort.

THE ORGANIZATION'S PROBLEM

It seems, from my experience, that another 30 to 40 percent of the work force will move toward long-term planning and self-development effort if properly encouraged, and if their efforts are rewarded reasonably well. The remainder of the population, another 30 percent or so, will make at least a modest effort at self-development whether or not the organization responds appropriately. These individuals may pursue a long-term educational program or self-awareness programs (including reading on subjects that interest them), but much of this effort may not have much to do with the organization and its goals unless the supervisor or others make an effort to connect the two. I have found supervisors who were surprised to discover that subordinates had been engaged in long-term educational or training programs for many years—without the subordinates ever mentioning the fact.

To be successful in getting employees into self-development, educational, and training programs that have at least some relevance to the organization seems to require at least five things:

1. A joint effort between management and the individual to explore the long-term needs and goals of each and to harmonize these efforts.

2. Some organizational support or encouragement of the individual in pursuing self-development efforts.

3. Information on present and future needs of the organization being made freely available to the employee.

4. A comprehensive human resource inventory system that keeps track of what the employee knows and can do, including courses taken and passed, certificates awarded, skills acquired, etc.

5. The actual use of the employee's self-development achievements so that people can clearly see that self-development pays off.

With respect to this last item, one organization with which I worked went further than merely announcing promotions in the house news organ. It gave a very detailed description of what the person had done to prepare for that promotion. Every promotee was interviewed—if no achievements were listed, the conclusions were inescapable. At least the articles showed that usually there was a payoff for self-investment.

OPPORTUNITY FOR GROWTH AND DEVELOPMENT

One of America's great strengths has always been its educational democracy and the relatively easy access to educational and training opportunities. It is easy to focus on the denial of opportunity for many people, such as women and black Americans in the past, but compared overall to other nations which maintained a small educational elite, America has had reasonably free access for those who wanted greater education and the development of their talents. Black Americans from the days of the Emancipation Proclamation created over one hundred institutions of higher education against great odds, and enriched the lives of millions throughout a very hard and difficult century. Women not only created their own institutions, but ransacked the nation's free libraries and brought learning and education into their families against great social resistance.

One reality that may be too close to us to appreciate is that the great thrust in productivity and national growth and development that occurred after World War II was fueled in part by the college and trade school graduates who were trained during the war under government programs or who later took advantage of the G.I. Bill. It is doubtful that our technological development of the 1940s, 1950s and 1960s could have occurred without the advanced training and education provided during and after the war through government programs that supplemented industry and individual efforts.

That impetus can still be felt, though it is being diluted by other factors. In many ways we are entering into a new phase of this training and educational development saga, and the dimensions of this development are not yet clear.

In the last decade, we increasingly heard people talking about lifetime learning. Until recently, a common question on application forms was, "How many years of schooling have you had?" This question is becoming increasingly irrelevant. People are no longer thinking merely in terms of years of education. In the United States and abroad we are gradually abandoning the notion of terminal education—the idea that a person goes to school for a certain number of years and then stops. We are also witnessing a growing number of instances where people who have halted in the educational process find a new interest in self-development and get fired up to go further. Unfortunately, such people are often at or approaching midlife, and have developed family or other commitments. The decision to prepare themselves further is often complicated by an organization's self-defeating behavior of overspecifying job requirements unnecessarily (a college degree, for instance, instead of a certificate covering job relevant courses) and failure to give adequate credit for job and life experiences. Increased flexibility in human resource development and use is needed if we are to maintain a viable society.

At virtually no age or stage of life can we assume there are not opportunities for human resource development. We have also finally arrived at the point where no group can be effectively excluded from opportunities for training and education. Though the war on poverty may have died as a crusade, training and educational programs for the disadvantaged (such as CETA) continue and probably will continue—for we can scarcely afford to waste any of our human potential.

NEW DIRECTIONS ARE REQUIRED

Something almost as fundamental as educational democracy is at work today with greater force than ever. The increasing complexity of jobs, the growing interdisciplinary nature of jobs, and the speed at which jobs change and become obsolescent dictate virtually perpetual ongoing training and educational upgrading to remain current. To even hope to run our complex society effectively, we have to become more educationally sophisticated and more finely trained in less time than ever before. To maintain our educational and training levels is to fall behind, and yet we have some evidence that we aren't even maintaining previous standards in some areas, such as reading, writing, and arithmetic. However, the world is shifting, and it is hard to tell where we are going. Without getting involved in the complex argument as to whether things are getting better or worse, we have to recognize that a number of hopeful signs are also at work and these good and bad aspects of training and education will greatly affect new employees for better or worse.

Training techniques are becoming more direct, more effective, and more sophisticated. Educational programs are being offered in more convenient forms—short courses, seminars, and conferences. More organizations are offering in-house training and educational opportunities. There is better integration of training and educational efforts through community service departments of local colleges and universities. More oganizations are offering supplemental support for self-development efforts, i.e., tuition refund programs, intern programs, and educational sabbaticals.

While many good things are happening, substantial problems in meeting our human resource needs still remain.

Obstacles to Supplementary Training and Education Part of the difficulty in promoting supplemental training and education above and beyond that which is required for technical or professional certification or for meeting entry level requirements, stem from past habits, outdated perspectives, and lack of vision.

A major utility that serves my area has an excellent tuition refund program with an adequate and revolving line of credit for each employee. The policy supports education and training programs which show a relationship to "any job in the commission." Therefore, according to the policy, an employee could in time, by taking college credit or noncredit courses, prepare for any job in the organization—not just to move up in her or his present line of work.

However, it has been very difficult to make that broad policy work in some areas because supervisors refuse to approve programs that are not specifically related to the employees' current line of work. Because of a lack of accurate information on the policy and its application, employees are often snowed by their bosses. The supervisors are often not being intentionally malicious (though that has probably happened in some instances), often they are merely ignorant, or they don't check out the policy or erroneously feel they are protecting the organization's money. If employees decide to fight a supervisor's decision, they may win a victory but it will probably be pyrrhic.

One sad example occurred when an employee wanted to take a course in statistics, which was required for a degree. Management decided that there were so few jobs requiring that skill that the organization would never get its money's worth. This false assumption only compounded the tragic reality that the $240 tuition was probably lost in lowered motivation by that one employee alone.

A large part of the organization's unwillingness (a decision often conveyed by the first-line supervisor) to look at the organization's long-term overall needs comes from not having clear-cut long-term objectives that are conveyed to all levels of management. The increasing social and technological complexity of any organization almost assures that sooner or later any bit of skill or knowledge can be used. A prime problem that most organizations will face in the future will be to bring to bear the expertise that is already within the organization on solving organizational problems. Personnel who are skimpy about investing in ambitious new employees will probably short-change their employers—intentionally or not.

DIRECT AND INDIRECT PAYOFFS

A primary example of the complexity of this human resource investment was encountered several years ago at Ford Motor Company. We were studying apprenticeship training in three maintenance trades and looking into problems related to upgrading semi-skilled production workers to the level of the maintenance trades—a much more complex type of work. We were asked to do the study because it had been ten years since the trades had been evaluated and many technological innovations made the maintenance tasks much more complex. Also, in the interim, training techniques had become more sophisticated and it was believed that the training could be made more efficient and effective.

We conducted task analysis on a sampling of 1,400 workers in twenty plants, and we came to some interesting conclusions. Not least among the conclusions was the finding that the equipment was becoming so complex that an effective journeyman sometimes had to master several crafts. For instance, an effective machine repairman had to be quite knowledgeable in the areas of electronics, electricity, hydraulics, and mechanics.

A spinoff of studying the apprenticeship process was the need to look at what Ford called "supplementary education." Henry Ford had established a junior college program (two years of college education stretched over a four-year period) to supplement the trades training. We found that only two or three courses in the junior college program related to apprentices performing on-the-job. Even though we found that the junior college program had little immediate effect on apprenticeship performance, its long-term value was enormous. Among other things, we found:

1. A high percentage of Ford's first-line supervisors came out of the trades and journeymen ranks. A good general education provides perspective, intellectual discipline, and social understanding for those who rise in management.

2. The understanding of scientific and mathematical principles was essential in understanding and handling the increasingly complex technology emerging in industry.

3. Social and economic changes were occurring not only in the industry but within the plants themselves, which required more educated managers and personnel for handling the increasingly complex problems of the future.

It was the broad application of education that often justifies an organization's investment in supplemental education. The need for continuing education has become a fact of life that Henry Ford in his wisdom and genius foresaw.

Management and staff personnel who too narrowly interpret the organization's need to provide supplemental training and education for its employees, may be buying a short future for the organization, or at least a lot of future grief.

One very large private firm decided to save money on training, and for five years it neither sponsored nor offered training for its management personnel. When the need for growth occurred, the organization had to go outside for managers—a move that demotivated current employees and caused a lot of expensive on-the-job learning to occur as each new manager "made a mark" on the organization. The organization nearly went under and would have if the public had not had a high stake in its continuance. For a few dollars saved over the previous five years the organization had virtually "fired its future."

MEETING ORGANIZATIONAL NEEDS

A great mystery to the world of adult education for several years has been why so few people take advantage of their organization's tuition refund and similar programs. At this point nobody can say for sure, though several studies hint at the answers.

Part of the reason seems to be that many employees fail to see any clear-cut relationship between investing time and effort (and in some cases money) in their own development and job-related payoffs for those efforts. In some trades and professions the relationship is clear, such as with teachers and nurses who have to take courses to keep their certification current, and with some police departments where portions of the pay scales are directly related to degrees and credits earned. However, for most employees, the connection is a tenuous one.

Another factor seems to be that the objectives and plans of the organization seem so obscure or vague that it is hard for employees to plan a course of study that will reliably meet the organization's future needs. Unless there is a specific certification program laid out for new employees, such as that for plant operators in the waste water treatment field, that specifies credits and courses required for each step of advancement, the employees often have no guidelines.

When the individual supervisor tries to encourage new employees (or any other employees for that matter) to take on a study program for self-development, the supervisor is justifiably cautious about making promises, and is often in as much doubt as others about future organizational needs. When professional counselors tackle the problem in the organization, they often suffer from the same disadvantages of lack of data and an uncertain future.

Increasingly what organizations are going to have to do, if they hope to have trained and educated people available to fill jobs in the future, is to become involved in a comprehensive full-ranged human resources development effort. This effort must have clear access to the organization's long-range planning effort and actually become an important part of that planning effort. Human resources are becoming recognized as the greatest constraint on economic growth and development and the most vital ingredient in productivity and organizational success.

However, since it can be truly said that the only real employee development is self-development, we must find ways to better involve the individual employee in the joint venture of meshing organizational improvement goals with individual improvement goals. Nowhere is this effective meshing of goals more important than when dealing with the fresh human resource of the new employee.

THE ESSENCE OF CAREER COUNSELING

Since every human being has at least some inherent need for self-actualization, recognition, and acceptance in the group, ways are needed to have all individuals take a hand in developing themselves and reaping the benefits of self-development.

Whether this effort to get new employees involved in their own destiny is conducted by their supervisor or by a professional counselor, we need to recognize the three basic rules of effective counseling: (1) provide information, (2) provide support (in the case of the supervisor, this can also mean to give *permission* when such is needed), and (3) never give advice. Most people do not have much trouble in applying items #1 and #2, but to not give advice seems alien to many who may reply, "After all I've given and received advice all my life—giving advice shows that you care!" Baloney!

There is a big difference between giving information (which you have and the other person doesn't because of the nature of your job or the access you possess to useful knowledge) and giving advice (you should do such and such because I know what's good for you).

Let's consider advice-giving in a personal frame of reference. You can give me information on job requirements, on course offerings, or on policies and procedures which I don't have because your job calls for you having that kind of data. You can share that with me as an equal because I have a legitimate dependency.[1] Sharing information is quite different from the parent/child relationship of telling others what they "should" or "ought" to do.

We have probably all been caught up in what Eric Berne calls the "Yes, but" game. You have probably encountered situations where you have been asked for advice and, after giving it, have received a reply like, "Well, that sounds like a good idea but I tried it before and it didn't work because. . . ." In your efforts to be helpful, perhaps you adjusted your advice to take into account the problem the person encountered in trying your last bit of advice and give a new suggestion. Again, you may hear, "That's a good idea but. . . ." Undaunted, you revise the prescription and try again, only to encounter another, "Yes, but . . .," with more reasons why your idea won't work. After thirty or forty tries, you finally conclude that the person doesn't really want help and you tell them in effect to "buzz off."

The trouble with that transaction is that you have been sending a subconscious message that you know the problem of their development better than the individual—which can never be the case since you are not living the problem. You imply by giving advice that you are somehow smarter or more clever, and that you can best prescribe for his or her needs, though in fact you know less about the problem than the individual does.

---

[1] Legitimate dependency is a reality of life and should be treated matter of factly. In other cases the legitimate dependency may be reversed, as when I tell my supervisor about problems I've encountered in doing the work. Often the supervisor has no other way of ascertaining that information.

The other person is also responding subconsciously and has all the information needed to shoot down your ideas. Subconsciously he or she resents the parent/child relationship your advice created. This brings us back to the cardinal rule of counseling: give information (which is factual, objective, and neutral), not advice.

Effective career counseling or any other type of counseling is based on mutual respect, acceptance of other people and their problems, and a belief that they can best solve their own problems.

New employees will be far more committed to carrying out a career plan if they develop it themselves than they ever will be committed to a plan developed for them by someone else. New employees should be allowed and encouraged to develop their own career plans based on the knowledge and support you can provide. They should be responsible for the results of the decisions only they can really make.

The primary tools of effective counseling are: (1) listening (with reflective feedback), (2) providing information, and (3) granting permission if such falls within the counselor's (supervisor's) realm.[2]

The art of listening is often an underappreciated skill. New employees will often express uncertainty when involved in career planning, and may need to work through some emotional blocks as they go along, especially if they are not in the habit of taking responsibility for planning their own future. By accepting their feelings and their problems and dilemmas as valid, and by reflecting those feelings back so that the new employees know that you not only heard what they were saying but understood what they were feeling, we can become effective helping agents.

PROBLEMS AND OPPORTUNITIES IN SUPPLEMENTAL TRAINING AND EDUCATION

For many organizations, it doesn't cost much to offer tuition refund programs to employees because so few employees take their employer up on the offer. There can be a variety of causes for this phenomenon, including restrictive policies on use (such as the requirement to stay with the organization for a period of time—usually a nonenforceable restriction anyway), employee apathy or hostility toward the organization, lack of clear-cut career paths, and the tendency to go outside the organization for key people. Yet, some of the problems must be within the employees themselves. In a speech presented at Rutgers in 1977, Gordon G. Darkenwald reported on research related to why adults participate in education.[3] Darkenwald's speech highlighted some motivational research findings on why adults participate in continuing educational programs.

---

[2]Permission in a counseling situation merely means such things as giving the OK to go to the personnel department or approving a course of action.

[3]Gordon G. Darkenwald, "Why Adults Participate in Education." Published in ERIC Reports ED135992. U.S. Department of Health, Education and Welfare, Educational Resources Information Center, Washington, D.C., 20202.

Darkenwald began with Cyril Houle's findings that adult learners tend to be goal-oriented, activity-oriented, and learning-oriented, and they use adult education (and training) toward a reasonably clear-cut end. Learning for goal-oriented people is pursued only if it can be put to use, however, not necessarily put to use in the work situation. The activity-oriented adult learner engages in educational opportunities for social reasons, i.e., to be with others, to engage in interesting activity, or to meet people. The educational content of the program is secondary. The learning-oriented adult learner seeks knowledge for its own sake and considers learning to be a natural and continuous part of living.[4] Research subsequent to Houle's indicates similar findings in several other nations.

Darkenwald also referred to research results obtained by Morstain and Smart at Glassboro State College in New Jersey.[5] They found six factors that motivated the adult learner.

- Social relationships
- External expectations
- Social welfare
- Professional advancement
- Escape/stimulation
- Cognitive interests

Social relationships. This motivator forms from a desire to make new friends, improve the ability to function socially, or to participate in group activities.

External expectations. This factor represents external compulsion or pressure on individuals to participate in educational requirements. This pressure may come from suggestions offered by a supervisor or by some organizational requirement.

Social welfare. Motivation from this source covers an altruistic concern for others, and often relates to such goals as community betterment, participation in community affairs, or service to others.

Professional advancement. This motivator is strongly related to acquiring useful knowledge, credentials, and job-related skills in order to improve one's occupational status or performance.

Escape/stimulation. This factor primarily represents an attempt to escape boring or frustrating situations and to attain intellectual stimulation.

Cognitive interests. As with Houle's learning-oriented participant, this person values knowledge for its own sake.

---

[4]Cyril O. Houle, *The Inquiring Mind* (Madison: University of Wisconsin Press, 1961).

[5]B. Morstain and J. Smart, "Reasons for Participation in Adult Education Courses," *Adult Education* 24 (1974): 83–98.

A fascinating byproduct of this research is the conclusion that individual characteristics such as sex, socioeconomic status, and age are only weakly related to the motivators. These researchers also found that learning for its own sake and professional advancement were the greatest motivators, while escape/stimulation and social relationships tend to be rated last. However, their findings also indicate that most adult learners participate in educational experiences to satisfy several of these motivators at one time.

Of some significance in trying to motivate new employees were the findings that:

1. Younger participants ranked somewhat higher on the social relationship factor.

2. Men scored slightly higher than women on the external expectation motivator.

3. Women tended to place slightly more interest on learning for its own sake.

4. Younger adults tended to enroll in adult education programs for external expectations reasons, while older people sought learning for its own sake.[6]

The principle value of this research to the career development of new employees, however, is to realize that new employees may have a variety of factors encouraging them to pursue self-development goals and a variety of ways to attain such goals. Career counselors, especially the supervisor when he or she is filling that role, should work to remove barriers to the successful fulfillment of those motivators, and to explain how such efforts can lead to career growth by meeting clearly identified organizational needs.

THE SELF-MOTIVATED ACHIEVER

Learning is an internal process and occurs most effectively when people want to learn. New employees are generally eager to learn and are often anxious that they will not have the opportunity to do so. David McClelland at Harvard studied the achievement motive at considerable length and concluded that while some individuals are challenged by opportunity and feel impelled to work hard at achieving, most human beings are not much interested. Since it appears that almost everyone has the natural desire to achieve something, this lack of evidence of a desire to achieve could mean that many individuals never experience the joy of achievement and therefore fail to develop a portion of their personality.

---

[6]R. W. Boshier, "Motivational Orientations Revisited," *Adult Education* 27 (1977).

McClelland believed that it was possible to develop the desire to achieve in people who exhibited very little such desire. His research provided the following conclusions about high achievers:

1. They set reasonable goals for themselves which required that they stretch a little to achieve.

2. They set such goals for themselves only if they could personally influence the outcome by doing (or supervising) the work themselves. They did not gamble recklessly, for that left the outcome to chance.

3. They enjoyed the work itself, not so much for the rewards for their success as for the success itself.

4. They preferred work that gave them concrete readings on how well they were doing.

In helping new employees engage in achievement-oriented training and educational programs, these factors need to be considered. However, there is an even more critical aspect to McClelland's work.[7]

Achievers (not so-called "overachievers," which is a libelous insult in many cases) often spend their time thinking about ways to do things better. McClelland says it appears that such people do not inherit this trait; they learn to express this aspect of their personality from the way their parents worked with them as children. These parents set moderate goals for them and provided warm, encouraging, nonauthoritative support in reaching those goals. People with high scores in the achievement motivation tend to get promoted more rapidly, make more money, and in a variety of ways do better than most people. These later results have strong implications for career planning for new employees.

I have seen supervisors and staff personnel counsel new employees by encouraging them to set reasonable but challenging goals, and by providing warm friendly support. In many cases, employees who had previously not shown any interest in achievement became highly motivated and eventually achieved goals that astounded them in retrospect. If we provide that kind of assistance to new employees, we are likely to reap great personal satisfaction from our own jobs by seeing such people gain the joys of solid achievement.

STUDY QUESTIONS

1. Why is employee passivity a primary problem when career counseling opportunities and needs exist?

---

[7]David C. McClelland, "That Urge to Achieve," *Think* (November–December 1966): 19–23. Also McClelland's *The Achieving Society* (Princeton, N.J.: D. Van Nostrand Company, Inc., 1961) and "Achievement Motivation Can Be Developed," *Harvard Business Review* (November–December 1965): 7.

2. Name five requirements for successfully getting employees into self-development educational and training programs.

3. Identify one primary obstacle to promoting supplementary training and educational programs within an organization.

4. Name the three basic *rules* of effective counseling.

5. Name the three basic *tools* of effective counseling.

CHAPTER 21

EXPECTATIONS AND ATTITUDES

The expectations that a supervisor holds for the success or failure of new employees is the single most important factor in determining whether they will succeed or fail in their new job. Unfortunately, the positive or negative assumptions we hold about other people, and what those other people are like, tend to govern our expectations of them. If we feel that people are lazy, selfish, and lack ambition, we will often treat them as such and hold low expectations of their performance. If we believe people like to work, will accept responsibility, and are self-directed and creative, we will expect them to behave that way. Considerable research and analysis supports the reality that we will usually get what we expect.

ASSUMPTIONS ABOUT PEOPLE

Frequently in seminars I give supervisors a sheet containing the following two groups of statements. I ask them to choose group A or B as a starting point and then edit the statements in that group to conform to "your personal view of people." Then I ask the participants to work in small groups to do the same thing. In the small group work, participants are asked to search for a consensus, but if such can't be reached then the reporter for the group can report on the unresolved disagreements.

ASSUMPTIONS ABOUT HUMAN NATURE AND HUMAN BEHAVIOR

Read the two groups of assumptions and decide which group comes closer to your beliefs.

Group A

1. The average human being has an inherent dislike of work and will avoid it if he can.

2. Because of this human characteristic of dislike of work, most people must be coerced, controlled, directed, threatened with punishment to get them to put forth adequate effort toward the achievement of organizational objectives.

3. The average human being prefers to be directed, wishes to avoid responsibility, has relatively little ambition, wants security above all.

Group B

1. The expenditure of physical and mental effort in work is as natural as play or rest.

2. External control and the threat of punishment are not the only means for bringing about effort toward organizational objectives. Man will exercise self-direction and self-control in the service of objectives to which he is committed.

3. Commitment to objectives is a function of the rewards associated with their achievement.

4. The average human being learns, under proper conditions, not only to accept but to seek responsibility.

5. The capacity to exercise a relatively high degree of imagination, ingenuity, and creativity in the solution of organizational problems is widely, not narrowly, distributed in the population.

6. Under the conditions of modern industrial life, the intellectual potentialities of the average human being are only partially utilized.

I have asked participants to do this exercise for many years. As time has gone on, I have noted a shift in the number of individuals who chose each group. About twenty years ago, 20 to 25 percent of the group of supervisors might pick group A; now the percentage is seldom more than 10 percent. In some groups a few individuals may look wistfully at group A, but indicate that overall they prefer group B. This shift I feel is a hopeful one.

However, a surprising number of people are unwilling to let go completely from group A, especially items #1 and #3. Some supervisors, especially those who oversee routine or manual tasks, not surprisingly tend to hold onto item #1. Some supervisors, and I've noticed this often in government agencies, seem to like the phrases "wishes to avoid responsibility" and "wants security above all," and work these items into their edited version of group B. I have long suggested that this affection reflects the individual's projection of their personal values onto others. However, it is in the small group discussions and reports on group B that the interplay becomes interesting. Disagreements most often occur when discussing the following items.

Statement #1. Many people find it difficult or impossible to relate work to play or rest in any fashion. They often describe work as, "that which I have to do in order to live and support my family," and see work as dull routine and nonrewarding except in a financial sense. The idea of enjoying work seems to be outside their realm of experience.

Statement #2. The issue of rewards are seen by many to be only monetary. Only after the concept of psychic income, such as recognition, enters the conversation are they able to go along with the statement.

Statement #3. Many are skeptical about whether people will *seek* responsibility even under the best of conditions. Much conversation is often generated about what would be "proper" conditions for ever accepting responsibility.

Statement #4. A surprisingly strong portion of many groups doubt that creativity is widely distributed in the population. Their experience, at least initially, tends to show a low level of creativity and imagination displayed at work. It is only after the conversation focuses on the word *capacity* are they willing to concede that much creativity might potentially exist, but that it is seldom made manifest. Many participants also fail to recognize that the employees they work with may be displaying considerable ingenuity, but in negative ways (goldbricking, goofing off, or getting even) and therefore it is discounted.

Statement #5. Some discussion goes on about the meaning of "modern industrial life," but seldom is there any serious consideration of arguing with point #5.

McGREGOR'S THEORY "X" AND THEORY "Y"

By now, many of you will have recognized this set of assumptions as Douglas McGregor's Theory "X" (group A) and Theory "Y" (group B).[1] McGregor developed these viewpoints after listening for many years to supervisors and managers talk about people. He found that many supervisors held the attitude that people generally could be described by those assumptions outlined in group A (Theory X). Other supervisors, however, were likely to use expressions like those in group B to describe people. McGregor used the terms *Theory X* and *Theory Y* to identify these two sets of assumptions just so that they would be labeled neutrally rather than to have "loaded" descriptions such as "autocratic" or "participative." At first, McGregor also regarded supervisors who subscribed to group A (Theory X) perceptions about people as likely to

[1]Douglas M. McGregor, *The Human Side of Enterprise* (New York: McGraw-Hill Book Company, 1960).

use the stick approach, and group B (Theory Y) as the carrot approach. Later he came to regard Theory X (group A) as both the carrot and the stick, for Theory X implies a negative view of people—they either have to be controlled and threatened or they have to be enticed and persuaded. Theory X assumes that people would not naturally be constructively oriented.

What has this got to do with supervising new employees, or any other employees for that matter? Just this—we tend to act as we think and if we have a negative view of people, employees—especially new employees—will pick up clues and cues as to this attitude and respond accordingly. Ask yourself: How would I feel if my supervisor assumed that people in general were basically lazy, preferred to be directed, have an inherent dislike of work, have relatively little ambition, and have to be coerced, controlled, and threatened with punishment in order to achieve organizational objectives, and I were part of the workgroup? I doubt that many of you would care to be included in that description and would object, perhaps strenuously, if you were.

If a supervisor holds those general group A assumptions about people, they are bound to surface from time to time, and the results will tend to be as we might expect—negative. New employees, because of their vulnerability, are likely to be the most sensitive to such attitudes and respond most negatively to them.[2]

THE POWER OF EXPECTATIONS

A long time ago I came to the conclusion that supervisors often get what they expect. If they have a low opinion of people, they get low performance, but if they treat people with the respect inherently implied in high, but realistic expectations, they get high results. I was consulting with a utility that had a practice of rotating supervisors among various workgroups. The same workgroup under different supervisors produced different results. I noticed that certain supervisors got consistently high productivity while others got moderate to low output from every group they supervised. When I talked to these supervisors about their results, the poor performing supervisors tended to complain about their subordinates, while the high producers described their subordinates in glowing terms and were not afraid to set high (but achievable) standards of performance.

At first I assumed that the difference was due to different leadership styles, and that was somewhat true. However, I discovered that the leadership

---

[2] I have found that the actual application of Theories X and Y to management is complicated by the reality that Theory X seems to be more of an emotional assessment of people, while Theory Y is more of an intellectual assessment of reality. Where this gets messy is that supervisors often subscribe to Theory Y when things are going well, but revert to Theory X assumptions in times of crises and when the going gets rough. They then revert to Theory Y when the air is clear. McGregor observed that many supervisors will state strongly that they believe in Theory Y, but then run their organizations as though Theory X was the total truth. Could it be that we think one way but feel quite differently?

style chosen was based on a more fundamental aspect of the person—that supervisor's perception of others.

When I talked to subordinates I found a common thread running through the conversation and one that comes as a surprise to some supervisors. To a remarkable extent, subordinates in describing the bosses they produced best for said, "He expects a lot but he gives a lot." When describing other supervisors and the poor results they got, the subordinates often shrugged and said, "What does he expect?"

THE SELF-FULFILLING PROPHECY

Dr. Robert Merton, sociologist and Columbia University Professor, long ago developed the concept of the self-fulfilling prophecy. This idea focused on the reality that "the expectation of an event can actually cause it to happen." He based his theory of the self-fulfilling prophecy on the very astute observation that people tend to behave in such a way as to make their expectations become reality, even if the results are to their sorrow.

Dr. Merton cites a "bank-run" as the classic example of the self-fulfilling prophecy. A bank may be solvent and well established, but if a rumor spreads that the bank is about to fold, customers will rush to withdraw their savings thereby ensuring the very thing they had come to fear. The same thing can be seen in times of reported gasoline shortage where customers rush to "top off their tanks" thereby bringing on the very shortage they fear. Historical examples of people hoarding food and other goods in anticipated shortages and thereby producing shortages are documented by the thousands. Merton points out that the basis of the self-fulfilling prophecy is that it starts with a belief that is false at the time it is initially held. However, when people act on a false belief, and do so collectively, they tend to produce a situation that then becomes true and meets their expectations. As he has said many times, "False beliefs tend to create true reality."

The self-fulfilling prophecy works to some extent when applied to virtually all aspects of human life. We are all familiar with the example of the psychosomatic patient who is prescribed placebo pills and told that they will make him or her feel better—and they do. We've seen examples of the child who is expected to turn out bad and does so. We've probably had the experience of anticipating an argument or unpleasant experience with a visiting relative or guest and finding that our expectations came true.

The self-fulfilling prophecy is not magic, however, it seems to operate at a subconscious level. We are not "aware" of when it is actually operating, and therefore it seems to be almost magical. This magical quality becomes obvious when we analyze the mechanism of a bank run, but it becomes less clear when we are dealing with specific human beings such as subordinates or supervisors with whom we have a close-knit relationship.

RESEARCH ON APPLIED EXPECTATIONS

How powerfully supervisory expectations of subordinate performance can affect that performance can scarcely be underestimated. Research indicates that workers tend to regard their supervisors as much more powerful than the supervisors rate themselves. The supervisor is often keenly aware of his or her limitations of authority, but subordinates often do not perceive these limitations. Consequently, messages sent by the supervisor, whether the messages are conscious or subconscious, affect subordinates more powerfully than the sender realizes.

Robert Rosenthal and Lenore Jacobson conducted a classic experiment with children in a California school.[3] They got the teachers to give an intelligence test to more than 500 students. The teachers were unfamiliar with this particular test. The researchers told the teachers that this test could identify children who were about to spurt ahead in their learning abilities and performance—that is, they were about to "bloom" scholastically. These students, the teachers were told, would show remarkable gains in intelligence in the next eight months. However, the researchers did not use the test results, but instead chose 20 percent of the students on a random basis. The names of these 20 percent were specially marked on the class lists turned over to the teachers. Since those identified as "bloomers" were chosen randomly, the only difference between them and their classmates was in the mind of the teacher.

At the end of the school year, a regular IQ test revealed that those children identified as "bloomers" had gained an overall average increase of four points in actual IQ over their classmates. This experiment indicated clearly that children responded to expectations. Those for whom expectations were high produced much, and those for whom nothing exceptional was expected produced nothing exceptional. The teachers involved in the study were, to say the least, surprised to find that their expectations had had such a powerful effect on the children, for they sincerely believed that they had treated all of the children the same.

Rosenthal has commented that one of the surprising results of this experiment has to do with the teachers' perception of the children—the more the children identified as "bloomers" gained in IQ, the more the teachers liked them and rated them more favorably. If the children who were in the group where no special gains had been expected, especially if they were in the slow track, then the more their IQ increased the less favorably they were received and rated by the teachers. These negative responses to unexpected achievers included not only intellectual variables, but also emotional and social ratings. Teachers seemed to prefer that others behave as they are expected to behave. Could it be that supervisors also experience the same situation when it comes to subordinates?

---

[3]Robert Rosenthal and Lenore Jacobson, *Pygmalion in the Classrooom* (New York: Holt, Rinehart and Winston, 1968).

This last point raises serious questions, not only about the tracking of students but of keeping dossiers on students and workers and on relying on other people's reports for our evaluation of the person's potential. Douglas McGregor said, "Underlying assumptions influence managerial behavior not only in respect to policies and procedures and techniques but with respect to subtle aspects of every day behavior."

Two other aspects of Rosenthal's experiment might also have considerable implications for new employees. First, the largest gain in IQ was made by those students that were in the first and second grades—those newest to the school system. Second, the effects of the teachers' expectations began to show up within the first few weeks, but the effects lasted after the experiment for periods ranging from several months to nearly two years.

EXPECTATIONS APPLIED TO THE WORKPLACE

Rosenthal and others have concluded that one aspect of the self-fulfilling prophecy—the ability to influence the performance of others—is not just a one-way street from supervisor to employee. Characteristics of employees are important in determining exactly what the effect of these expectations will be. Young workers, especially those new to the job, are likely to be most susceptible to the supervisor's expectations. These people have relatively fewer preconceived notions about themselves in a work environment, have less of a track record to sustain their self-image, and are anxious to live up to the manager's goals and desires.

Lest anyone discount Rosenthal's and Jacobson's work when the results are applied to adult workers instead of school children, consider the following study. Dr. Albert King conducted an experiment at a vocational training center for the hard-core unemployed. He told the welding instructor that tests showed that five of his trainees had an exceptionally high aptitude for welding. The five men, however, had been chosen at random. During the six-month training course these High Aptitude Personnel, HAP's as they were called, showed significantly different behaviors than their fellow trainees. They were absent less than the control group, they learned the fundamental welding process in little more than half the time of the rest of the group, and on a comprehensive welding test they scored an average of ten points higher than their co-workers. Dr. King also asked the whole group to rate the other members as to who they would rather work with, be with, and socialize with. Without exception, the workers singled out the HAP's as those they most liked and respected.[4]

In a similar study by A. Bavelas, foremen were led to believe that some of the women under their supervision had scored high on tests of finger dexterity and intelligence, when in reality they had gotten low scores. The foremen were also told others had scored low when actually they had scored high. Bavelas found that regardless of the test scores, if the foremen expected high performance, the production records showed high output for these people—higher than those of other workers. When low expectations were held (based on assumptions made by the foremen from the erroneous reporting of test scores), productivity was low. In reality, as with other similar studies, the foremen did not know who would be the top producers but thought they did, and therefore implemented the self-fulfilling prophecy. As Rosenthal and Jacobson have said, "People, more often than not, do what is expected of them."

From a study of over thirty experiments, Rosenthal and his colleagues have developed a four-factor theory on how expectations may be transmitted to others through very specific behaviors.

1. Climate. This is composed of all the nonverbal messages from the person in a position of authority, including eye contact, tone of voice, facial expressions, and body posture. Warmth and acceptance in communication seems to be the most critical factor in creating a climate for positive expectations to bear fruit. However, as in all four factors, climate can communicate negative as well as positive expectations.

2. Feedback. A manager will provide the employee with more (or less) feedback depending on the supervisor's expectations of the employee. It is almost as though the supervisor draws satisfaction from giving feedback to people toward whom he or she is positively inclined, but doesn't bother with those for whom he or she has low expectations.

3. Input or information provided to the employee. When the supervisor has high expectations, there is a tendency to give the employee considerable training and job-related information. To employees where there is low expectations, the supervisor again seems to "not even bother." In a perverse way this lack of data makes sense since the point of view of the supervisor is "What difference will it make?"

4. Output. The amount of output or production which the supervisor encourages from the employee also seems to be closely related to supervisory expectations.

IMPLICATIONS OF EXPECTATIONS AND NEW EMPLOYEES

In most cases, supervisors have optimistic expectations for employees they hire, and generally their expectations work out well—at least in the early months (or perhaps years) of the relationship. However, what is likely to happen when employees are, in effect, hired by someone else such as through a selection panel, or to meet EEO requirements, or in response to an affirmative action effort? Also, what happens if the persons made available to the supervisor (as when selecting from a list of three) have a substantially different life style than that approved of by the supervisor? What happens if a new person dresses differently, speaks differently, or perhaps practices a different approach to grooming than that common to the supervisor and the organization? There is a strong tendency, expressed by many supervisors, to expect low results and negative behavior—consequently there is a good chance of producing just that!

The most frightening aspect of such a situation is that the research related to the self-fulfilling prophecy indicates that if those people for whom the expectations are low begin to perform better than expected, the supervisors will not like them. Supervisors, as with teachers and others, seem to have an innate need to be able to predict accurately. If people do not meet our expectations, we often punish them for not behaving as expected. Conversely, people are often rewarded when they perform as expected, even when the expectations and the performance is negative. We seem more tolerant of those who produce expected incompetence, and we even make statements like, "Old Joe doesn't do much but at least he's loyal." "Old Joe," knowing very well on which side his bread is buttered, goes along doing what is expected. Could it be that we often foster incompetence and poor performance by not periodically reexamining our expectations of people and trying to develop a set of positive expectations and behaviors?

Could it be that we are often unwilling to just set aside our previous assumptions about an individual, provide the person with as much information and positive support as possible, and see what happens? In order to develop positive expectations, we have to carefully and honestly examine our feelings about a person and decide where those feelings come from. Often, our expectations for another are so entangled in a long emotional relationship that this is hard to do. However, with a new employee, where we have a merciful lack of data, we have the rare opportunity for a truly new beginning.

STUDY QUESTIONS

1. Which group of assumptions, group A or B, did you feel most comfortable with or which seemed right to you when describing other people?

2. How would you edit your preferred group in order to make it conform to your beliefs about the way people are by their basic natures?

3. Which items on the list of your choice, if any, gave you a problem in the way it was written?

4. Sum up a definition of the self-fulfilling prophecy that meets your needs.

5. Why are supervisory expectations and the self-fulfilling prophecy such potent factors in the job success of the new (particularly young) employees?

6. List Rosenthal's four-factor theory on how expectations may be transmitted to others through very specific behavior.

CHAPTER 22

PRODUCTIVE NEW EMPLOYEES

*The most powerful force loose in the world is the idea that all people
are somebody.*   (Andrew Young, 1979)

The primary goal, from the beginning of this book, has been to achieve the full
use of the abilities of new employees by the organization. Insofar as that can
be accomplished, it is hoped that in equal measure the satisfactions, rewards,
and accomplishments commensurate with this outpouring of talents can be returned to new employees. Only thus can we avoid exploitation by either side.

Daily we can find examples in the press and elsewhere of employees ex-
ploiting the organization for their own purposes, through pilferage, retiring on
the job, or wasting time or resources. Likewise, we find organizations taking
advantage of employees through the unfair use of power by unnecessary restrictions on employee development or advancement and by discrimination. If
the organization and the supervisor are to receive a full measure of performance, they must give a full measure of fair and effective management. To do
this, both sides need to put aside past negative practices, harmful and retali-
atory behavior, and outdated grievances, and begin to work more closely together to achieve mutual ends. Nowhere is this fresh beginning more feasible
than in the case of new employees working in what they consider a new organization.

FUTURE ISSUES

Unfortunately, new employees and the organization's management personnel
may be burdened by past generalizations about "what organizations are like"
or "what employees are like." These past notions and concepts are not useful
attitudes on the part of either party to a relationship. They tend to set in
motion the self-fulfilling prophecy and set up the relationship for a mutual
lose/lose outcome. We need ways to look at this new employee/new organiza-

tion relationship in a new light, to free ourselves from the burden of past assumptions, and to get on with meeting mutual needs. The "human use of human resources" should become a battlecry—not because it is a nice thing to do, but because it is the only way that each party can develop or contribute to a win/win relationship.

Of equal concern is the need for deeper exploration of the concepts inherent in the phrase, "Quality of Life Work." What affects the quality of life work for each person is a unique combination of things for each individual. Though we share many motivators with other people, there is an optimum situation and combination of satisfactions for each person in each period of their life. We need to explore those things that will provide the highest quality of life work for each individual while meeting the organization's goals (and indirectly our own goals, for the health of each organization, be it government agency, institution, or private firm, affects the quality of life in our society). None of us can fully escape the effects of our own behavior, even if we decide to do nothing. If I goof off on the job, if I supervise ineffectively, if I allow waste in the organization, these behaviors or lack of behaviors hurt us all and myself in turn. We all know that fact, but making the concept of working for our mutual benefit a living reality in our daily activities is difficult.

Part of the problem involves getting each of us to "own our own job" in a somewhat different way than in the past. Jobs have long been regarded as property, but often thought of as something to be possessed and exploited rather than nurtured and developed. Throughout history, because jobs of any kind were scarce, they were valued and fought over. Much of significance in human history, at least in recent centuries, can be seen as a fight over jobs. Political appointees, receiving safe sinecures, often went to extremes in using their offices for personal gain or sloth and thereby triggered the movement for a civil service system. In a like manner in the industrial revolution, firms often regarded their creation of jobs as power, a tool for their own ends, and they often used people arbitrarily—thereby giving impetus to the rise of unions. In both these cases, at stake in the combat was the ownership of jobs. In any such combat each side is likely to see the other side as an enemy, and this attitude perpetuates distrust and dysfunctional behavior.

Admiral Hyman Rickover discusses another type of job ownership. He believes that if you own your job you ought to take full responsibility for it. Rickover says if an individual feels ownership of the job, he or she "need not worry about their next job. He should exercise a devotion to his work as if his children were the direct beneficiaries of what he is doing, as indeed they are." This sense of investment and personal responsibility must be matched by an equal commitment of the organization to the *full* well being of that individual. It is only when both parties to the employment contract are committed to the welfare of each other can the employee feel secure enough to concentrate on the present job and maximize its potentials—confident that the future will take care of itself because the organization, through its management and professional representatives, truly cares. It is this lack of caring that worries most people about organizations today, and yet it is only by all of us doing our jobs to their fullest can an organization really care. As Pogo once said, "We have met the enemy and they is us." Let's stop blaming others and take responsibility for our own behavior—you and the new employee will benefit mutually.

The question still remains. How far do we go until our needs are optimized for a given time and place? One employee may reach a level of personal comfort and security, feel satisfied, and then just live for the daily social interaction the job provides. The employee may not feel the need for esteem and self-actualization à la Maslow—yet if that person is properly placed in the organization, she or he can be highly productive. Only individuals can determine their level of needs satisfactions. The organization also must establish its level of needs satisfaction. Today, the best method of matching needs satisfaction between employees and the organization seems to be through mutual goal setting in some form of a Management by Objectives system. This chapter will describe one type of MBO approach that seems particularly well suited to dealing with new employees.

THE PRODUCTIVITY PLANNING CONFERENCE (PPC)—APPRAISAL AND BEYOND

There is nothing more likely to turn an untried rookie into a battle-scarred veteran than the performance appraisal system applied in most organizations. This type of evaluation system generally consists of a form where the supervisor rates (by sliding scale or other method) all employees and gives them feedback on their "report card." I regard this approach as worth a little more than nothing since it *does* force the supervisor to talk to employees about job performance at least once a year. Aside from the fact that I've yet to see this type of evaluation form get rid of arbitrary subjectivity or to be well thought of by almost anyone, its use doesn't seem to diminish.

I will grant that such rating systems have tended to become more objective, more sophisticated, and less one-sided over the last thirty years since I first encountered them. But I feel that no amount of doctoring is likely to redeem them. The very notion of one-sided appraisal is destructive, though most managers recoil in horror at such a suggestion for they consider the only alternative as being that of providing no feedback at all.

I can certainly understand an organization needing a managed system of feedback to employees on how they are doing on the job. The employees need this information too, especially the new employees who may lack other benchmarks. I also acknowledge a need for a fair system of rewards so that those who perform well get their just due and those who don't, won't. It is also quite clear that there is unquestionably a need to discourage negative behavior and encourage productive behavior. My primary objection is to virtually all formal evaluation forms which are cast in some type of standardized rating form. The systems I've seen, whether they are called fitness reports, employee rating forms, performance review forms, or merit rating forms, either don't actually achieve those goals or they encourage nonsense games to be played in the organization which destroy the value of the feedback.

My purpose here is not to attack general performance appraisal rating systems—their almost universal unpopularity speaks well enough for that. I do not expect those systems to be abandoned, for there are too many people who have a vested interest in their continuation. Also, since those systems have been around so long and seem to fill such a widely held psychological need to evaluate others, few organizations would feel secure in giving up these systems.

My primary objections to conventional performance appraisal rating systems are:

1. They are backward looking. The poor performance has already occurred and cannot be corrected. We can only warn or punish the person in the hope that future behavior will be improved.

2. People don't like to be evaluated. They often respond negatively to the experience (even praise has its problems for some) and they would rather experience success. Performance ratings often damage self-esteem.

3. People need day-by-day feedback, and this they can best get when they know how well they are doing the job. Performance ratings often create anxiety and produce surprises because many employees only find out once or twice a year how well their boss considers their work performance to be.

4. Management games are often played with performance rating systems, such as setting quotas on certain ratings in order to match the money available for raises. Such quota systems destroy the integrity of the appraisal concept.

5. The psychological problems related to halo effects, prejudice, preconceived opinions, and the supervisors' own perceptions of themselves as "having high standards" or "being generous" can lead to many distortions—that is, the ratings often tend to be subjective rather than work-related and measurement-oriented.

6. Ratings tend to get people uptight and produce peculiar nonproductive behaviors, such as "working for grades," distorting facts, covering up (commonly known as CYA), destructive competition, and apple polishing.

7. Because people are being judged, they tend to argue about the fairness of the evaluation, at least in their minds, and tend not to hear the

supervisor's efforts at counseling. I've observed that the appraisal conference seldom motivates the subordinate to achieve positive change, only to be more clever and devious.

What I'm going to suggest as an alternative to the performance appraisal system is that supervisors at all levels, but particularly first-line supervisors, consider using the productivity planning conference as a method of assessing performance. I also suggest, since your organization is not likely to give up its current system, that all persons carry out their job requirements and fill in those conventional rating forms as a separate activity. However, the productivity planning conference will provide objective data for such evaluations, and can be used to justify ratings more precisely.

The productivity planning conference is a forward-looking focus on accomplishing worthwhile objectives and developing a pattern of employee success. Unlike some MBO systems, however, it focuses on the goals of only a given workgroup and need not be applied across the whole organization. It is, in effect, a way of managing work and people, which any supervisor can use.

Generally I prefer to conduct the productivity planning conference with the whole workgroup. I mean by the term *workgroup* those people who report directly to you regardless of their rank (whether you are a first-line supervisor or a manager of other supervisors or managers). However, with new employees, there are so many new and special considerations in the relationship that the first time through the productivity planning conference is generally a one-on-one session, and it takes place about six months after hire.

The general purpose of involving all subordinates in the productivity planning conference is to take advantages of the improved communications offered by group work.

PREPARING FOR THE PRODUCTIVITY PLANNING CONFERENCE

When working with new employees, the appropriate preparatory steps are to:

1. Notify the employee in advance that you would like to plan out a program of job accomplishment for the next six months and invite the new employee to prepare his or her own tentative agenda for such a meeting, i.e., what that person would like to accomplish in the coming period.

2. Ask the employee to prepare a list of "task contribution" statements covering their job; that is, what she or he does that adds value to the organization. Employees often are startled by this request, but with help and guidance they usually develop enthusiasm for the task. In a way, they are justifying the existence of their job and at first they may not be too sure about its ability to be justified. Often though, as this exercise proceeds (assuming the job and its duties are justified), they

usually warm to the task and frequently develop a new respect for the importance of their job and for themselves.

In order for this exercise to be accomplished, the new employees must understand the difference between a "task statement" and a "task contribution statement." The latter not only deals with qualitative aspects of the task, but couches it in words that indicate the output or result and the value of that output or result.

An example of a task statement and task contribution statement is given below.

Receptionist Position

Task Statement	Task Contribution Statement
• Handles incoming calls	• Receives and responds to incoming calls so that caller receives a favorable impression of the organization
	• The caller is helped to achieve his or her objective whether it is information or contact with an employee
	• When the caller is unable to reach the party sought, a "return call" slip is prepared, making a return call possible when appropriate
	• Whenever possible, the information on the caller and his or her purpose can be relayed to proper person
	• Calls are sometimes screened to prevent untimely, inappropriate interruptions
	• The person being called is alerted to the caller and his or her purpose so that the respondent can be prepared to deal with the conversation
	• Telephone calls are correctly and effectively routed

The task contribution statement is often somewhat lengthy when compared to a task list, but it also deals with the consequence of the task and to some degree establishes its value. However, this piece of work need not be arduous for the task list previously prepared for the new employees can be used as a base. Often the qualitative or value factors can be attached to some of the KSAD's as appropriate. Most important, these contribution statements need only be prepared once and then need only be refined or updated as the job changes. This list is also an excellent orientation tool for the new (subsequent) employees who might assume this job in the future. The task contribution statements are far more detailed and results-oriented than the usual job description.

It is usually a good idea if the supervisor independently prepares his or her own list on the new employees' job so that perceptions can be checked out.

3. Then the supervisor gets together with the subordinate, and they compare the two lists. At this time the purpose of the comparison is to prepare one mutually acceptable list. It is not to quibble over wording or to prove one person right and the other one wrong. It is a check on each person's perceptions of the job, on how effective job goals and values have been communicated, and on whether or not the supervisor and the subordinate are headed in the same direction. These lists are a communications device and, as such, the goal is clear understanding and agreement. No one else need see the resulting list, nor should the list necessarily make sense to an outsider as long as the supervisor and subordinate understand.

4. The supervisor and the new employee should then discuss future goals and plans for the new employee. The supervisor should also have a written list of goals he or she envisions for the new employee, but should allow the new employee to take the lead for often the supervisor's list will be largely covered and the employee will feel most committed to goals personally developed. The supervisor can then suggest other areas for development, if appropriate, and see how they can be added to the list.

For people currently employed, the task contribution statement will generally cover the *routine functions* the employee has been doing for some time. Therefore, this list is a check on how effective interpersonal job-related communications has been. The point here, however, is that recriminations for misunderstandings are quite useless. The important issue is that both parties agree *now*—for the future.

The resulting list will hopefully reveal future plans and the anticipated needs of both parties. This is where the supervisor can communicate future needs and the subordinate can deal with his or her aspirations.

5. Each party should then negotiate agreement on how performance is to be measured and reported for each item on the lists. Often the routine items will be fairly obvious. Feedback should be continuous so that

both parties know what is going on and they can check out their perception of results quickly and easily. On developmental goals and new objectives this measurement and feedback may be more difficult and more critical. The primary point is to make the measures as specific as possible and the results as visible as possible. Many excellent books on Management by Objectives give concrete suggestions as to how this may be done in detail. The primary concern is that measures and results be mutually understood and agreed upon.

6. Implementing the decisions made in the productivity planning conference is the next and most critical step. It is here that the payoff comes, for the key is to have the new employees take responsibility for appraising their own performance and insofar as possible develop answers to their own performance problems. The supervisor can then be cast in a supportive role, a person who makes things possible and who provides the resources for accomplishment. The productivity planning conference becomes a way to delegate authority and develop the fullest possible (within the job context) capabilities of new employees.

Obviously the key to the successful implementation of the productivity planning conference procedure is a *trust* that the subordinate wants to do a good job and wants to accomplish goals in which he or she has had a hand in setting. With new employees we are not often handicapped by past patterns of mistrust which may pervade the atmosphere. With new employees we have a fresh start and a chance to build mutual respect and trust based on mutual accomplishment.

Where I have been able to use this approach, I have found that:

1. Subordinates are highly motivated by working on *their* goals.

2. The job gives them more self satisfaction and they become more involved in meeting the needs of the organization.

3. Subordinates become less dependent and more willing to do what needs to be done even where risks are involved.

4. My job becomes easier and I get more time to do more constructive things than overseeing.

5. Problems in the organization get solved more effectively and I personally benefit from the results.

6. Creativity flows more freely.

7. The atmosphere has less tension and people (including myself) are more relaxed.

8. *Useful* productivity flourishes.

Such goals need to include targets that are clear, specific, realistic, measurable, somewhat challenging, and achievable within a given period of time (usually the next six months).

Once the productivity planning conference is being implemented, we can begin to regard new employees as regular employees. Performance is measured by objective results, the new employees know how well they are doing, and corrective action can be taken as needed, not a year late. The new employees begin to take responsibility for the results attained and begin to "own" their job.

THE PRODUCTIVITY PLANNING GROUP

As stated earlier, I have a preference for including all subordinates in a productivity planning conference (after the preliminary work has been done with each individual subordinate) because it enables the supervisor to lay out new goals and objectives on organizational needs and to get the group working cooperatively and supportively on achieving these goals. Such an approach shares knowledge of problems, permits each person to contribute what they can, and builds team spirit.

I have found this group planning approach particularly useful when we were working in a project-oriented environment. Even though each person had a specific job they ordinarily performed, I found them willing and often eager to cross job lines to help out an associate or to fill a gap in expertise whenever they could. Since the focus was on getting the job done, instead of protecting turf, my associates often contributed valuable ideas and knowledge, worked extra long hours willingly, and took responsibility for things which were far in excess of their job requirements. The principal advantage was they could see what needed to be done overall and could figure out ways to achieve our objectives.

New employees often found this type of environment unfamiliar, but they soon warmed to the participatory nature of the group's activities. The group was supportive and extremely sensitive to the problems and needs of new employees. Soon the new people felt comfortable enough to begin taking part, and in virtually no time they became full-fledged members of the group.

FINAL CONSIDERATION

A responsibility the organization owes to new employees as a return for investing their talents, creativity, and productive effort on the organization's behalf is opportunity—real opportunity insofar as the organization can possibly supply it. The organization, as represented by a collection of management people, has a responsibility to apply managerial talents to meeting employee needs as well. We all need to continue the search for better ways to meet each other's needs.

One need that I perceive as the key to meeting other needs is a way to reinvigorate each person's learning curve from time to time. It is often said that twenty years of experience for most people really means six months of experience repeated forty times. This is the tragedy of dead-end jobs, discrimination, and a punishing environment, as well as the result of faulty assumptions we may make about ourselves and others as to their potential and creativity. The problem with an "old" job is that it is seldom challenging, seldom really rewarding, and seldom invites new thoughts or ideas. An "old" job is often a dead-end that does neither the employee nor the organization much good. In a challenging world, where there is a perpetual need for improvement of all types, we need to look at jobs to see where the learning stops. See Fig. 22.1.

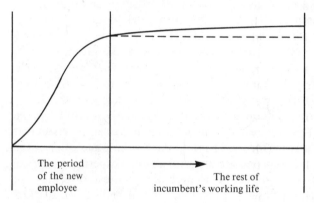

The period of the new employee

The rest of incumbent's working life

Fig. 22.1
Learning Curve

There is a period in any new job when the person's learning is at a very high level—this is generally when the employee is new or the job is undergoing substantial change (in effect creating a new employee as far as that job is concerned). This period may be two weeks long (as with a clerk) or two years long (as with a research analyst), but it seldom exceeds two years even in the most professional of positions. At the end of this rapid learning period, learning may still continue but at a much slower rate. This is often where a new employee becomes a "regular" employee. This is where boredom sets in and productivity levels become routine. This is not necessarily bad if the employee is satisfied and performance is still high, however, for many this is where they begin to get careless, indifferent, and less effective.

For more and more people, few jobs are truly satisfying in the long run. Employees need the stimulation of new learning to make their maximum contribution to the organization. There are a variety of ways we can make jobs more interesting if we have the intelligence to do so effectively. Job enrichment and job redesigning are just two of the ways. Promotions and transfers often revitalize the learning curves, as do new projects and new ventures. Cross training and rotating jobs are other possibilities.[1]

THE PERPETUALLY NEW EMPLOYEES

In some ways we are dealing with the concept of rebirth and new beginnings. The Peace Corp's "In, Up, and Out" concept, where a new employee was inducted and trained effectively, promoted rapidly, and then left the organization for new fields after about five years (presumably when they were likely to become stale), was one innovative government effort to apply these principles. While many people will be shaken by the idea of spending only a few years with an organization and then moving on, the growing approach to mobile pensions may make the risk of such a venture less drastic and more acceptable.

Our society is no longer one where many people expect to hold a single job all of their lives (unless they feel very insecure) and routinely grind out the same product or service at the same rate forever. Our society is becoming too complex and the needs for innovation too demanding to permit very much of that type of stagnation. While the choice is an individual one to make, many people are suddenly becoming aware that they have a choice between "standpatism" and challenge. How this will come out in the long run no one can be sure, but in a dynamic society where new learning means new opportunities and a new chance to solve society's complex problems, I suspect that great changes are in the wind.

With a new focus on improving "the quality of life work," I suspect that we will increasingly see a focus on "the perpetually new employees" who will move to where their unique talents and interests will be utilized most fully.

STUDY QUESTIONS

1. Identify the key to avoiding exploitation of the employee and of the organization.

2. Define and explain the basic concepts underlining the productivity planning conference.

---

[1]Some people argue that unions will not permit them to cross train workers, rotate people in jobs, or in any way threaten the status quo. I have not found this to be true and I suspect such statements, in many cases, are self serving "cop-outs." I have seen such job adjustment plans adopted where the toughest unions held sway. Unions were first created to protect employees and their jobs by achieving equity for employees when dealing with employers. All of us can be shortsighted, at times, but if employing organizations are not arbitrary and meet employee needs, the employees will insist that the union change—as is happening in many situations—to meet their members' needs.

3. List several primary objections to conventional performance appraisal rating systems.

4. Briefly sketch the six basic steps to managing a productivity planning conference.

5. Identify several (of the eight) benefits listed as resulting from the use of the productivity planning conference.

6. Think of the learning curve on the jobs you have had or know a great deal about, and project the point at which new learning greatly diminishes (the curve tended to flatten out).

BIBLIOGRAPHY

ARTICLES

Boshier, R. W., "Motivational Orientations Revisited," *Adult Education* 27 (1977).
Darkenwald, Gordon G., "Why Adults Participate in Education," Published in *ERIC* Reports ED 135992, U.S. Department of Health, Education and Welfare—Educational Resources Information Center, Washington D.C. 20202.
McClelland, David C., "That Urge to Achieve," *Think* (Nov./Dec. 1966): 19-23.
McClelland, David C., "Achievement Motivation Can Be Developed," *Harvard Business Review* (Nov./Dec. 1965): 7.
1 OSS Assessment Staff. "A Good Man is Hard to Find," *Fortune Magazine* (March 1946): 62.

BOOKS AND PAMPHLETS

Booker, David, "How to Structure Job Tasks for Training the Disadvantaged," National Civil Service League's Reference File No. 7: Public Employment and the Disadvantaged, 1970.
———, "Training and Testing the Disadvantaged," a Manpower Press Publication of the National Civil Service League, 5530 Wisconsin Avenue, N.W. Washington, D.C. 20015.
Bray, Douglas, *The Assessment Center Method Training and Development Handbook,* 2nd ed. (New York: McGraw-Hill, 1976), Chapters 15, 16 and 32.
Houle, Cyril O., *The Inquiring Mind* (Madison: University of Wisconsin Press, 1961).
McClelland, David C., *The Achieving Society* (Princeton, N.Y.: D. Van Nostrand Company, Inc. 1961).
McGregor, Douglas M., *The Human Side of Enterprise* (New York: McGraw-Hill Book Company, 1960).
Peter, Lawrence J., and Hull, Raymond, *The Peter Principle* (New York: William Morrow, 1969).
Prince, George M., *The Practice of Creativity* (New York: Collier Books, Macmillan Publishing Company, 1976).

Rosenthal, Robert, and Jacobson, Lenore, *Pygmalion in the Classroom* (New York: Holt, Rinehart and Winston, 1968).

1 OSS Assessment Staff, *Assessment of Men* (New York: Rinehart, 1948).

U.S. Department of Labor, *A Handbook for Job Restructuring* (Manpower Administration, 1970, Superintendent of Documents, U.S. Government Printing Office, Washington D.C. 20402).

FILM

"The Pygmalion Effect—Productivity and the Self-Fulfilling Prophecy," McGraw-Hill.